SHADOW OF WAR

D1143547

'At that moment the foundations of the house shake with the force of an explosion. Instinctively people cover their heads with their hands. Within the split second before the light goes out, I see that Mother is not with us . . .'

Shadow of War tells the story of a teenage girl's horror in the midst of conflict; of a family torn apart; of the privations of post-war Germany. It introduces a British soldier's young bride, and follows a personality and a faith as they are gradually rebuilt.

This book is an intensely personal account of how ordinary people's lives are devastated by war. It shows that the healing of mind and spirit can take a lifetime.

Copyright © 1990 Gerda Erika Baker

Published by
Lion Publishing plc
Sandy Lane West, Oxford, England
ISBN 0 7459 1873 5
Albatross Books Pty Ltd
PO Box 320, Sutherland, NSW 2232, Australia
ISBN 0 7324 0214 X

First edition 1990

The quotations from *Four Quartets* by T.S. Eliot are used by kind
permission of the publishers, Faber and Faber Ltd.

British Library Cataloguing in Publication Data
Baker, Gerda Erika
    Shadow of war.
    1. Germany. Social life, 1933-1945 — Biographies
    I. Title
    943.086092

    ISBN 0-7459-1873-5

Printed and bound in Great Britain
by Cox and Wyman Ltd, Reading

SHADOW OF WAR

Gerda Erika Baker

A LION BOOK

Oxford · Batavia · Sydney

Contents

'. . . for the growing good of the world is partly dependent on
unhistoric acts; and that things are not so ill with you and me as
might have been is half owing to the number who lived faithfully a
hidden life, and rest in unvisited tombs.'

George Eliot, *Middlemarch*

Dear Sandy

Here it is at last: the account of my life that, ever since the day when we walked in the mountains of Austria, you have unceasingly urged me to write.

One hundred years ago this year saw the birth of Adolf Hitler, and this year sees the fiftieth anniversary of the Second World War. Immeasurable suffering for millions has resulted from both these events, and yet without these two events you and my other grandchildren would not be here now.

Writing about some of my experiences has been painful but at the same time liberating; and, once begun, the writing became compulsive because, I suspect, there is in all of us an unconscious longing for some kind of permanence — *non omnis moriar*.

Memory is selective and once evoked becomes more so. Objects, actions, characters emerge; pictures and images flicker through the mind, some extraordinarily vivid, clearly defined, others as insubstantial as dreams, unrealistic and yet familiar. In reconstruction the cameo shots, the fragments, become part of a pattern. Fading ink on yellowing paper, cuttings and clippings from newsprint send signals to the brain, reactivate memory, and slowly the pieces fall into place to create a whole, though there are yawning caverns into which events have vanished without trace and thus the picture cannot be complete.

I decided to record my memories in a kind of diary and, since I am no longer the carefree little girl, the bewildered, lonely teenager, but an old woman, a spectator, describing the events of those years from a distance, I am to a certain extent interpreting the thoughts of childhood. I can recall certain conversations not from memory of when they took place but because they were recounted in later years by those who had been present at the time.

Grandma

PART ONE

The Magic of Childhood

Germany, 1928-37

1

The Innocent Age

Earliest memories are cameos, circumscribed but detailed. I recall the round face of a child with enormous blue eyes and a shining helmet of silver-blond hair from an oil painting that hangs in drawing rooms of successive homes. The solemn-looking child in the heavy gold frame is I, Gerda Erika Maria, nicknamed Peterle. The word is a diminutive of Peter. It clings to me into old age and causes embarrassment because it always necessitates explanations, so in the end I spell it Peta.

The room is large and lofty, the glossy parquet floor blissfully slippery, an ideal slide when Anna lets me wear the huge felt polishing slippers that she uses to keep it shining like a mirror.

Anna is one of the people who are important in my life because she is always there to answer my many questions when Mama is not around. Her boyfriend, Hans-Georg, is Papa's batman. He fascinates me because he makes Papa's riding boots shine like lacquer by spitting on the long shafts and rapidly turning the brush from wooden frame to bristle, spit and polish, spit and polish. When I try to imitate him by using this technique on my black patent-leather pumps, Anna is cross. 'You have even got the stuff in your hair,' she scolds, 'and goodness knows how I'll get it out.'

More important than Anna is Papa, devastatingly handsome in uniform, with jingling spurs and sword in pommelled sheath, and I am thrilled when he takes me to the stables in the barracks and the sentry outside the box springs to attention and presents arms.

But most important is Mama. She is love and warmth and total security and happiness.

Aunts and uncles come and go. I learn to distinguish between friend aunts and uncles and relation aunts and uncles. Aunt Mia, best loved of the relation aunts, is the innocent instigator of a nightmare that is to haunt me for years when, unaware of my presence behind a couch where I am playing with my doll, she talks with a friend about the battle of Verdun in which her youngest brother, Leo, died.

Mama and Papa have gone out. Anna is standing outside the door talking to Hans-Georg. I can see them because I have pushed a chair up to the window and am leaning out. This is strictly forbidden, but I am careful. The walls of the barracks are flushed rose; in the warm glow trees and house tops stand stencilled dark against a gold-green sky. Lights twinkle in the streets. The horses in the stables neigh drowsily, and the bugler is getting ready for 'lights out'. Carefully I detach two sticky lumps of sugar, purloined that afternoon from the silver sugar basin, from the inside of my pyjama pocket. Leaning as far out as I dare, I push them to the end of the window ledge for the stork that stands on the stable roof, one bright red leg tucked under his white wings. If he finds them, he will bring me the longed-for baby brother.

In bed I pull the duvet cover up to my lips where I can nuzzle its comforting softness. I make strenuous efforts to keep my eyes open, for I want to stay awake to see the stars cascading over the black roof tops. As always I am afraid of missing something wonderful by going to sleep. As always sleep overtakes me. *Soldaten müssen schlafen gehn und nicht zu lange bei den schönen Mädchen stehn, der Hauptmann hat's gesagt.* Tonight the familiar tune of the bugler, previously always associated with Anna and Hans-Georg kissing each other goodnight under the lamp-post, swells and becomes a hideous roar. It sets in motion images evoked that afternoon by the account, overheard and imperfectly apprehended, of booming guns, grenades, explosions, bayonets, pools of blood, men screaming in pain, crazy-eyed men laughing and a monster caterpillar rearing. And then there remains only the corpse of Uncle Leo, whose head has been blown off and is never found again.

Awake with the screams echoing in the dark room, I lie rigid, waiting for the corpse now faintly outlined in the starlight at the far end of the room to advance. Then suddenly the room is flooded with light, and I am safe in Mama's arms, rapturously sniffing the familiar scent, pressing my hot cheek to hers, fluttering wet lashes against the cool softness of her skin in butterfly kisses as my sobs subside until, in the delicious warmth of her tender embrace, I drift once more into sleep.

Friday is market day and special. The *Schönwälderinnen*, apple-cheeked peasant women in voluminous skirts and billowing underskirts, have come to sell their wares. Their stalls are piled high with boxes of brown eggs, great primrose slabs of butter, cans of foaming buttermilk, smaller ones of thick yellow cream, and pyramids of snowy curd cheese, and the women coax with soft, lilting voices. *'Kommen Sie, junge Frau, Hähnchen, weich wie Rosinen.'* Delicious smells of the dairy mingle with those of soup greens, lovage, parsley, marjoram. Best of all are the bonnets covered in starry flowers, exquisitely embroidered by the *Schönwälderinnen* in rainbow-coloured silks. They are so beautiful that I bury my nose in them, half expecting to smell their perfume. Mama buys two for me, a red one for weekdays and a white one for Sundays. Above the ears the corners bend upwards like wings. I am enchanted.

Each season has its own magic.

'Easter is late this year,' says Mama. I am impatient. It should be here now, for I am eager to go to my beloved birch woods where the translucent blue sky peeps between slender branchlets that hang gracefully from pearly silver trunks, and fragile pointed green leaves and yellow cat-kins tremble in the breeze. I want to look among the dewy scented primroses for the chocolate, marzipan and nougat eggs that the Easter bunny has hidden for me to find.

May spells pomp and pageantry. Dressed all in white, I struggle with the silver button hook to fasten my white strap shoes.

'Let me,' Anna says. 'They are too tight because they are new.'

Papa wants me to learn to do things for myself. 'There is no such thing as can't,' he says. 'It's buried in the church-yard, and next to it lies won't.'

Mama comes in singing, *'Maria, Maienkönigin, es soll der Mai Dich grüssen.'* She brings a basket full of flower petals for me to scatter in the path of the procession in which the Queen of Heaven is carried past houses decorated with young saplings, foliage and flowers. The air is heavy with the scent of lilies and incense.

As I pass Anna kneeling by the roadside, she whispers, 'Be careful of wasps.' A short while ago, while putting my hand on a flower, I was stung by a wasp and had to go to hospital, where Mama was told that I am allergic to wasp stings.

My favourite flowers are lilies of the valley and lilac, but in summer I pick big bunches of deep blue corn-flowers, starry marguerites and scarlet-faced poppies in sun-drenched, billowing cornlands that are an ocean of splendour beneath a blue, blue heaven. I wear dresses that Mama has embroidered with garlands of them. They are for special days and for watching parades and the grand march-past.

'Which do you want to wear today, the sky-blue or the cream?' Anna's cheeks are flushed: Hans-Georg is coming back from manoeuvres. The sun is reflected in shining boots marching in rhythmic step, bounces off yellow brass instruments. Men and women, boys and girls line the road, feet tapping to the rhythm of the band, lips parted, eyes sparkling.

At the head of the platoon ride Papa and Colonel von Bartsch, a dearly loved friend uncle. When he sees me he calls out, 'Hello, Gerda Erika Maria,' and the next moment I am sitting in front of him on his frisky horse and among the cheers of onlookers enter the barracks in triumph.

Mama is beautiful, slender and straight as a young birch tree. Her hair, of the glossy red-brown of chestnuts when first they burst from their spiky green shells, is smoothly parted and drawn back, coiled low on her fragile neck in a heavy silken knot; her green eyes sparkle and dance as she holds out a huge cartwheel hat — her new hat for the garden party. That never-to-be-forgotten garden party: the music of Kalman, Léhar and Strauss floating on blue radiance, the fragrance of roses tumbling over garden walls, sunlight falling in showers on uniform tunics, gossamer dresses, clanking spurs, bright sword hilts.

The smiling bandmaster hands me tl · silver-tipped baton. With all eyes upon me I stand petrified, incapable of movement until galvanized by the opening bars of the favourite piece, the Radetzky march, I raise my head, my eyes. Copying every remembered movement of the bandmaster, intoxicated and carried away by the rousing music, I look from player to player and imperiously direct their instruments in the music that is to fill my heart with a warm rejuvenating glow for years to come.

The leaves that drift in showers of russet and gold from autumn trees rustle and whisper under my feet. Autumn bonfires crackle and spit in fields prickly with stubble. Potatoes roasted in the glowing embers, raked out and eaten black and searingly hot, taste more delicious even than the nursery rice pudding floating in pools of brown butter under a crust of sugar and cinnamon. The days are drawing in and it is getting colder but, enfolded in the cosiness of the loved stables, I am wonderfully warm. Under the rafters fragrant heat radiates from the horses' bodies, and through the cobwebbed windows I see uniformed figures drilling, hear the voice of the handsome young lieutenant: 'Sta-and easy, grou-ound rifles, di-s-miss.' When I grow up and am beautiful like Mama, I am going to marry him and will live with him and Mama for ever and ever.

Mama and I are gathering fir twigs for the advent wreath. Behind a ridge of cloud the setting sun flames blood red. It is the red-hot glow of the heavenly baking oven. The angels are very busy just now, mixing and rolling and baking the spiced honey *Lebkuchen* for Christmas. Anxiously I gaze at the fiery glow. They might get their lovely wings singed. As the glow fades, I breathe a sigh of relief, the danger is past for today.

In the morning the windows are magically transformed by a tracery of ferns and flowers. My warm breath makes smoky clouds in the air and leaves a clear patch on the window pane. No snow yet, but frosted boughs and twigs glitter and sparkle in the sunlight. Breath steams from the nostrils of horses, and the sentry outside his box stamps his feet and claps his hands.

Next morning, when Mama draws back the curtains, snow is falling silently outside the window, drifting softly and dreamily, transforming the whole world. Dustbins and coal bunkers are hidden under a gleaming white coverlet.

Leise rieselt der Schnee,
Still und starr liegt der See,
Weihnachtlich glänzet der Wald,
Freue Dich, Christkind kommt bald.

My favourite Advent carol speaks of softly-falling snow, frozen lakes and sparkling woods decked out in Christmas splendour to await the Christ-child. But how soon is soon? Will Christmas ever come?

When it comes at last, I try hard to sit still while Papa turns the pages with pictures of the manger, angels and shepherds and little lambs. With half an ear I listen to the well-known story of the birth in the stable. With the other half I anticipate the longed-for tinkling of the small silver bell that will tell us that the Christ-child has come, has lit the candles on the tree and has placed the presents under it. Then both wings of the large doors connecting dining room and drawing room are flung open, and I stand speechless before the glory of the tree that reaches from floor to ceiling. Rapturously I sniff the pungent scent of fir, melting candle wax, apples, marzipan and *Lebkuchen*.

Before we open our presents we sing, concluding our carols with 'Silent Night'. In the manger under the tree sleeps the heavenly babe, and in my arms I cradle the baby doll that the Christ-child has brought for me. I croon gently to it, pretending that it is the baby brother that the stork still has not delivered.

I am not yet allowed to go to Midnight Mass. The bliss of taking the sledge ride under the stars, of waiting in the great silence in which the whole world is held for the jubilant, exultant voices to proclaim the miracle of Christ's birth, of watching the incense drifting in fragrant clouds that form haloes around bowed heads is yet to come.

Endless days of light, of music and laughter; but in the shadows always the monster, formless and dark, rearing its hideous head, ever ready to spring and destroy. Everywhere I see men without arms and legs, each one a reminder of Uncle Leo's mutilated body. War is a constant topic of conversation among those who remember it vividly, and sometimes in the music of the gay marches I love I think I can hear the mutter of guns, and it fills me with sick horror. Then I hide in my secret world, a world of flowers and birdsong that I drift into when Mama sings to me in a voice that is sweet and low.

There comes the day when Anna, who is hanging up the washing in the drying loft, lifts me up to the skylight. The evening is already alive with stars. From the ground they look infinitely remote, but here they swing and tremble so

17

near! I feel that by reaching up I can gather the crystal points of light in my arms, and as I gaze I become aware of a joy so great that I chuckle with delight, for quite suddenly I know that God is here.

'*Lieber Gott, mach mich fromm, dass ich zu Dir auf den . . . komm.*' It is a childhood prayer in which I ask God to make me good, so that I can come to him. But that night I make a change, using the word 'loft' in the place where I should have said 'heaven'. This leads to a long and serious discussion with Mama during which I tell her about the joy, and also about the funny ache inside me that I cannot understand because it so often comes when I am very happy, when I listen to the buzzing of the bees, smell the flowers, look at the loveliness of the stars or at snowflakes. Mama has explained how each little flake is made of thousands of shining ice crystals, of stars and arrows. Every one of them is unique, she says, and God, who has created all things, has made each one of us unique and special. He loves us and everything he has made, and he especially loves me and cares for me. But why war? Why does he, who has made us and loves us, let war happen and allow people's heads to be blown off? Mama says it is too late and we shall talk about this tomorrow. Sleepily I think of the love by which I am surrounded and happily give myself up to comfort and safety.

2

Family Gathering

Grandpapa lives in a big house on the outskirts of Hindenburg, where I was born. The town is named after Generaloberst Paul von Hindenburg, Reichspräsident and head of state, the celebrated hero of Tannenberg. Mama's papa is a giant of Olympian stature, erect, straight as a ramrod, with a melancholy face, shaggy eyebrows, snow-white hair and beard. Each morning and evening he reads the Bible to the members of his household in a voice of profound doom. Today is his birthday, and Anna has put out my party frock of white spotted muslin, high waisted with little puffed sleeves and a sash of sky-blue satin tied at the back in a butterfly bow.

Seated in a large armchair garlanded with flowers, Grandpapa receives his guests. We, the grandchildren, approach timidly, the girls curtseying and the boys bowing from the waist. Mama and the aunts and uncles use the formal '*Sie*' when addressing their father or Grandmama, who is really Step-Grandmama because she is his third wife and has had no children of her own.

Neither Grandpapa nor Grandmama like children. Aunt Therese has brought her last born, a very new baby boy. Grandpapa stabs a finger at the lacy white bundle. 'More cannon fodder, eh?' Aunt Therese is offended but says nothing. Aunt Mia, the fearless, protests, but Grandpapa laughs derisively. 'We are on the brink of civil war, with riots and fighting every day. Six million unemployed. *Six million*,' he repeats, and then continues. 'Every few days people are killed when the Communists and that other lot, what do they call themselves, the NSDAP, come to blows.'

Uncle Joseph, the youngest son, raises his eyes defiantly. 'The NSDAP are finding more supporters every day. We could do with a strong authoritarian government, one that can deal with the menace of communism and can wipe out the shame of Versailles, which the *Nationalsozialisten* have promised to do.'

'And open the way to dictatorship,' Grandpapa thunders.

'You'd rather Germany was left without army, defence and honour?' The final slogan rings powerfully around the room — *heerlos, wehrlos und ehrlos* — an appeal to national pride.

Before Grandpapa can reply, Mama, behind whose skirt I have taken refuge, places me firmly on a stool in front of Grandpapa's chair. At once he swells and towers ten times life size. I begin to recite the poem that I have had to learn in honour of his birthday, speaking very fast for fear of forgetting the lines. Then a dreadful thing happens: a crystal drop appears at the end of Grandpapa's nose, and I am stuck. He knits his brows and looks ferocious. Hypnotized by the dew drop, I stand speechless. Only when it drops do I hear Mama's whispered prompt and am able to continue and finish with a gusty sigh of relief.

Cousin Heinz is next in line. His bow is so exaggeratedly low that he is in danger of toppling over. 'Your cousin is a holy terror; I pity Fräulein Gross,' sighs Anna on days when Heinz comes to stay. Anna is very pious and outraged by Heinz's irreverence. He once found her telling the beads of her rosary during a thunderstorm and shocked her by telling her that there was no need for her to be frightened: all the noise and water were due to the good Lord upsetting his bathtub.

Gross is a most inappropriate name for his nanny, who is tiny and spare. She was engaged for Christa, Heinz's older sister, who has been ailing from birth. She wears a high-necked blouse with a man's tie and on her nose are *pince-nez* that tremble when she is angry. Because Christa is a semi-invalid, Aunt Mia, so clear-sighted in everything else, has a blind spot where her youngest offspring is concerned, and she molly-coddles him despite his outstanding robustness. Unpredictable from the start, Heinz arrived in this world before there had been time to summon midwife or doctor and he has turned it upside down ever since. I, who cannot bear anyone to be cross, regard him with a mixture of disapproval and admiration.

We are allowed to go with Nanny to see Aunt Mia's cook make ice-cream. I walk sedately beside Nanny, avoiding the cracks in the paving stones to escape the unimaginable consequences that Heinz has told me will follow if I tread on them. The young man himself runs on ahead, using the elastic chinstrap of his sailor hat, which he has ripped off, as a catapult.

Cook is enormous. Neckless and waistless, she resembles the snowmen that I build in winter, even to her eyes, which are small and dark like pieces of coal. We adore her, for she is immensely kind and fills our pockets with goodies from her store-cupboard. I watch spellbound as she begins to turn the handle of the ice-cream machine at great speed. I am alarmed when she starts to pant and great drops of perspiration run down the sides of her nose, along the curves of her cheeks and on to her trembling chins, but the end result of her exertions is delicious.

We lose the chance of a second helping when Nanny comes to collect us. Heinz is to have his daily dose of cod-liver oil. The sight of the tendered spoon sends him whooping upstairs, with Nanny in hot pursuit.

I wait, sitting on a chair in the drawing room, gazing at a full-length painting of Aunt Mia. She is dressed in white, full busted, hour-glass waisted, her luxuriant gold hair piled high on her head, a sheaf of flowers in her round, bare arms. Self-confident, independent, despotic, generous, loving and loved, she, the eldest of six, effortlessly slipped into the role of mother to her brothers and sisters when their mother died. She forfeited Grandpapa's respect by marrying into trade. Her husband's business, already successful at the time of her marriage to him, prospered exceedingly after she brought her acumen, vitality, creative energy and efficiency to bear on it. Her husband, Uncle August, mild, gentle, fastidious and somewhat timid, gladly abdicated when his forceful, energetic wife took over.

Back at Grandpapa's, the talk is still of crises, but this time I am interested in the topic, for I like to hear about the time when money was not counted but weighed in suitcases and washbaskets, and packets of biscuits cost 400 milliard marks.

At dinner we children sit together with Nanny at the lower end of the table. We are not allowed to speak unless spoken to and have to content ourselves with making faces at each other. I cry out when Heinz kicks me under the table, but fortunately Grandpapa does not notice. He is congratulating himself on having put most of his capital into real estate, where it is safe. Heinz, who hero-worships the father of one of his friends, a flying ace in the war, electrifies us by directing his impudent gaze at Grandpapa and announcing in his clear, high voice, 'Anyway, Karl says that in the next war all the houses will get bombed.' He accompanies this announcement with appropriate gestures and noises intended to indicate the nosedive of a plane about to drop an invisible bomb into his soup. Grandpapa's eyes flash angrily under jutting white brows.

Then Uncle Joseph, suppressing laughter, turns to his father. 'You see, sir,' he says, 'the phrase "safe as houses" can no longer be applied.'

We are staying overnight with Aunt Therese when I am woken by frightening sounds. After a while I pluck up my courage and run to the window. In the street below me a seething multitude, from which issue threatening noises, ebbs and flows. Street lights glint on helmets and, as I become accustomed to the half-light, I see hands wielding truncheons and fists raised to strike. Then Mama comes and carries me to a room at the back of the house. When I return in the morning to collect my clothes from the room the duvet has been stuffed into the window embrasure. 'To stop the bullets,' Anna explains when I tell her about it.

I long to go to school, partly because of the customary cone of sweets that I will be given on the first day, but mostly because I long for the company of other children. The school year starts at Easter but, because I shall not be six until July, I have to wait another year. I have an imaginary playfellow who makes up for the fact that I have few real playmates. There are fine shades of class distinction, and I am only allowed to play with carefully selected children.

Anna, who is beating the long red hall carpet that she has flung over the carpet rail in the courtyard, will not let me help her because of the dust, but out in the meadow the bed- and table-linen that she has spread out to bleach in the sun is dry and will have to be sprinkled for further bleaching. Mama and I set out with watering cans. Overhead a plane circles, and then to my delight innumerable white doves flutter down. Most of them descend on the barracks, but one or two drift in our direction. I run towards them and find that they are printed sheets of paper, which Mama, to whom I hand them, crumples up and puts in her pocket. I keep one for Anna, who later helps me to read what is printed on it. 'Unity, solidarity, peace, order and work,' and below this, 'Give Adolf Hitler your vote and he will give you work and bread and freedom.'

Anna sighs, 'It's what we need all right.'

The name Hitler is becoming familiar. Paul von Hindenburg has been Reichspräsident since I was born. I hear snatches of subdued conversations held behind closed doors. Grown-ups are mostly unaware of the acute hearing and perception of children. I am in love with words, hoard them and store them so that I can take them out at a later stage and re-examine them. There is a party that Papa cannot — no, *will not* — join. 'Not even as a mere formality,' he says, 'because in doing so I would lose my liberty of conscience.'

The advertising pillars carry posters on which appear the names of Hindenburg and Hitler. Hindenburg is very old and, though he reminds me of Grandpapa, I passionately want him to win because subconsciously I connect the name of Hitler with the party that will take away Papa's 'liberty of conscience'. I don't know what this is but feel that it must be precious. Hindenburg is re-elected. Shortly afterwards the Reichstag is dissolved and another election campaign starts. The word *Nationalsozialismus* and the names Hitler, Goering and Goebbels are heard more and more frequently. Uncle August, whose home town is Hamburg, comes to tell us that a friend of his has been killed in street riots there along with eighteen others, and that in the same night three hundred people were injured.

On the kitchen cupboard stands the wireless. The needle in Anna's fingers flies backwards and forwards while I watch. She is making a pinafore for 'big dolly', drawn threadwork embroidered pink. 'A pinafore fit for a princess,' she says, but I reflect that princesses don't wear pinafores because they never get dirty. From time to time I touch the 'snails' over my ears. Anna has plaited my hair, wound the plaits round and round over my ears and fastened them with hairpins.

The music from the wireless is interrupted by the voice of the announcer. 'The chancellor Adolf Hitler will in a few minutes issue an autonomation to the German people.' The statement is repeated in English, and I wish that Papa, who is an ardent anglophile and is always reading *The Times*, were here. I store away the word 'autonomation', repeating it to myself several times. This morning my teacher has told us about Hitler, who is to save Germany from Bolshevism, and has called him a prophet sent by God to wipe out the shame of Versailles.

These words 'the shame of Versailles' remind me of what Uncle Joseph has said. When Hitler begins to speak, I am relieved that the message is not as obscure as the word 'autonomation' has suggested but seems to consist mostly of a request for four years of time. Anna switches off when the transmission to America begins, and I am sorry, for I am fascinated by the sound of foreign languages. Papa often calls Mama or me 'sweetheart' or 'darling', and I know that this is English and like it.

3

Disturbing Changes

The date is 5 March 1933. Mama, Papa and I are listening to the wireless, from which emanate the ecstatic cheers of a multi-thousand voice bursting into great roars of *'Sieg Heil'*. From the window I watch men in brown and black uniforms moving forwards as one, their jackboots hitting the ground in perfect unison. I watch the torchlight parades of the SA and SS forces with their waving banners and hands raised in the Hitler salute, while Mama weeps.

Almost since birth I have been aware of danger outside, in the streets, but home has always been a haven of safety. Now I am conscious of an element of disturbance, a subtle change in the once-happy atmosphere, of mounting tension, sentences left incomplete, whispers behind the hand, behind closed doors. I store away the words 'denounced', 'demoted', notice a difference in Papa's shoulder strap. Mama, who has always gone about singing, is quiet and withdrawn. Her eyes are no longer bright with laughter; they are more often red and swollen. My immature mind is struggling to comprehend what is baffling and puzzling, trying to fathom why my world, once so safe and happy, has changed.

We are to move from Gleiwitz. Herr Goldstein, my piano teacher, looks sad when I tell him that I shall be back to visit him. 'Bad times, bad times!' he sighs. I lie on the back of Gerda Erika Maria, the mare named after me by Colonel von Bartsch, my cheek pressed against her silken

26

neck, stroking the mane, the soft ears and sob my heart out. To feel secure I need permanence, and in Miechowitz, the town to which we move, my insecurity manifests itself in recurring nightmares in which I am constantly looking for our old home, familiar landmarks and the people I miss and never find them.

By now Hitler's face is becoming familiar. The newspapers are full of photos of him, looking kind and benevolent, surrounded by adoring, cheering crowds, by children waving banners. People in the streets no longer greet each other *'Guten Tag,' 'Guten Abend'*. Instead they call *'Heil Hitler'* and raise their arm in the Hitler salute.

My new school is a state school. I loved the convent, where the nuns were kind and gentle, even though I was badly frightened by end-of-term plays depicting hell and purgatory. Now all of school is torture. Even though I am ahead in some subjects, I am hopelessly behind in others and, however hard I work, I do not appear to be able to catch up. The worst subject of all is *Leibesübung* — physical education. Though I enjoy riding, skating, skiing and ballet, I am useless at gymnastics. The horizontal bars, parallel bars and vaulting horse inspire me with fear. My wrists are weak, I lack control, balance and, so I am told over and over again by the irate teacher, nerve. When I am forced to climb up to the top of the gym on frames fastened to the walls, I am overcome by dizziness. I cling to the bars with ice-cold, sweating hands while waves of weakness and nausea wash over me. One day I shall drop and this will at least be punishment for the hateful woman who calls me coward.

I have no friends among my new classmates and when, after desperate struggles with my shyness, I try to make friends, every attempt is brushed off by girls who are already pally with one or more others and resent my overtures. Most of them belong to the *Jungmädel*, the junior branch for girls of the Hitler Youth, the *Hitler Jugend*. I feel that if only Papa and Mama will let me join, all will be well. I also covet the uniform: brown skirt, white blouse, black triangular kerchief drawn through its braided leather knot, and the smart little imitation-suede jacket with leather buttons. When in December 1936 a law is passed to make membership compulsory, I am ecstatic. In my room I walk proudly up and down in front of the full-length mirror, stretching out my hand in the Hitler salute and softly calling '*Sieg Heil*' and '*Heil Hitler*'. I speak softly, because by now I know, even though they have never said so, that Mama and Papa disapprove.

My enthusiasm soon peters out. At first I enjoy the singing, the marches, the outdoor celebrations — especially at the time of the summer solstice, when piles of wood are lit on surrounding hills and we carry blazing torches. I feel moved to tears when I join in the mighty chorus of ardent young voices pledging their allegiance to *Fahne*, *Führer* and *Vaterland* — the flag, Hitler, and the fatherland. But soon I tire of marching, and I detest the contests in the stadium where I am made to feel excluded and ashamed because I do not excel in physical exercises, am never commended, never receive a certificate or pin. The purpose of athletics, we are told, is to steel our bodies and minds. My body and mind remain sadly unsteeled.

Papa is determined that I shall learn to swim. I have been swimming for a long time now, but always with a cork float around my middle that no one can persuade me to part with. Papa is angered by my mulish obstinacy and is losing patience. When, on my way to the changing rooms, I hand my float to Mama, he lures me on to the diving-board, allegedly to watch him dive; and then, turning round, he suddenly pushes me off the board.

The terrifying sensation of drowning is as nothing to the panic I experience when, spluttering and gasping, I manage to reach the safety of the aluminium ladder and, wrapped in Mama's protecting arms, hear the frightening edge to Mama's voice as she accuses Papa of trying to kill me. Papa's reply is sarcastic and scathing. To see the two people I love and who are always kind and loving to each other quarrel over me is more than I can bear. A pain inside my chest swells intolerably and, with the courage born of despair, I tear myself from Mama's embrace, run straight back to the diving-board and, without stopping, jump. This time I feel triumph instead of fear as I rise to the surface, because I have suddenly realized that I can swim without a belt; and the triumph changes to gladness when I see Papa putting his arm round Mama's shoulder and smiling.

By now Hitler is universally acclaimed as Germany's saviour. In 1935 the people of the Saarland, as agreed by the peace treaty of Versailles, are allowed to vote after fifteen years of French rule and thus to decide whether they want to remain part of France, return to Germany or exist under the rule of the League of Nations. The result of the plebiscite, run by the League of Nations with English soldiers ensuring the secrecy of the ballot, shows that 90.3 per cent of the electors are for the reintegration into Germany. We receive letters from friends abroad expressing their admiration for Hitler's achievements. In view of all this I am considerably puzzled by Mama's and Papa's silence on the subject of Hitler. I am once again conscious of sentences cut short or left incomplete whenever I enter the room, and instinctively I feel that their completion might spell trouble and that my parents want to spare me sorrow; but why and wherefore I cannot comprehend.

I have stopped calling my parents Mama and Papa because my class-mates think that it is babyish and un-German. Mother hardly ever goes out to parties, concerts or the theatre now. She, who has never had a day's illness for as long as I can remember, now often suffers from violent headaches and then lies, white as marble, in her darkened bedroom.

I love Sundays; no school, no physical education, and the deep joy of having Mother to myself when we sit together in church. On our way home she asks me if I would like to make my first communion at Whitsun. I am surprised, because I have previously been told that I will do so in just over a year's time, but I agree joyfully.

In the evening I am so excited that I cannot sleep and decide to go to the kitchen for a glass of milk. On passing the door to the drawing room I am arrested by Mother's voice pleading with Father. 'People no longer believe in God,' she cries bitterly. 'Their religion is *Nationalsozialismus*. Let her go now, before they stop us from going to church altogether.'

Who are 'they'? She has mentioned National Socialism: that means Hitler. Hitler would not stop people from going to church, of that I am sure. Does he not in every one of his speeches invoke the name of the Almighty and even end some of them with the word 'Amen'? However, these questions are replaced by others that soon occupy my mind to the exclusion of all else.

In order to receive communion I shall have to go to confession, and the thought of kneeling outside the confessional and whispering my sins through the grille into the ear of the priest terrifies me beyond measure. I revere the old priest, who I am sure is sinless, and the thought of telling him my sins fills me with shame and humiliation. Instructed by nuns and brought up in the Catholic faith, I have from an early age been made aware of the fallibility, the sinfulness of human nature. There are among the questions in the list I have been given for self-examination some that worry me, because I cannot understand them. Have I been unchaste? I dare not ask the priest and finally decide that I would know what it meant if I had transgressed in this way; but I feel uneasy nevertheless.

As the great day draws near I become totally obsessed with the conviction of my sinfulness and utter unworthiness, and am plunged into such misery that even the sight of my bridal dress, the wreath of white roses, the lace handkerchief, the candle garlanded with myrtle and the prayer book bound in white leather with its gold cross cannot relieve my morbid fears. On the day I kneel for hours before daring to approach the confessional where, cold and sick, I force myself to repeat through dry lips the list that I have rehearsed for days. When I stop, overwhelmed by the enormity of my sinfulness, I cannot believe what I am told. God loves me, has forgiven my sins before I confessed them, wants me, yes, even needs me. Incredulously I listen to the kind voice telling me to 'go in peace and love the Lord'. At home I kneel down by my bed to praise and give thanks, but I am overwhelmed by relief and fatigue. My head drops on to the duvet and I fall asleep; and this is how Mother finds me.

Next morning the room is lit by radiant sunshine that matches the happiness in my heart. All things are bathed in glory and the pure light of love. *Corpus Domini nostri Jesu Christi custodiat animam tuam in vitam aeternam.* The words of the liturgy promising eternal life through Jesus Christ echo through my mind. Thanksgiving and praise fill my heart with such joy that it seems impossible to contain it. The roar of the tremendous storm which breaks that afternoon holds no terror for me — I who am usually so frightened of thunderstorms can look calmly at the dark, tormented sky, the terrifying bolts of lightning, secure in the love that will never let me go.

4

Rumours of War

The summer is unusually oppressive, and it is during another thunderstorm that Father is carried on a stretcher into the infirmary. When I come home from school, I meet the six-year-old son of one of the stretcher-bearers. 'Your father is dead,' he announces importantly. 'They've just taken him in there.'

'Concussion,' says Anna. 'Thrown by his horse.'

Mother is with him, and all I can do is wait and pray. When Mother comes home to see me to bed, he is still unconscious. We pray together until I am overtaken by sleep.

When I wake it is dark but, as my eyes grow accustomed to the darkness, I can see that Mother is still kneeling by my bed. 'What time is it?'

She passes her hand gently across my face. 'Go back to sleep, darling, I'm just going.'

Father has come home to convalesce. Because of the oppressive heat, all the doors and windows are open to create a draught. I am reading in my room when I hear Mother's voice from the adjoining study where Father is resting on the couch. 'No, Bernd, no!' Then the thud of a heavy object falling to the floor. Then Father's voice, dull and toneless. 'He said it was the only way left to me.' And Mother's voice, hushed now, 'The child!' Dragging footsteps . . . a door closing gently . . . silence.

For a few moments I remain motionless, then cautiously

I approach the open door to the study. The room is empty. On the floor by Father's desk lies his revolver. I stare at it in disbelief as the full implication of what I have heard hits me. Later that afternoon Mother goes out. I have never seen her looking more elegant. The address she gives the driver is that of a very important person.

A new name begins to dominate the media: Mussolini, the *Duce*. In the geography lessons we learn about Eritrea, Somaliland, Abyssinia and Addis Ababa. Somehow the events connected with these names add, without my knowing why, to my growing sense of insecurity. Father seems to have recovered, but Mother suffers increasingly from migraines that keep her confined to her room for days on end, until one afternoon she is taken away in an ambulance.

'An overdose,' Anna tells the maid next door. Father has been called and has gone straight to the hospital. Once again I am left alone with my fears. It is then that I decide that the only way in which I can conquer them is to train myself to be indifferent. I do not know what stoicism is, but instinctively I feel that self-pity is despicable and cowardly and that I must be courageous and overcome my fears. It is very hard to fight anguish when the person one is anxious about is the person one loves most in all the world and, when Father comes home and takes me in his arms, I cry as though my heart must break. 'Poor child,' he says, 'poor, poor child.' Then he explains that it will be necessary to send Mother away for a while to where she will have peace and quiet and that, if I would like to, I can go with her.

In the days that follow Father spends a great deal of time phoning, and I learn that Mother is suffering from severe depression and a nervous breakdown.

Two weeks later we sit in the little mountain train that is puffing and groaning like an asthmatic old man as it

33

climbs higher and higher into the Riesengebirge mountains of Lower Silesia. Mother, sitting opposite me, looks pale and very fragile, but I am happy — happy to have her to myself, happy because the sound of the chugging engine, begging us to 'push and shove', and the acrid smell of coal dust remind me of the first time I travelled in this train. Then I imagine the glowing sparks of the engine to be coming from a fire-breathing dragon. They remind me also of the winter when the scrubby hillsides were so deeply blanketed after a heavy fall of snow that only the tops of trees and signposts were visible, and Opa's house was so completely snowed in that we had to ski out of a first-floor window. And I remember watching the sun rise on the high peak of the Schneekoppe, when crimson flags blazed across a sky of palest opal as the sun like a flaring bonfire lit peak after peak, dipping each into gold and rose, saffron and lilac. It had been a moment of sheer magic, and I am longing to repeat the experience.

I call Father's father Opa to distinguish him from Grandpapa in Hindenburg. His family left the Austrian Tyrol during the persecution of the Protestants and came to the Riesengebirge. They called the village where they settled Zillerthal, after the place they had to leave. He has come to meet us. Tall and erect, his back as straight as the trunks of the tall fir trees that surround his house, he resembles the legendary giant Rübezahl. His eyes, at first sight disarmingly round and blue, are shrewd and resolute and can snap alarmingly under the bristling brows of snowy white that match the hair on his head, his magnificent whiskers and his small, fiercely projecting beard. When he smiles, which does not happen very often, he reveals a magnificent set of strong white teeth which he cleans with soap and occasionally salt, dismissing toothpaste as a totally unnecessary refinement.

While Mother is having a rest, I am left alone with Opa. I fidget and wonder how I can get away. Opa, who watches me intently from under his bushy eyebrows, puffs at his

34

pipe and says nothing. At last, indicating a chair opposite him, he commands, 'Stop fidgeting and sit down.' I subside apprehensively and nervously clasp my hands in my lap. 'So your mother's had a nervous breakdown. I told your father, right at the start, beautiful women are usually useless.'

'Mother is not useless, and she has only been ill since . . . since . . . '

'Since that fellow Hitler came.'

Bewildered, I stare at him. 'No. . . Why. . . ? I mean Hitler is all right, he has done a lot, he's given people . . . ' I falter, then the words first read out to me by Anna, and since then heard and read many times, come to my aid, and I repeat them in one breath: 'Unity, solidarity, freedom, peace, order and bread.'

Opa sucks his pipe and glares at me. When I think I can stand his silent scrutiny no longer, he spits out one word: 'Brainwashed.' I jump as he thumps the table with his fist. 'Freedom! Who is free? Are the media free to write, to broadcast? Are you free to assemble with others? What books are you allowed to read? Are you allowed to read Heine, Kästner, Mann? They burned *their* books. Hitler!' he snorts contemptuously. 'A little Austrian corporal, a megalomaniac.'

At night I toss restlessly on my bed. Opa's denunciations echo in my mind. I am totally confused. I remember the riots, the street fights, the queues outside food shops and banks. Since Hitler came they have ceased. People look contented. New houses, roads, factories and cars are being built. Opa is the first one I have heard speak out against Hitler. Then I remember the secrecy with which the subject of Hitler is surrounded at home, our sudden move, the frightening, still-unexplained incident with the gun. I am deeply disturbed and frightened, and very relieved when two weeks later we move on to Austria.

Austria, the country of my ancestors! I am enchanted with everything — the mountains, the towns and villages, the gaiety and the people. The topic most frequently discussed here is the *Anschluss*. The remarkable change that Hitler has brought about in the economic situation in Germany in four years seems miraculous, and those to whom we speak want him to do the same for Austria. They wanted the *Anschluss*, they tell us, after the war, but the Allies not unnaturally refused to agree to a measure that would have extended the borders of the defeated Reich.

I have become an avid reader of newspapers and see that military service has now been introduced in Germany. This, we are told, is necessary in order to safeguard the peace. The Russian army has increased its force and France is about to introduce conscription. On the day of the army, the *Tag der Wehrmacht*, Hitler declares that only strong peoples are blessed by peace. The fact that Germany is once more strong is due first and foremost to its highly-trained and newly-equipped soldiers. When I next open the paper, I read of the formation of the Rome-Berlin axis.

Mother is well again and missing Father but, when she writes to tell him that we are ready to return, he replies by urging her to stay a little longer as there are certain developments that make it inadvisable for us to return just now.

There has been a meeting on the Obersalzberg between Dr Kurt Schuschnigg, the Austrian federal chancellor, and Hitler. We are told that the Austrian chancellor has endeavoured to find with Hitler a way that is in the interests of the German people, whose sons they both are.

A few weeks later the German government issues an ultimatum. The federal president is to reform his government according to suggestions from the German government and appoint as chancellor a candidate named by them. Failing this German troops will march into Austria. Schuschnigg orders the army not to resist, and on the following day German troops cross the German-Austrian borders, among them my father. The missiles the troops encounter are flowers thrown in greeting by a rapturous population.

PART TWO

Momentous Events

Austria, 1937-46

5

A Meeting with Hitler

On 15 March 1938, in Vienna's Heldenplatz, Hitler addresses an ecstatic crowd of more than 100,000:

Ich kann somit in dieser Stunde dem deutschen Volk die grösste Vollzugmeldung meines Lebens abstatten: Als Führer und Kanzler der deutschen Nation und des Reichs melde ich vor der deutschen Geschichte nunmehr den Eintritt meiner Heimat in das Deutsche Reich!

As leader and chancellor of the German nation, I am announcing in this, the greatest hour of my life, the entry of my homeland into the German Reich.

Carried away by the emotion, the enthusiasm, the hysteria, I too want to cry and cheer and shout 'Sieg Heil'. I remember Hitler's words at the beginning of his book, *Mein Kampf*, which we read at school, in which he states that he considers it fortuitous that he should have been born in Braunau on the Inn, situated close to the border of the two states, and regards it as an essential task to reunite German Austria once more with the great German homeland, and I feel happy and proud that German troops have brought about this reunification.

When Father joins us, we are appalled to see that during

our separation his hair has turned white, but we are happy to be reunited.

In April posters appear everywhere bearing slogans: 'Bit by bit Adolf Hitler has torn up the dictate of Versailles'; 'The whole of Germany acknowledges her liberator, Adolf Hitler'. A referendum is to take place in which Austrians are to express their agreement or disagreement concerning the reunification of Austria with Germany. Of an electorate of 49,493,000 people, 49,279,000 go to the poll and 99.7 per cent reply with a resounding yes. Austria's enthusiasm for her son is boundless. Wherever Hitler appears he is greeted by stupendous ovations.

I never hear anyone express Opa's opinion of him here and feel that, as he is very old and somewhat grumpy, it is to be expected that he should harbour queer notions. I have also come to understand that Mother has some kind of phobia which is connected with Hitler and that I must therefore be careful lest she become ill again. When I once try to question Father about his reticence concerning Hitler, he is totally non-committal and immediately changes the subject.

Everywhere I see pictures of Hitler surrounded by cheering crowds, ecstatic, adoring youngsters, and I am beginning to envy those to whom he speaks, little realizing that before long I shall come face to face with him myself.

Graz is preparing for the great event. Banners with the slogan *'Ein Volk, ein Reich, ein Führer'* stretch across the roads, proclaiming Austria's commitment to unity with Germany under Hitler. On public buildings red swastika flags ripple in the wind. One by one flags begin to emerge from the windows of private houses. Excitement grows to fever pitch. Hitler is coming, and I learn that I am to be one of the lucky ones who will have a chance to meet him.

I have a sleepless night. Father is away, but there is Mother. Is she going to expect me to stay with her? I am so preoccupied with my problem that I fail to see that she looks pale and ill. Only when I notice that she leaves her breakfast untouched do I become alarmed. My heart contracts: *No, no, please God, don't let her get ill again,* I plead; *I'll stay here with her if it will prevent her being ill*. When she smiles and tells me that she is going to lie down to stop a headache developing, I struggle with my conscience and, though I feel deceitful and ashamed, I cannot resist temptation. Surely it cannot be wrong to wish to see him. In her room I draw the curtains, kiss her and, after making sure there is nothing she wants, hastily and guiltily withdraw.

As I open the door, I come face to face with the caretaker. I jump guiltily when he asks if I am going to watch the ballyhoo. Instead of replying, I ask, 'Are you?' He laughs: he is not such a simpleton that at his age he is going to stand for hours buffeted by a hysterical, flag-waving multitude to see a man he can see any time he likes on the newsreel. I go back in and listen once more at Mother's door. No sound. With madly-beating heart, I run out of the house through deserted streets, through the park where the red squirrels who love to fetch nuts out of my pockets when I stop at a seat on my way home from school are today standing up in vain to beg, and on to the parade route, which is already lined with people standing five and six deep.

No traffic, no trams; a sound truck driving slowly between the police and SA cordons broadcasting announcements and leading the cheering, the singing, the mighty chorus demanding to see our Führer. At last, frightened and elated, I arrive at the place of the assembly. Here uniforms of every description abound. Then the intolerable waiting starts.

To pass the time we sing. Fleetingly I think of Mother lying on her bed in the darkened room, and then a sound, blotting out all thought, reaches my ears and steadily increases in volume. In my mind's eye I see the motorcade, pennants flying, slowly progressing. Hitler is standing in his car as I have so often seen him on the newsreel, hand outstretched, smiling at the waving multitude. Throats are choked with excitement, eyes blinded by tears of emotion; in a delirium of joy and happiness hands are raised to jubilant heights in the Hitler salute. At this instant everyone present feels that this is the moment in history to be talked about to children and grandchildren in years to come.

Then, as in the close-up of a film, everything fades and there is only a fair-skinned face, a wing of fine dark hair falling across a broad forehead, the compelling gaze of hypnotic blue eyes, the firm grip of his hand, a flash of gold as he laughs at something I have said in reply to his question, something to do with school, I think. I am aware of my madly-pumping heart and the blood roaring in my ears when he smiles kindly, pats my cheek and moves on to the next child in line.

What follows is of little interest to me, for the memory of the brief moment when I was actually speaking to the Führer, an event so momentous that it almost seems like a dream, makes all else pale into insignificance.

When I arrive home, Mother is lying as I have left her. Anticlimax! There is no one I can talk to about the stupendous happening of this day.

The house that is intended to be a temporary home for us is situated in a pleasant tree-lined avenue and within a few steps of beautiful countryside. I am blissfully happy. Mother and Father reunited, Mother completely recovered. I have a horse, Graziella. Our evenings are spent entertaining friends, among whom are actors from the playhouse and opera singers. Each week we go to concerts, plays or the opera. I spend a great deal of my time playing the piano and singing the arias of whatever opera we last saw. At weekends we drive into the mountains, walk and picnic or swim in the ice-cold water of a mountain lake.

School is the cloud that casts a dark shadow on an otherwise idyllic life. Though advanced in subjects such as Latin, French and English, I am sadly behind in Mathematics. English is not taught in my new school, and I don't know Italian, which is. Father, who is a brilliant mathematician, decides to take me in hand. He is soon thoroughly exasperated with my lack of comprehension and finds it difficult to believe that a child of his can be as dull as I appear to be. For the first time since the swimming incident our temperaments clash seriously, and I feel resentful. He has always been strict but, being compliant and anxious to please, I have rarely given him cause to be angry. I still try to please but become increasingly convinced that I am educationally subnormal. Mother acts as mediator, but my coaching lessons are torture nevertheless.

Leaving aside certain lessons, I like my new school because my new class-mates are fun. The Austrians are a happy people, pleasure loving and easygoing. 'The Germans say, first work, then play; but we say, first play, then work.' So runs popular sentiment. The summer seems endless, a succession of sunny days with, here and there, a thunderstorm that quickly blows over, and afterwards the sun shines as brilliantly as ever.

In the autumn a meeting takes place between Hitler and the British prime minister, Neville Chamberlain, to discuss the position regarding the Germans in the Sudeten who demand autonomy and eventually the annexation to Greater Germany. Czechoslovakia does not accede to the demand. It appears that the British prime minister is on our side, for he warns the Czechs not to mobilize and gives them an ultimatum, with twenty-four hours in which to reply. As a result over half a million Sudetendeutsche and 10,800 square miles of territory join Hitler's new Germany.

It seems reasonable to me that Germans in the Sudeten, like the Austrians, should want to belong to Germany; and, as Mr Chamberlain tells his people, Herr Hitler has to champion other Germans. Moreover, once this question is settled there will be no other territorial claims in Europe.

6

Declaration of War

Our house is one of three houses built around a central courtyard. The people who live in our block are, for the most part, elderly. Below us are a solicitor and his wife; above us, a *Frau Generalin* — the widow of a general — with an unmarried middle-aged daughter, a doctor, another solicitor, and a younger man with his wife and two very noisy boys; opposite us, an opera singer. I rush on to our balcony whenever his voice is heard through the open windows of his flat, irrespective of whether he is practising scales or singing arias.

On one such occasion I see on the balcony in the inner corner of the block a very old man sitting in a cane chair. An elderly woman spreads a rug across his knees, and presently a slight young girl comes out to chat with him. Hair as lustrous as Mother's and, like hers, parted in the centre surrounds her face in lovely half-moon curves. Though small of stature, she has a beautifully-proportioned figure, and I wonder how old she is. There are no children in the block of flats apart from the two boys, and I am therefore very interested in her.

One day when I am staring across to where she has just emerged, she turns and waves. I wave back delightedly. 'Come on down!' she calls. I nod and immediately make for the stairs. I am enchanted with what I can now see clearly: enormous eyes of a soft, pansy brown, fine dark eyebrows, a straight small nose and full lips, tilting upwards at the corners. Her name is Beatrice and, though she can be no more than five feet two inches tall, she is a year older than I.

'You are *Reichsdeutsche*, aren't you?' I incline my head. By now I am used to this question about my origins. Some of those who ask it do so in a tone suggesting admiration, others sound slightly condescending. The former regard those who have come to Austria from the Reich as superior beings; the latter consider themselves superior since they are natives of the country that gave birth to the Führer. I am relieved because Beatrice's tone of voice is neutral.

She lives with her grandfather, a retired navy admiral, and his housekeeper. After both her parents were killed in a car crash they moved from Trieste to live in Graz. We quickly become friends and, according to Mother, who takes the young orphan to her heart, inseparable.

Before long she confides in me. Her grandmother was Jewish. 'So you see, that makes me a quarter Jewish, both Grandfather and Father being Aryan and Mother half Jewish. Do you mind?'

I am bewildered, for there is in the tone of her voice a mixture of pleading and defiance. 'Why?' I ask.

'You are supposed to hate Jews.'

'But I don't, why should I?' She does not reply; just takes my arm and squeezes it, and her smile is joyous.

Tennis is the game at which she excels but at which I am, at best, mediocre. On the other side of the avenue are several tennis courts, and she invites me to play with her. I have to give the game my full attention, and it is not until I go to bed that I recall our conversation. I remember that Jews are forbidden to marry Aryans and know that I am Aryan because Father has had to research into his ancestry and provide proof of it. I also remember seeing posters telling the population to boycott Jewish shops and that Goebbels, the propaganda minister, has denounced Jews as 'world enemy number one, parasites among nations, the incarnation of evil'. I have had Jews pointed out to me in

45

Silesia: little oily men with sideburns, long black locks, long bony noses, flowing beards and caftans, invading Silesia in large numbers from Poland in order to escape from the terrible pogroms there. Grandpapa has nothing but contempt for them and describes them as glib tongued and quick brained, slick and secretive, men with a keen, uncanny instinct that sniffs out hidden sources of profit, so that they quickly become rich by cheating 'honest Christians'. Grandpapa, who has spoken so scathingly of the *Nationalsozialisten*, is now, so Aunt Mia tells us, a supporter of them. Is that because of the Jews, I wonder? What about Christ, the man whose teaching he professes to follow: wasn't he a Jew too? Beatrice doesn't look at all like the Jews I saw in Silesia. What is wrong with them as a race? It is a long time before I eventually fall asleep.

For some time now I have heard rumours about Czechoslovakia becoming German but have taken them to refer to the Sudetenland. However, in March 1939, Joseph Goebbels, in a proclamation to the German people, announces that German troops have entered Bohemia and Moravia and that the area is now a *Protektorat* under the auspices and protection of Greater Germany. Czechoslovakia has ceased to exist.

On our way home from school, Beatrice and I stop at 'our' seat in the park to feed the squirrels. They sit up prettily on their feathery red tails, their paws folded over their breast, waiting for the nuts, which they nibble daintily. When their cheek pouches are empty, they whisk their tails and climb the seat to explore our pockets for remnants.

Beatrice, who is emptying the last broken bits from a packet, startles me by saying, 'Grandpapa says we shall be at war within a few months.'

I freeze. War has been the threatening monster waiting to pounce ever since I heard of Uncle Leo's death. Mother was thirteen when the last war started, and Father was fighting in it at the very end. During my early childhood, when all the talk around me was of unrest, street fighting and economic crises, war was frighteningly close. Of late, the spectre of it has receded further and further until this moment, when Beatrice's words suddenly bring me face to face with it. But Hitler is a man of peace! Has he not declared over and over again that Germany will never go to war against any other nation? I try to convince Beatrice of this, but she only shakes her head. She believes implicitly in her grandfather's judgment.

We hear that the president of the United States of America has requested Hitler and Mussolini to take part in an international conference and answer questions regarding the aims of their policies. There are very many questions in my mind. I cannot talk to Beatrice, who has gone to Italy to visit relations. I miss her very much. Never before have I had a close friend and her friendship is very precious. Through her I am discovering things about myself; I am beginning to grow up.

When she returns we go for a long walk up the nearby Rosenhain. On our right we pass a building which is a home of recreation for the élite of the SS, young men in their early twenties, all over six feet tall, who have been selected for their physical perfection. On the wide sill of one of the windows a strikingly handsome SS man is sunbathing. He waves to us and smiles. Beatrice hurries me past.

'Don't look at him.'

'Why ever not?'

'You know what they are doing in there?' I don't, and wait for her explanation. 'Producing babies for the Führer.'

With the exception of a brief spell in Germany, I have been taught mostly by nuns. Babies and how they come about are something of a mystery to me. One of my classmates whose mother is expecting a baby has told me that the baby would emerge from her mother's navel, which would open up when the time came. This was news to me, for up to then I had always ascribed the increased size of an expectant mother to the milk accumulating in her body. I now tell Beatrice that she must be mistaken because I have never seen either expectant mothers or babies in there. The babies, she informs me, are not born there, and the girls who are to give birth to them have to go to a special home for unmarried mothers called a *Mutterheim* to have them. I am not totally convinced, the idea seems rather fanciful, but henceforth I give the house a wide berth. I am a little uneasy because of a mural I have once glimpsed through the open door, depicting muscular, firm-jawed soldiers and rosy-cheeked girls with long blond plaits marching hand in hand through cornfields, and somehow this seems to fit in with Beatrice's story.

Hitler's reply to President Roosevelt, as reported everywhere, has once again affirmed his abhorrence of war, and I tell Beatrice that it is possibly her grandfather's great age that is responsible for his gloomy prediction. She is offended and invites me to meet him so that I can see for myself that he is not senile, but when I at last see him we are already at war.

The summer holiday has started. Brilliant sunshine fills each day and, while the shadows of doom lengthen and the hellish sophistry that is to produce war is continued, Beatrice and I laugh and play. To improve my weak wrists that are responsible for the fact that I often throw the tennis racket after the ball when I hit it, I wear a leather strap; and when even then my playing improves only marginally, I tell her that for the sake of my self-esteem it is essential that I should teach her to ride. Later on, when the season starts, Mother encourages her to accompany us when we go to the opera, to plays and to concerts, and we spend more and more time together.

While we are away on holiday in Velden, Germany cancels her naval agreement with the UK and the non-aggression pact with Poland. England and France are trying to get Soviet Russia to give certain guarantees in case of an attack by Germany.

By the time we return, Germany has concluded a non-aggression pact with the Soviet Union. The Russians, whom Hitler has described as the Bolshevist oppressors of the world, the incarnation of the force of destruction and who, he has always insisted, are the one nation with which he will never make contact, are now our friends; the evil Slav monster is our close ally. All Germany, so Hitler tells us, welcomes the pact with Soviet Russia. The British were hoping to win Russia for themselves; we have beaten them to it.

We are still reeling under the impact of this news when we are informed of the general mobilization of Poland, of atrocities being committed against Germans. Names well known to me are in the news. The transmitter in Gleiwitz, where we once lived, has been attacked by Poles; the names of Ratibor and Kreuzburg are mentioned. I recall people speaking about a time when the Polish army was much in evidence in the Polish corridor and along the East Prussian border, and there had been fears of a Polish attack. Shortly afterwards the prophecy of Beatrice's grandfather is fulfilled when Great Britain and France, in accordance with their pact with Poland, declare that they are at war with Germany.

The spectre of war and death that for so long has menaced my security has drawn closer and closer, and now that the incredible has happened I try to accept it and its unimaginable consequences with as much stoicism as I can muster. This assumed stoicism fails me for the first time when, on 4 September 1939, a fighter squadron appears in the sky above the Adolf Hitlerplatz, the main square in Graz. With trembling legs and racing heart I prepare to run for shelter, expecting bombs to drop at any moment. The word *Stukas* pronounced by a man standing next to me causes the blood to rush to my face. I have very nearly made a fool of myself. I am, however, surprised that the sun still shines in the sky, that the pigeons wheel around me, hoping to be fed, and that everything looks exactly the same as before.

Now that what I have dreaded for so long has actually happened, I realize with a sense of relief that it is less terrible than I had imagined, and slowly the sense of doom that has settled on me begins to lift. There is even a certain feeling of anticlimax. Apart from special announcements on the wireless, apart from searchlights that play in the sky at night, crossing and recrossing like the thrusts of practising swordsmen, nothing seems to indicate that we are at war. Life goes on much as usual: we eat, sleep, work, and go to the theatre and concerts. In the pavement cafés perfumed women sit, chat and drink coffee and the elegant shops are as enticing as before.

Within days Warsaw is taken and Poland divided between Germany and Soviet Russia. Hitler announces that the Germans in Poland have been liberated.

By October the campaign in Poland is over. I breathe a sigh of relief when Hitler turns to the Western powers with the offer of peace, but am indignant when it is rejected.

Father is in the west where German troops are facing the French at the Maginot Line. He writes that nothing is happening there and that this period of silent confrontation is referred to as *Sitzkrieg* by our soldiers, *drôle de guerre* by the French and *phoney war* by the British. He is looking forward to coming home for Christmas.

On the morning of Christmas Eve I plod along to the shops. Snow is falling in thick feathers. On either side of the road the snowplough has left a wall of snow so high that I cannot see the vehicles driving along the road. In town the shop windows glow with colour, heat rises from iron braziers and the delicious scent of roasting chestnuts competes with that of apples, oranges and *Lebkuchen*. Last-minute shoppers hurry through streets that are garlanded with fir, and in the square, standing under the immense tree, children look up at the crystal points of light, their eyes sparkling, their voices raised in joyful song.

Back home I pick my way through branches of fir and boxes of fragile silver baubles to my room, where I shall wrap the presents that I have worked on for several weeks in an atmosphere of secrecy and excitement. By the afternoon the streets are deserted, the shops closed. The German broadcasting corporation has been transmitting festive music, carols and poetry since early morning. Time is passing intolerably slowly now, but at last the clouds turn from pink to a deep and fiery red, and then suddenly all colour is gone: it is evening.

After the meal, the carols and the present-giving, I curl up with my new books. The busy outside world is hushed, and inside the room is peaceful and fragrant. In the open grate of the large-tiled stove the flames of the scented logs whisper and dance and light up the silver and gold of the tree. I read and doze a little, and then it is time for Midnight Mass.

The wind is blowing powdery snow into our faces, and our boots crunch on the hard-packed snow. An occasional car drives along the muffled road, its headlights sparkling on frosted trees. All edges are blurred, all angles softly moulded in snow. In the arc of the sky the stars are shifting points of diamond, like the sparklers on our tree.

The church is crammed with a crowd of people who are motionless with expectation, their eyes fixed on the candles flowering on the trees that stand either side of the altar and reach right up to the vaulted ceiling. Uniforms are very much in evidence this year, but the joy is not yet muted as it will be in years to come. Twelve o'clock strikes, each stroke echoing in the hushed silence. Choir and clergy enter in their festive robes preceded by the cross-bearer, and at the final stroke of midnight an angelic voice sings out the first clear notes of 'Silent Night'. Gradually the congregation joins in the singing, and the music swells, reaching a jubilant crescendo with the words, 'Christ the

Saviour is here'. At 2 a.m. I snuggle under my duvet. The first Christmas Eve of the war is over.

Heinz has come to spend a few days with us. I have not seen him for some time and am amazed how tall he has grown. Though now in his early teens, he seems very young, and my attitude to his pranks has changed to one of tolerant amusement.

We ski during the day and in the evenings we skate on the *Hilmteich*, a large pond just outside Graz. While Heinz races along the frozen surface, skates flashing, arms flailing like windmills, Beatrice and I skim gracefully in and out of the shadows of the trees or circle the lake, performing intricate arabesques on the ice that in the moonlight becomes a shimmering sheet of iridescent silver. Both downhill skiing and skating induce in me a feeling of physical and spiritual weightlessness that is intoxicating. When the music coming over loudspeakers changes to a slow waltz, Beatrice and I move in time to it in a fairytale world of glittering snow and ice. Beatrice skates with flying grace, her skirt swinging out and revealing her straight slim legs. We cut figures, pirouette and spin, and sometimes just glide hand in hand. At night, glowing and tired, we fall into deep dreamless sleep.

In the new year we start dancing lessons. The dancing master, a Hungarian, speaks a mixture of French and German with a pronounced accent that delights us greatly. We are hilarious when, on introducing us to the quadrille, he solemnly announces:

> *Schönstes Danz is das Quadrille,*
> *kann man danzen wie man will.*

> Nicest dance is that quadrille,
> Can you dance as you will.

Our enjoyment of dancing the quadrille is immeasurably enhanced by the gleeful chanting of this ungrammatical, mispronounced phrase, and we collapse with helpless laughter when at last he raises his hands imploringly and cries, 'Please, please, ladies and gentlemen, a little more sobriety, *s'il vous plaît.*' This even produces a smile on the faces of our unfortunate chaperones.

On the way home we compare notes on our individual partners and their scintillating conversation.

'What did he say to you?' Beatrice enquires.

'He asked me if I like cheese!'

All the way home we giggle at the recollection of their performance. Some of the boys, whose ages range from fourteen to seventeen, are painfully shy and *gauche*. Though they have to wear white gloves to protect our dresses, we can often feel their sweaty hands through them. We polka, tango, waltz, foxtrot, quickstep and try to put up with sweaty hands and clumsy feet. To our delighted surprise we find after the first ten lessons that some of us are turning out to be excellent dancers, and even the boys acquire some social graces. One in particular, a slightly older boy, has very soon become an accomplished dancer. His name is Wolf, and Beatrice thinks he is aptly named. He is a leader in the Hitler Youth and very handsome. Most of the girls adore him, and he concentrates on them the full force of his ego, knowing himself to be irresistible. He reminds me of the SS men in the Rosenhain and Beatrice's remarks, and so I avoid him. I suspect that this piques him and offends his inflated ego, for he often singles me out and tries to impress me with his charm.

Before long stark reality once more intrudes into this carefree lull. In April Denmark and Norway are invaded and occupied by German troops. Fierce fighting breaks out around Narvik, a port in the north of Norway. A month later German troops attack Holland, Belgium and Luxembourg.

Beatrice and I are out in the country on our bikes and discussing this latest development. 'So much for observing the neutrality of states,' Beatrice snorts.

I am deeply troubled, and repeat to her what the announcer has said. 'England and France decided to attack Germany from the north; they are now trying to reach the Ruhr via Holland and Belgium. Surely,' I plead, 'we were forced into taking action.'

Beatrice stops abruptly, letting her bike fall into the grass by the side of the road. 'Do you really believe that?' When I do not reply at once she swipes savagely at the blades of the young green grass, 'Lies, all lies.'

'How do you know?'

She shrugs her shoulder: 'Propaganda!'

After a moment's silence she continues, 'You don't really believe that Poland attacked us, do you? Hitler needed an excuse for his aggression, so he pretended that we were being attacked. He thinks he can make the whole world part of his Great Germany.'

This seems to me so wild an exaggeration that I once more express the opinion that her grandfather's age is responsible for the extremist views he imparts to her. But she maintains that it is because he is old and because of his military experience that he can see through Hitler and his tactics.

I remember Opa calling Hitler a megalomaniac, a word stored away at the time but not forgotten. In the dictionary it is explained as 'insane self-exaltation, mania for big things'. Opa too is very old. Is it right to discredit the judgment of these men just because they are old?

Beatrice is looking at me speculatively. 'You ought to listen to the other side some time.' I stare at her. Anyone caught listening to foreign news stations is sentenced to hard labour. The slogan 'Beware of curiosity' appears on walls everywhere.

'Beatrice!' In my agitation I pull at the string of her blouse. 'You know it's strictly prohibited. They'll put you in prison if they find out.' She remains impassive. Then memory comes to my aid. 'What about *their* propaganda then? Do you believe every word *they* say? You know what they said in the last war, don't you? They said that the Germans in the territory they occupied gouged out the eyes of children and cut off their hands. Do you believe that too?' But what she has told me continues to haunt me, and so does my worry that what she and her grandfather are doing may be found out, and I am terrified of the consequences that this would have.

We are asked to hand in our skis for the soldiers in Norway. Sadly I watch my skis being taken away by a transporter, only to learn a little while later that since they are downhill skis they are of no use in a country like Norway.

7

Gathering Clouds

For some time now I have been uneasy about Mother. She has become more and more withdrawn. Of late it is Frau Trapp, who is housekeeper to Beatrice's grandfather, who has to chaperone us at our dance class, for Mother has become too apathetic to care and does not leave her room. She no longer prepares any meals, and when I urge her to eat something she shakes her head. She is getting very thin and her eyes are lustreless. Her skin, which when she is well has the sheen of ivory silk with just a faint tinge of pink, has become dull and tired looking. She hardly speaks and spends long hours in prayer.

I remember the time before, when she was taken away in the ambulance, and tremble. At school I am unable to concentrate, but I cannot talk to anyone about my worries because in people's minds the idea of a nervous breakdown is invariably associated with mental illness. I sense that especially now, with all the talk about a pure race, sound in body and mind, this is something dangerous, something to hide, something to be ashamed of.

When Mother does not seem to know me any longer, I am badly frightened. Beatrice comes to see me and together we enter the room where Mother is kneeling. She does not respond to my questions, does not even seem aware of our presence. Though for my sake Beatrice strives for calm and composure I can see that she is deeply troubled.

'We've got to get your father here quickly.'

I look at her helplessly. 'It will be days before he receives my letter.' And as the days pass and there is no response to my urgent request, I am at last forced to call the doctor.

When he enters her room Mother, who has not spoken for a long time, has shown no reaction to my coming and going, retreats in terror. She puts out both hands in a gesture of repulsion. 'Go away, go away,' she repeats over and over again. As she will not allow him near her there can be no question of an examination. He retreats, shutting the door behind him quietly.

'Are you the only relative here?'

I nod.

'Your father?'

'I have written some time ago but have had no reply.'

'I see.' His manner is brisk. 'She needs treatment, and urgently. I'll be back.'

I lie down on my bed, my face buried in the pillows. Several hours pass, and then he returns with two men in uniform. Through the window I see the ambulance.

'We've got to take her to hospital, you understand.'

'No, no; please don't take her away.'

He is not looking me in the eye but staring at a point somewhere just below my chin. With a shrug of his shoulders he turns and opens the door to Mother's bedroom. She is sitting on her bed, dressed only in a pair of pink silk camiknickers. His voice is brusque. 'Ask her to get dressed.' I look at him imploringly, hoping that he will leave the room; but he only retreats a few steps into the next room, leaving the door ajar so that Mother can see the two men behind him.

Her eyes widen, and I am appalled by the stark, naked fear in them. I try to put her dressing-gown round her, but she pushes me away. The doctor, tired of waiting, motions to the men to come forward. One of them holds something in his hand, and suddenly I understand. They are going to take her away by force and the thing he carries is a straitjacket.

I fling myself at them. 'No, no, no! Please don't, not that, please, please not that.'

For a moment they stand irresolute, then I hear Mother's voice, toneless but firm. 'I'll come.'

I pick up the dressing-gown that has slipped to the floor and she slides her arms into the sleeves and stands motionless while I button it up. Then, moving like a marionette controlled by strings, she moves forward and precedes the three men out of the room down the stairs and through the door that one of them has hurriedly thrown open, into the street and into the ambulance.

'Can I come?' I plead, but they are already locking the doors.

The doctor shakes his head. 'Not now, later. We'll tell you what to bring for her.'

Motionless I watch the ambulance disappearing in the distance, assailed by the feeling of bereavement that I will feel years later when I follow the hearse that is to take her away for ever. When eventually I turn to go back into the house, I see faces in the window of the ground floor flat and know that what they have witnessed will soon be common knowledge.

In Mother's bedroom I stand and look at the bed where she has been sitting such a short while ago. A heavy silence fills the room and seems to beat in my ear. I feel forsaken, and overcome by a great desolation such as I have never known before. I fall on my knees and pray. Through the open window drifts the scent of jasmine that for ever after remains a symbol of heartbreak and loneliness.

I must have fallen asleep, for when I next look around me, it is very dark. I don't know where I am and there is a feeling of unreality all about me. Then memory comes flooding back, and with it the terrible pain of bereavement. The doctor has promised to ring me from the hospital. Have I been so deeply asleep that I have not heard the bell? I pull out the directory and look up the number of the hospital. The voice at the other end of the line sounds sleepy. As best as I can I explain the situation and am advised to ring again in the morning.

After a restless night I wake once more to the same fierce pain. Stoicism is no help; instead I hug self-pity to myself. For days I have managed on my own, and this is going to continue. I am all alone and not yet fifteen. Desperately lonely, I want to be comforted, I want love, I want Mother. The thought of Mother makes me feel ashamed, and apprehension and worry take over from self-pity. What is happening to her? I must find out, must act. I must also cease to regard myself as the centre of the universe around which all must revolve, must face the fact that I am no longer a child, that a sense of security is an illusion that I can no longer cling to. Above all I must develop stoicism, for if I do not, I too will crumble and will have to be taken away.

When I phone the hospital again I am told to ring the *Nervenheilanstalt* — the mental hospital. Fear flickers, for the name recalls rumours, sentences overheard in whispered conversations, pictures of people considered unfit for life, the word 'euthanasia', the sudden inexplicable deaths of people considered mentally unstable.

Resolutely I focus on practical matters. I shall buy some presents to take to Mother. By now she must have had some treatment and will undoubtedly be better, will be able to talk to me.

Clutching my purchases, some pink and white carnations, a bunch of grapes, and an exquisite bedjacket quilted in white silk and embroidered with tiny rose-buds, I follow the nurse along the grim corridor. From a room ahead of us a woman emerges. She moves quickly towards us on very high heels, then stops and with her heels executes a rapid tattoo on the spot. The nurse motions me past her, but I turn and encounter a look of such panic in the woman's eyes that I know I shall never forget it.

In passing I notice that there are small spyholes in the doors and, when the nurse takes a key from a bunch hanging at her waist to unlock the door in front of which we have stopped, I am convinced that I have come to a prison and not a hospital. Before I have time to speak she has disappeared, locking the door behind her.

Mother is kneeling on the floor, looking up at a barred window. The room is small and almost bare. In a corner stands an adult-size cot with sides made of strong wire mesh. Putting down my case, I kneel down beside Mother and hold out the flowers to her. I open my mouth to speak, but the drone of aircraft drowns my voice, and for a moment several fighter planes flying in formation are framed in the window. Mother grabs my arm. 'There he is, do you see him? He's come to destroy us all, to destroy the whole world!' Her voice is rising higher and higher as she shrieks, 'Hitler, Hitler, the Antichrist.'

I throw my arms around her and am holding her as she struggles and screams, imploring her to be calm. Then the nurse is back, in her hand a syringe. In one swift movement she pushes up Mother's sleeve and inserts the needle. When Mother has become quiet, the nurse asks me for help to lower her into the cot. After fastening the side and securing it, she takes me by the arm and leads me out of the room.

I feel as though the life has been shaken out of me, and in the corridor I lean weakly against the wall. My demand to see someone in charge is rejected. When I question why Mother is locked in, has to be in that horrible cot, the nurse replies that Mother tried to walk out the previous night and, as I have seen for myself, is violent, and that the cot is to stop her from falling out and hurting herself. The answer to my question about whether she has had any treatment is negative, and further questions are brushed aside. I am obviously regarded as too young to ask questions and I leave feeling if anything more desolate than I did the previous night.

Beatrice rings. Her grandfather has bronchitis and Frau Trapp has flu. She cannot leave them and is horrified when she hears my news. When she rings off I realize that I have eaten nothing since last night. In the pantry I find two potatoes and one egg. Tomorrow I shall have to buy food. There is not a great deal of money left, for the bedjacket has been extravagantly expensive. It is now lying beside the white and pink carnations on the bare linoleum floor — that is, unless the nurse has done anything about them, which I doubt. Despite my resolution not to give in to self-pity, I break down and cry bitterly.

Mother's condition does not change and, whenever I try to see someone in charge, I am put off. Every time I visit, I see the woman who is ceaselessly running up and down the corridor, and each time when she sees me she stops and beats the same rapid tattoo on the floor with her ridiculously high heels. Her run reminds me of a sewing machine adjusted to the smallest possible stitch, and it makes my scalp and spine prickle with cold. I avoid her eyes because I cannot bear the look of abject terror in them. On my third visit I pass an open door and see into a room with padded walls. The room is empty, but my overwrought imagination fills it with frenzied creatures, tearing frantically at the padding that holds them prisoner.

I wake each morning to the same wild pain of bereavement. Sometimes I even think that it might have been easier if Mother had died because it would have spared me the agony of seeing her become what she is now, someone less than human. Then I feel bitterly ashamed of my wicked and sinful thoughts and wish that I could pray. The words 'Today if ye will hear his voice harden not your hearts' drum in my ears, but my heart is frozen. The barrier erected to shut out self-pity is also shutting out his voice. The complete trust and belief in a loving and omnipotent God is gradually and almost imperceptibly giving way to doubt and unbelief.

As a child, such a long time ago now it seems, my faith

was strong and unshakeable. Now that I am losing it, I am left in utter darkness and loneliness. God, if there is one, I reason, must be a heartless tyrant, unmoved by the idiocy of men, killing and destroying. I have been deceived and have prayed either to a vacuum or a God of wrath. The stoicism into which I try to retreat cannot replace the peace of my former happy certainty, and I am left with the stifling feeling that I am living in a nightmare.

Just when I think that I cannot bear the horror any longer, Father comes. I run into his arms, my relief at seeing him so great that I become completely incoherent, and it takes several minutes before he realizes what has happened. When at last he detaches himself from my embrace and lowers me into an armchair, his face, indistinct through my tears, looks white and haggard. He only has three days, but he is going to make arrangements and I am not to worry. While he is here I do not have to go with him to see Mother, and I feel guilty because of my relief at hearing this.

Our last maid left some time ago, and just before Father goes back he thinks of the housework. He looks so ill and strained that I quickly assure him that I can manage. As I watch his car disappearing down the road, I am seized by a feeling of unspeakable desolation. The papers carry whole pages with notices of those killed in action. I have worried about his being killed since the war began, but what would become of us now if he did not return?

To break the oppressive silence in the room I switch on the wireless. A fanfare precedes a special announcement. 'Here are all German broadcasting stations. We are transmitting today's report of the supreme command of the army as a special announcement. The great battle in Belgian and French Flanders is nearing its end with the destruction of the British and French armies. Since yesterday the British expeditionary force has been in total disintegration. Leaving behind vast material resources, the enemy is trying by swimming or on small boats to reach the British ships, which are being attacked by our air force with devastating results.'

Hastily I switch off, but I cannot switch off the pictures invading my mind: pictures of men desperately trying to reach the coast, of corpses floating in the surf, of men drowning, shot down in boats and ships by the attacks from planes which are bearing down on them, accompanied by the eerie howl that I have so far heard only on the wireless or when watching the newsreel. It isn't our fault, I tell myself. We are the ones who have been attacked. Hitler is declaring over and over again that he is a man of peace. Beatrice thinks otherwise. Can she be right?

There are definite signs of improvement in Mother's condition, and she is speaking to me. Beatrice is trying to persuade me to resume dancing classes. At last I agree. The summer holidays will shortly begin and then the dancing school too will close down until the autumn term.

I have missed quite a few classes and have fallen behind. I seem to be behind with everything. School has become an ordeal because I have missed so much. To my surprise I find that I enjoy the dancing and even laugh at times, but it is a superficial enjoyment. In the day-to-day routine of work and during these hours of outward gaiety, I can temporarily find forgetfulness, but the knowledge of what has happened and might happen again is ever present, a nightmare and a pain that cannot be shaken off.

Wolf, looking taller and even more handsome and self-assured, asks me for several dances and at the end asks Frau Trapp for permission to see me home. Captivated by his easy charm she gives it, and we set out. He tells me stories about our dancing master and, even though I do not care very much for him and think him conceited, I am in the mood to be amused. When we arrive at the house and I am searching in my bag for my key, he suddenly puts his arms around me and begins to kiss me. I try to push him away, but he is strong and pins me against the wall with his body. I struggle wildly but in vain until the sound of voices and approaching footsteps causes him to let me go. Furiously angry I raise my hand and strike him as hard as I can across the face. The voices are now quite close and he turns abruptly and leaves. My lips feel sore and I am trembling violently. In the bathroom I scrub my mouth and brush my teeth. I am disgusted with males. 'Beasts,' I say to the flushed face in the mirror. 'That's what they are, beasts.'

When I tell Beatrice what happened and that I slapped Wolf's face, she is pleased. 'Good for you!' she exclaims. 'That young man needs to be put in his place. I guess he'll leave you alone from now on.' But Wolf has his revenge. At the next and last dance class before we break up, when during a break he is as usual surrounded by adoring girls, he declares in a voice audible throughout that he approves of the policy of the government to sterilize men and women of unsound stock, as this will prevent the birth of physically and mentally handicapped children. While he speaks he looks pointedly in my direction, and several boys and girls turn to stare at me. I have difficulty in restraining Beatrice from attacking him, but at last manage to persuade her that he would love a confrontation and that this would only make matters worse. Nevertheless I am troubled. When, some time later, I come across a newspaper report stating that persons with venereal disease, mental or other hereditary diseases are forbidden to marry and will be sterilized, I am haunted by a new nightmare.

Mother is coming home. Before collecting her, Beatrice and I have stopped for a quick cup of coffee in the Café Herrenhof, when the music transmitted by a loudspeaker is interrupted by a special announcement from the headquarters of the Führer. 'This is the Greater German broadcasting network with all German broadcasting stations, incorporating the stations of the *Protektorat*, Bohemia and Moravia, and the repeater stations of the general governments in Poland, Brussels II, Kotweijk and Lux-embourg.' There follows the report that the total collapse of the French front between the Channel and the Maginot Line near Montmédy has frustrated the original intention of the French to defend the French capital, and that at this moment victorious German troops are entering Paris. Beatrice and I gaze at each other in consternation. The French asking for an armistice, beaten within a few weeks — it seems incredible.

That day I meet Beatrice's grandfather for the first time. He hardly ever stirs from his room now. There is noble dignity in his gaunt features, and the penetrating gaze of the dark sunken eyes is levelled on me. Remote and wraith-like he lies back in the wheelchair, his gnarled hands rest-ing limply on the rug that covers his knees. I feel uneasy under his gaze. Does he know that I have questioned his judgment? As though in reply to my thoughts he smiles tolerantly and gently says, 'I am a valetudinarian but not yet senile.'

Guiltily I blush, suddenly conscious of my youthful arrogance.

'Though I am weak physically,' he continues, 'I think I can boast that the mind's keenness is unimpaired and memories are crystal clear.'

Has he heard the news, Beatrice enquires.

The old man sighs deeply. 'The victor and the van-quished, turn and turn about, history repeating itself endlessly: 1871 Germany, 1918 the French, now it is once again Germany's turn to triumph and nothing is ever learnt from history, nothing.'

Beatrice is convinced that the next country to be invaded will be England. For me this is unthinkable, and my hopes for the cessation of all hostilities rise when Hitler appeals to Churchill to end the war. Despite the intervention of the King of Sweden and the endeavours of the Pope, Churchill rejects negotiations, and soon everyone is humming the refrain of a rousing new marching song:

Denn wir fahren,
Denn wir fahren,
Denn wir fahren gegen Engeland, Engeland.

Its insistent repetition of the words 'for we're sailing to conquer England' fills me with fear and foreboding. In September of the same year a pact already concluded between Italy and Germany is signed by Japan, and in the following year by Bulgaria.

Gradually I have become used to being on my own. Mother is now in Badgastein recuperating, and I am getting quite good at washing and ironing, though some of the clothes have shrunk and some are singed. One evening, while twiddling with the knobs of the wireless in search of a station transmitting a concert that I want to listen to while darning stockings, I am startled by an English voice exclaiming 'Oh isn't love wonderful.' In my haste to turn off the sound, I nearly send the set flying and then sit petrified, listening for the knock that I am sure will come. Half an hour later I pluck up enough courage to switch on once more, and this time I listen to the report of a speech by Goebbels in which he states that the world is to be divided anew, that we have, in previous centuries, been the losers and will now make up for what we have missed out on and change the face of Europe. I am no longer in any doubt but that he must be mad.

When Father comes home next time, I tell him how unhappy I am in school because I have missed so much. He listens and then suggests extra lessons from private tutors and promises to make enquiries. The outcome is that I am to leave my present school and go to a special school that will prepare me for university entrance. He has also enrolled me for evening classes in typing and shorthand. I look at him aghast. 'But I don't want to learn typing and shorthand.'

He is adamant. Shorthand, he tells me, will be very useful when I go to university. I know that it is useless to argue and I also know that my failure to keep up in school has made him suspect that I am not as bright as he had hoped, and he thinks that if I can type and do shorthand then I will at least be able to get a job in an office. Without intending to do so, he has by his action and my interpretation of it become the catalyst that fires me with the resolve to prove him wrong.

I master typing and shorthand in record time and then devote myself to my studies for the *Matura* that will qualify me for university entrance. Since I can start each subject at exactly the point where I am, I proceed rapidly, with the result that in the end I take my examinations a year earlier than I would have done had I stayed at my old school and so become one of the youngest to qualify for university entrance.

At the *Matura Schule* I make a new friend, Hetty, who is round, placid, brown as a nut, with deep-set dark eyes. She is full of fun. I often spend a weekend with her at her home in the country when Mother is away at a rest home. My visits to the castle where she lives are light-hearted interludes. I ride out on Graziella and eventually stable her in the castle stables. Riding in and out of soft tree shadows, the horse's hoofs beating a steady rhythm along summer roads that are filled with the aromatic fragrance of sun-warmed pines, the distinctive smell of the horse in my nostrils, I forget Mother's illness, war and my nightmares.

Long before I graduate from the *Matura Schule* another graduation takes place. We have finished our course with our little dancing master at the *Tanzschule* and the date for the ball that we have looked forward to with a mixture of apprehension and excitement has been fixed. I stare critically at myself in the mirror and, though I have had to resign myself long ago to the fact that I shall never change and become beautiful like Mother, I am not entirely displeased with what I see. My tanned shoulders rise smooth and golden out of white tulle, and my waist, to which I fasten a spray of miniature roses, is really quite dainty.

67

Beatrice, lithe and fawnlike, is vivid in a gown of dull gold. She looks just like one of the graces in a painting by Botticelli, I tell her.

The ball is an unqualified success. For one night we forget all about war, fear and destruction. The boys overcome their *gaucherie* and behave with impeccable courtesy. We are allowed one glass of pink champagne each, but it is the music and the sight of sparkling eyes and glamorous gowns that goes to our heads and even transforms each pink-faced youngster into a handsome escort.

After the ball the days settle down to a fairly dull routine until Christmas, the second Christmas of the war. Father is unable to come home and Mother and I spend the season very quietly. I think of the families who have lost a father, son or brother, and for the first time I am glad that I have never had the brother I always longed for.

8

Confusion and Turmoil

The war drags on. By now it has become almost common-place, an accepted part of everyday life. What I have feared for so many years has happened and has not turned out to be quite as horrific as anticipated. So far I have not seen any fighting except on the cinema screen, and somehow seeing it there, sitting in a comfortable seat in the darkened room, gives one the feeling of things happening in another world.

Hitler has now conquered nearly all of Western Europe and is acclaimed as a military as well as a political genius. We hear and read that, being surrounded by enemies, not self-sufficient in food, lacking land for expansion and farming, we are driven to fight. The general opinion is that Germany is the victim. Other countries have been jealous of Germany's swift return to prosperity after Hitler came to power. We have suffered unprovoked attacks and have been forced to fight back. When, after having been vic-torious on all fronts, we magnanimously offered peace, the offer was rejected. I feel trapped. My mind revolts at the idea of death and destruction and is numb.

Mother has withdrawn from communication with every-one except me, but I am happy because she talks freely to me. Occasionally she even comes shopping, but most of the time she spends at home in prayer or in keeping every-thing immaculate.

She is happiest in the woods and the mountains. As we

walk along moss-grown tracks where the light is cool and green, gather chanterelles and wild strawberries, climb through forests and meadows where the only sounds to be heard are the joyful song of the birds, the gentle soughing of the trees, the chime of cowbells and the whirr of insect wings, she also is at peace.

Once, we rest together on a plateau, where a lake lies deep blue with a tiny island that seems to reflect a single cloud suspended in the sky. Mother talks to me of her childhood, of her own mother, whose hold on life had been tenuous, and of her distress when, as a six-year-old, she realized how desperately ill her mother was. She had crept into the room when no one was looking and had sat at the bedside, keeping her eyes fixed on the gentle face she loved, trying to will her to get well; but she had been sent away, never to see the beloved face again. God had wanted her mother, she was told. She could understand that, but she wanted her too, needed her most desperately, and she prayed to God that he would let her have her back. When her prayer was not answered, she grieved silently and uncomplainingly, and the others had assumed that, being so young, she had soon forgotten the loss that to her was too great to bear.

Aunt Mia, the eldest sister, had looked after her, Therese and baby Joseph, and she had continued to do so even after her father had taken a third wife. But before long Mia had become engaged to be married and Mother, feeling forsaken, had followed the couple about wherever they went. On one occasion, when Mia and her fiancé had gone skating, Mother had climbed up to the loft, where she unearthed some rusty skates, and had run across crunching, frostbound fields to the frozen pond. There, among the shouting, laughing, gliding and swirling crowd, Mia found her, coatless, hatless and gloveless, struggling with stiff fingers to attach two left skates to her boots.

Mother laughs at the recollection of that escapade, but I feel for the abnormally sensitive little girl. I remember

Grandpapa's stern and joyless religion and marvel that, far from driving her into unbelief, it engendered her deep, unshakeable trust and belief in a loving God, a faith that has not been weakened by sickness or adversity. I am about to question her about this when a cow, her patient eyes framed by long, graceful lashes and clung about by flies, comes sniffing gently, nudging us with black, moist lips. We jump up and the chance has gone.

In June, 153 divisions of the German army, supported by Rumanian, Finnish, Hungarian, Slovak and Italian units, commence operation 'Barbarossa', the start of the offensive against Russia. Goebbels tells the nation that the operation is necessary to safeguard Europe and the entire world against the Bolshevik threat.

By August German troops have taken the West Ukraine and surrounded Odessa and Nikolajew. A month later they do the same at Wjasma and Briansk. Russia, we are told, is finished. A few days later our allied forces stand before Leningrad, and in October the battle around Moscow begins. Father is in Russia.

I am woken by a cry of terror, and with fearful apprehension I rush to Mother's room. She is sitting up in bed, and in her eyes I see the look I have come to dread. I sit down beside her and talk softly to her as to a frightened child. After a while I feel her relaxing in my arms. 'Your father,' she sobs, 'has been shot.' I stroke her hair and rock her gently in my arms, telling her that she has had a nightmare. She drinks the infusion of camomile that I prepare for her and takes two of the tablets that the doctor has left with me. When she falls into an uneasy sleep, I collect my duvet and lie down on the floor by the side of the bed.

The next morning she seems quiet, though listless, and in due time we learn that Father has been wounded and will come home after his discharge from hospital. Though I dismiss the event of the night as coincidence, it seems to be surrounded by an air of the supernatural and sends shivers down my spine.

Beatrice agrees. 'Gives you the creeps,' she says, and shudders.

Beatrice is in love. Smiling dreamily and secretively she tells me that his name is Günter. He is a young lieutenant home on leave. His father is the admiral's godson. They met ten days ago and will get married as soon as possible. I am aghast. Only a few days earlier we had discussed the situation of Monica, a girl of eighteen, who is a war widow with a tiny baby. We couldn't understand anyone so young getting married, and then reasoned that all these young boys and girls were rushing into marriage after knowing each other for only a few days because they were afraid that the war was cheating them of love. Either that, or they were afraid that war made death inevitable; they feared that they would never see each other again and had to live as fully as possible while they could. Beatrice, looking thoughtful, had announced that the whole world was upside-down. In the end we had decided that what was happening was nature's way of redressing the balance, but at the same time we concluded that, though we could understand what had driven those poor young things into an early marriage, it could never happen to us.

Beatrice is eighteen, but I do not remind her of Monica or of our conversation. She is radiant and amazingly beautiful, but I am pierced with a sense of loss. Could it be that I am jealous? Someone has come into Beatrice's life who from now on will have a greater claim to her affection and understanding than I. I have made a new friend myself, but Hetty can never take Beatrice's place. The ties that bind us are strong. I am closer to her than I have ever been to anyone except Mother. I have always been grateful for her unfailing support and companionship. But it is only now that I realize fully how much she means to me. The thought steals into my mind that Günter is going back in three days' time and I shall have her once more to myself, but I know it is an unworthy thought and scold myself severely for being mean and selfish. I think of the fighting, the death and destruction to which he has to return and the anguish that Beatrice will suffer while waiting for news, her dread that one day the telegram might arrive to tell her that he has been wounded or even killed.

Father has come home. He looks pale and ill. He has not yet recovered from the multiple wounds he received and, though we rejoice that no vital organs have been affected, the injuries he has sustained will be for years to come the cause of severe pain.

He is totally exhausted after five weeks of campaigning without let-up, without sleep. The wounds are slow to heal, and he seems to be on the verge of a total physical breakdown. He does not speak much of what is happening, but once he mentions that Ukrainians, Finns, Estonians and others are fighting on the German side. I question him about this, for surely Ukrainians are Russians. I learn that they regard the Germans as their liberators.

'The Bolsheviks,' Father says, 'wanted collective farms, so they confiscated everything in the name of the people, and millions who opposed Stalin's dictatorship and agricultural policies were starved to death. We have handed back their property and re-opened their churches. Now they are prepared to do whatever is asked of them.' He frowns: 'There are those among our men who take advantage of the situation, even officers.' His voice hardens: 'Have you seen Frau K's new fur coat?' The implication is clear. 'War,' he continues bitterly, 'brings to the fore the baser instincts, greed, lust . . . ' He pauses, then in a voice so low that I can barely catch the word, he adds, 'brutality.'

9

Interlude

I am on my way to Aunt Mia, where I shall stay while Father and Mother are at Badgastein. The train journey through the *Ostmark*, as Austria is now called, is fairly comfortable, but soon after we enter the *Protektorat* the train becomes crowded. I give up my seat to a young mother with a baby and go out into the corridor where I stand wedged between an overdressed, much bejewelled woman of ample proportions who chain-smokes and complains loudly about the lack of space, and a tall, slim man who with folded arms leans in an attitude of easy elegance against the door of the compartment.

The last rays of the sun light up eyes of unusual clarity and a deep gentian blue. His face, bony and sharp edged and deeply tanned, relaxes into a rueful smile as the woman launches into another angry tirade. He turns to me with an expression of humorous chagrin. Fascinated by his eyes, all the more striking in someone of his colouring, for his hair is black except for white wings above hollowed temples, I gaze at them with an intensity of which I am unaware until the jerking of the train brings me to myself and I avert my eyes in embarrassment. I wish I could move far away but that is impossible, wedged in as I am between him and all the others on either side.

Darkness falls and people are trying to get more comfortable by sitting down on cases or on the floor. My cases are in the compartment, and the tall stranger, who has folded his coat and put it on his case, courteously offers me a seat. At first I refuse, but he points out that there is room for both of us. The case is indeed a very large one, a fact that disgusts the angry woman. I see from the label that he has stayed at the Schloss Hotel in Velden. It is a place I know well, and this provides us with a topic of conversation. We talk about sailing on the Wörthersee and about mountains and other lakes in Carinthia until I feel sleepy.

I must have dozed, for when next I open my eyes I can hear the porter calling 'Hindenburg!'

'Could you. . . ? Would you. . . ?' I stammer, gesturing towards the compartment.

He is already wrenching open the door to it while I try to make my way to the carriage door, apologizing as I stumble over protesting, prostrate forms. The train is beginning to move when I jump on to the platform and race back to the window, through which he hands me one of my cases.

'There's another one,' I shout.

'Don't worry, I'll get it to you somehow.' His voice, floating on rushing air, is carried away in remnants of sound.

Aunt, who is there to meet me, shakes her head when I explain. She obviously does not believe that I shall ever see my case again. In the car, driving along dark, deserted streets, I feel the colour rushing to my face, for I suddenly remember that, when I woke, my head was resting on the stranger's shoulder and his arm was encircling me protectively. Yet even while I tell myself that it does not matter, for I shall never see him again, I am surprised at experiencing a vague sense of regret.

We are going to collect my case. The stranger has contacted Aunt with the help of the address that Father, as a precaution against just such an event, had printed on the case. He has offered to deliver it personally, but Aunt has to go on business to Gnesen within the next few days and we shall collect it on the way. It appears that he is a friend of friends of hers, and she has accepted an invitation for both of us to lunch with him. He is a 'man of substance', she tells me, and she is looking forward to meeting him.

The house is very beautiful. Aunt's eyes approve everything: the wide, gracious staircase, the elegantly proportioned dining-room, the Persian rugs on gleaming parquet floors, roses massed in bowls and vases, the table sparkling with fine porcelain, silver and crystal, and on the panelled walls portraits of distinguished ancestors, and wall lights in triple-branched gold brackets.

Herr v. G. is the perfect host, courteous and considerate. I am amazed to hear that a programme for the day has been agreed by him and Aunt. While she goes on to Gnesen, I will be shown over the estate, and in the evening we shall accompany him to the opera.

I assume that some employee will have been detailed to show me over the estate, but this is not so. Herr v. G. has ordered a trap in which he will personally drive me. I am shy and tongue-tied until the distinctive ammoniac smell, the stamp of hoofs, the champing of teeth and the rattling of chains tell me that we are nearing the stables. When we stop to inspect them, I forget my shyness in my delight in the sleek animals standing in their loose boxes. Asked whether I ride, I laugh and tell him that I have been riding from almost before I was able to walk. 'Then let's ride,' he says, but I glance ruefully down at the smart silk dress that Aunt has procured for me through her 'connections'. 'No problem,' I am told, and a short time later, dressed in an outfit belonging to his niece, I see the groom lead out my mount: a beautiful thoroughbred bay mare.

Herr v. G. pushes open the gate with his crop, and we canter out into the still, golden afternoon. We do not speak much. Every now and again he lifts his crop to point something out to me or explain. Once, looking across to him, I see him watching me intently, and startled I break into a gallop. I lean forward in the saddle, lying along the mare's neck as she bounds, her hoofs barely touching the ground, revelling in the exhilaration, the sheer delight of handling her. At last he shoots past me, wheels in his tracks and, leaning over, seizes my rein. I know then that he easily could have outdistanced me but has refrained from doing so in order not to spoil my pleasure.

He points to a slight incline. 'Shall we ride down to the river?' I look in the direction he indicates, patting the mare's blowing muzzle and stroking her heaving flanks. Before us the country spreads in one great sweep, fields of wheat, oats and rye rippling in the breeze in waves of burnished gold, outlined by dark forests. When we reach the curling silver line of the river, I am reluctant to stop, I wish we could ride on for ever. We draw rein and the horses edge close to each other. Our shoulders touch and, for the first time in my life, I am aware of masculine attraction. All is still, drowsy and peaceful, but I feel nervous and excited. This solitude and his nearness are at once wonderful and alarming, and time ceases to exist as we merge with the scents, the gentle field noises and the sunlit landscape in poignant, intimate enchantment.

Since we are staying on to go to the opera, we have booked into a hotel and, while changing for the evening, Aunt wants to hear all about the afternoon. She is most impressed by Herr v. G.'s breeding, his great charm, his impeccable manners and his distinction of appearance.

In evening dress, which he wears with an easy naturalness, he looks even more distinguished. He takes my hand in his firm hold, lifts it to his lips and kisses it. Once or twice since I have been considered to be growing up, men — for the most part family friends — have raised my hand to their lips in greeting with the customary *Küss die Hand*, but in this general salute the lips barely touch one's fingers. Herr v. G.'s kiss is as firm and warm as the grip in which he holds my hand, and my heart misses a beat. He has brought a corsage for each of us: freesias for Aunt, lilies of the valley for me. I bury my face in their scented loveliness to hide my tremulous delight.

'They are my favourite flowers,' I stammer. 'Nobody has ever given me flowers before. . . I mean . . . not like this. . . ' I feel my lips trembling and stop in despair. Is he laughing at me, seeing how confused I am, not knowing what to say?

When I raise my head in painful embarrassment I encounter his grave eyes. 'I am glad,' he says gently.

We enter the box just as the overture begins, and at once the music that tells of the tender love story of the young Goethe and Friederike and embodies all the sweetness, the delicacy and foolishness of youth takes hold of me. Under the spell of it, utterly contained in the present moment, all the agony, the fears and the sorrows of the past months vanish as though they have never been, and I know that whenever or wherever I shall hear this music again, it will bring back not only this evening but the whole of this enchanted day, and I feel strangely elated and expectant.

The next day, when we are getting ready to leave, a bell boy delivers two baskets of flowers: roses for Aunt and lilies of the valley for me. 'Where on earth,' Aunt exclaims, 'does he get lilies of the valley from at this time of year?'

When I arrive home after my brief holiday, Father phones to say that he and Mother are staying on in Badgastein for a few more days. Will I be able to manage? Am I quite sure that I'll be all right? I assure him that of course I shall manage: have I not spent days and weeks on my own while Mother was in hospital? I am restless and on edge, aware as never before of my youth, of life surging within me, tremulous and waiting. My thoughts return to the past few days but are interrupted by the renewed ring of the phone. When I recognize the voice, I grip the receiver so hard and press it so tightly to my ear that it hurts.

After a few preliminary enquiries regarding the rest of my stay with Aunt and my homeward journey, he asks if he may come and see me. I am struck dumb — first of all by the request itself, and then because I feel that such a visit would be impossible. He does not know, of course, that I am alone, but even after my parents' return it will be impossible for him to come. Haltingly I try to explain and end by saying weakly that I shall write. He is very gracious and makes me feel terribly awkward, unutterably *gauche*.

After replacing the receiver, I lie back in the chair, remembering the look in his eyes as they rested on me. What is happening to me? I feel different, the world is different, there is confusion in my heart and mind and I am both troubled and thrilled. I am reading mostly poetry these days and, inspired by the music of the verse, I am often sad and moved to tears or wildly and unaccountably happy. Always I am filled with a deep and undefined longing.

I have told Beatrice about the episode with my case and have briefly described Herr v. G. to her. Jokingly she warns me to be on my guard with men who have reached *l'âge critique*, For the first time I feel that I cannot share what is moving me so deeply, even with her.

Several times I have started the letter to Herr v. G. but have always torn it up. My last attempt is more than conventional and satisfies me not at all, but I send it off nevertheless. His reply comes by return of post. He tells me about his work, the mare I rode, another visit to the opera, this time to *Don Giovanni*.

My next letter is easy. I have been to *Madame Butterfly* and can talk about the production. I tell him about Graziella, about weekend excursions into the mountains with Mother and about Father's return to the front.

Letters are beginning to fly to and fro between us. I find myself telling him more and more about myself, about Mother, about my fears and anxieties and hopes, and I look forward eagerly to his replies. It is, I think, like talking to an older brother, someone who understands and is in total empathy with me.

One of his letters contains a photograph, taken of him sailing on the Wörthersee. I study it and realize that I have almost forgotten what he looks like. In my next letter I enclose a photograph of myself on Graziella and he replies by telling me that he has the picture on his desk. Then one of his letters is delayed. I feel restless and run to the door every time the postman comes. It arrives just before Mother and I are due to leave for a holiday with Opa.

Opa has aged since we last saw him. He is no longer quite as upright, but seeing my searching look he straightens and becomes his old bristling and defiant self: shoulders back, chin out, his beard quivering aggressively.

The USA have entered the war and Opa, who has been warned by Father not to talk about Hitler in front of Mother, is impatiently waiting for an opportunity for us to be alone so that he can give vent to his feelings. For the first time since the beginning of the war, the German army has had to retreat. According to Hitler, it is solely because of the arctic conditions in which our soldiers have to fight. As soon as we are alone, Opa erupts. Snorting contemptuously he heaps abuse on Hitler and Mussolini, a corporal and a private who are paraded as military geniuses to fools who have been too easily hoodwinked by the victories of the first war years and by Goering, whom Opa describes as 'that fat effeminate fellow', who fawns on Hitler and calls him *Du gottgesandter Mann*'. Opa spits at this phrase and viciously denies that Hitler has been sent by God. He denounces Hitler's adversaries for not being ready to oppose him in time. The sparks that rise from his clay pipe compete with the sparks issuing from his diamond-blue eyes as he puffs furiously. 'Styling himself *Oberster Befehlshaber der Wermacht*,' he growls. 'Supreme commander of the armed forces indeed! Ha! And men like your father, who can run rings round him when it comes to military strategy, have to swear on oath to support him, a miserable little Austrian corporal.' His pointed beard juts out and quivers truculently. 'An oath of loyalty,' he continues. 'The only one to whom we pledged our allegiance was the kaiser. He thinks of himself as more powerful than the kaiser, *allmächtiger Gott*, he's made himself more powerful than the kaiser ever was.'

His pipe has gone out and he is trying to fan it back into life. Hypnotized I watch his rosy, wrinkled cheeks pop in and out between wrathful exclamations. 'Poor fools . . . obliged to carry out orders . . . orders of a madman . . . slaughtered in their thousands. . .' I am disconcerted by his outbursts and glad when Mother's entry puts an end to them.

The snow falls densely, softly, blotting out the hills and forests, weighing heavily on roofs and trees. I stand outside, revelling in the utter stillness. The hush is profound, nothing stirs, not even the wind. Nothing is heard, not even the piping of a bird. After the first heavy falls of snow the sun shines with a dazzling brilliance in the illimitable blue sky, imparting to the hills a light of crystal splendour in which they stand out so clearly that I feel I can touch them by putting out my hand. Icicles hang and glitter in the brilliant light, and the snow blows like powder in the breeze.

I ski every day and am feeling extraordinarily well, revelling in the exercise and the firmness and strength of my body that at times stirs me in a way that is disturbing. While skimming down the mountain slopes, I delight in the pure breathless intoxication of movement and feel the blood singing and tingling warmly through my body.

I love the village nestling between mountains. They are not as spectacular as those in Austria but are beautiful nevertheless. I love the onion tower of the old wooden church and the tranquillity, undisturbed by cars and broken only by the bells of horse-drawn sleighs. I can ski on slopes that encircle the quaint houses, and there are long gentle runs through the meadows that are summer pastures and a few exciting long steep ones covered in moguls, where it is necessary to turn and jump constantly.

On the Monday of the last week but one of our holiday, I stand on the summit; and, when I straighten up after adjusting my skis prior to making the descent, I see a tiny speck advancing from below. I push off and stop at a distance. I can make out the figure of a man but am still unable to see his face. He raises one of his poles and waves it, but makes no move to climb any higher, so I set off once more. As I draw closer my heart lurches. 'I've come to join you for a few days,' he says, smiling up at me. 'May I?'

Feeling coltishly awkward and overcome by another crisis of shyness that sends the hot blood rushing to my face, I stammer, 'Of course you may,' while thinking desperately, oh, I wish you hadn't come. It is so very much easier to talk to you in a letter than face to face with you when I feel so terribly young and immature.

But as the hours pass, tension and strain vanish and there remains only the delight of hearing his voice and seeing the gladness in his eyes. Then I too am glad.

I wake in the morning to joyous anticipation, released for a brief spell from all care. Here there is no war, not even an aeroplane is seen or heard. Out on the slopes we are the only inhabitants of a world that is peaceful and serene.

With my shyness at last dispelled, I am no longer as disturbingly conscious of Lutz's — I have at last brought myself to call him by his Christian name — masculine presence. Like children we swoop down the mountain slopes, free as the exhilarating air that surrounds us. There are no ski lifts, no brightly-lit restaurants here; but there is an old wooden chalet where after a day of fresh air and exercise we clomp tiredly towards a beautiful old free-standing tiled stove, and wait for a glass of hot mulled wine that a sloe-eyed, raven-haired girl hands us.

We have snowball fights and labour hard in building an enormous snowman. When it is finished we cover his breast with medals and write 'Goering' in the snow, laughing so much at our magnificent creation that tears roll down our cheeks. Lutz is, in one glorious week of warm, bubbling happiness, releasing all the fun, all the laughter and joy that are part of normal childhood and that have been suppressed and overshadowed by Mother's illness. I have found life a very serious business and have therefore taken myself seriously to the point of tragedy. From the time of Mother's first breakdown, I had guiltily thought of indulgence in any kind of fun as frivolous. Now Lutz's sense of humour and fun brings forth from me a response in which I delight. I look back in surprise at my life so far, amazed to find another me emerging that I did not know existed. Sorrow and pain are forgotten, and the security and happiness that were mine as a small child are mine once again. The beauty surrounding us, the mountains, the sky, the sparkling snow, the trees with their fairy-tale blossoms of hoar-frost are all part of my joy.

One morning, looking up at the slopes of virgin snow, I suddenly imagine the snow in Russia, see it defiled by the tracks of tanks, by craters left by the explosions of grenades, by deep scars made by artillery shells and stained with the blood of the wounded and dead.

I know that among Lutz's closest friends is a general who knows the Führer well. Emboldened by the close companionship of the last few days, I decide to ask Lutz about his friend's opinion of Hitler and his actions. I start by stating my conviction that Hitler's attack on Russia was sheer madness. He reminds me of the triumphant campaign in Africa, the victories of Dunkirk, Norway and Greece, the incredibly fast advance in the east and the breakthrough to the Volga, all proof to Hitler that the German army is invincible and the speedy destruction of the Soviet army assured.

Lutz has never spoken to me about Hitler, and I wonder what he himself feels about him. Is he in agreement with the majority who consider Hitler to be our saviour? I know of only a few who do not share this opinion: Beatrice and her grandfather, who listen to foreign broadcasts of what is undoubtedly propaganda; and Mother, with her pathological phobia concerning Hitler, whom she has called the Antichrist; and Opa, whose contempt for Hitler seems inseparable from his cantankerous old age. And then there is Father, who is preserving absolute silence on the subject. I decide to be completely open but still dare not ask a direct question of him. What do those who know him well think, I ask; is he really the monster of iniquity that some whom I know think he is?

Lutz turns quickly with a guarded, nervous movement and a shadow passes over my mind, a dread that I tell myself has no substance. Then slowly he replies. 'His generals,' he says, 'though scornful of his antecedents, his lack of culture and education and often exasperated by his ignorance of military strategy, nevertheless admire his quick intelligence and his gift of oratory.'

I wait for him to continue, and when he remains silent I insist, 'Is he evil?' Then, half afraid of an affirmative reply, I tell him of my brief meeting with Hitler, of my own reaction to his powerful magnetism, of his apparent kindness and of how I can see that he can inspire affection and loyalty. But then I repeat my earlier question, 'What about those who know him quite intimately?'

'It is true, he is genuinely fond of children and he can exert considerable charm.' He pauses and his brows contract.

Intuitively I know that he is debating how to reply honestly to the question that is so important to me and quietly I repeat, 'Is he evil?'

He looks at me with intense gravity, then slowly, like a man cautiously feeling his way along a tightrope, he replies that it is his opinion that no one is totally evil. Hitler, he thinks, is a sick man with a mind deranged by his pathological hatred of all foreigners and especially non-Aryans, by delusions of grandeur that have been fostered and nurtured by the sycophancy of some of his immediate *entourage* and the limitless adulation of his people in the early days. Then abruptly he drops his ski poles, takes my hands and smiles into my eyes. 'We have a long climb, shall we start?'

I feel resentment welling up inside me. Is he being patronizing, treating me as a child? But seeing in his look the protective love to which my immature being responds so joyously, I surrender and determine that during these last two days left to us, I shall shut out all my worries and give myself up to joy.

On the day preceding his departure, Lutz and I are resting in the sun outside an old and disused mountain hut. I have started to doze in the warmth of the sun, when suddenly I sit bolt upright, electrified by his words. Eight years ago, he tells me, after only two years of marriage, his wife left him; and since then he has lived with his widowed sister who is keeping house for him. He is divorced! Since childhood divorce has in my mind been associated with adultery and disgrace. Before I have time to absorb the information, to sort out my feelings, he shocks me out of them by telling me that after he leaves this place, he is going to Russia. Because of the injuries he received in the first year of the war, and because what he is doing at home is important for the war effort, he was given to understand that he was exempt from further service; but he has now been re-examined by a medical commission and declared fit for duty. He has been given command of a regiment and is going to Kiev next week.

He is holding my hands, clasping them tightly in his and, when they begin to tremble, he raises them to his lips. He tells me that he loves me, that he has not wanted to talk to me of his love until much later, for he realizes that I have had to grow up too soon, that there has been no time for the transition from childhood to womanhood, that I am still very much a child even though the responsibilities I have had to bear since childhood have made me serious and wise. But now his recall has changed everything. He does not want me to commit myself in any way now, but he will come to me as soon as he comes back.

The physical disturbance of his touch, his words and his look move me strangely. Whatever is happening to me fills me with a strange confusion, a turmoil of emotions, bliss mingled with terror. A smile softens his grave eyes. 'Little one,' he says, 'do you know that ever since I saw you for the first time that night on the train, I have not stopped thinking of you?' He pushes my hair back from my forehead, and stroking it gently he murmurs, 'I love you so much,' and very tenderly he kisses my eyes and lips.

Surely what I feel must be love but I cannot say the words, cannot tell him that I love him too. Then brightly he talks about the future. 'We shall ski in St Anton in winter, sail on the Wörthersee in the summer and dance on the terrace of the Schloss Hotel in the evenings.'

'But when,' I ask unhappily, 'when do you think it will all be over?'

He smiles reassuringly, but I sense the effort behind the cheerful assurance when he says, 'We have conquered Western Europe, most of North Africa and half of Russia. This year should see the end of it.'

At night before I go to bed, I look searchingly at myself in the dim, old mirror that hangs on the wall of my bedroom. For the first time I try to see myself through his eyes, becoming aware of my skin, hair and eyes as he sees them. I remember the night at the opera and a woman to whom he introduced us, remember the drift of perfume in which she gracefully descended the stairs, the beautifully manicured hand gleaming with rings, extended for him to kiss. I remember the elegance, beauty and charm that she had used with consummate skill and the mocking way in which she had looked at me, and I marvel that he should prefer me, in my immaturity and childish naivety, to someone like her. When I drift into sleep it is with the memory of his tenderness and love, which fills me through and through with warmth and sweetness.

In the cold light of morning the glow has faded. The sun, which has climbed each morning from behind the mountains and touched the frosted trees with diamonds, remains hidden, and the low-hanging grey clouds are pregnant with snow. When we meet, we walk through the village and a short way into the woods, where a path has been cleared by the woodcutter.

I am devastated to find how short a time we have before his train is due to leave. He pulls a box out of his pocket and hands it to me. From it I take a ring, a ruby in a plain gold setting. 'It is not an engagement ring because I do not wish to tie you in any way; it was my mother's.' Wordlessly I hold out my hand and he slips it on my finger.

With my head nestled beneath his chin and one of his hands holding the back of my head, we stand for a long time. I hear the hard, quick beat of his heart, and in an agony of the most poignant tenderness I cry soundlessly, 'I do, I love you too,' but still I cannot say it out loud.

Then he steps back: 'I am leaving you here, my dearest, please don't come to the station.'

I nod, looking up at his lean bony face, taking in every detail, for I have to get it by heart, engrave it upon my memory for ever; but it is the expression of love and sadness in his eyes that I am to remember with seeringly painful clearness. He cups my face in his hands and kisses once again my eyes, my forehead and my hair. Then he is gone. Was it only yesterday that I felt uplifted, transported? Only such a short time ago?

I remain motionless until my feet turn numb and the first snowflakes begin to drift. Then I take the ring off my finger to hide it from Opa's inquisitive eyes, but my fingers are stiff with cold, and it falls out of my hand and lies in the snow, a living thing, a crimson drop of blood. With trembling hands I pick it up and put it back on my finger. In the distance I hear the whistle of the departing train.

10
Cataclysm

A few weeks after our return from the Riesengebirge, I am alone in the flat when the doorbell rings. In the dim light stands an old man, dressed in rags, his haggard, unshaven face deeply etched with fatigue lines, his eyes sunken. It is only when he staggers into the hall, addressing me by name, that I recognize Father.

When Mother returns from church he is asleep. I look up at his portrait, painted in 1927, at the high, unlined forehead, commanding deep blue eyes, square, determined chin and full, smiling lips. I wonder at the change that a few years have wrought. It is true that his hair turned white some years ago, but on his last leave, at least after the period of recuperation at Badgastein, his face had still been unlined and his colour good. Even after he has bathed and shaven and changed into clean clothes, he looks shrunken and old. He spends most of the time during the ensuing two days sleeping the sleep of total exhaustion.

As always when he comes on leave, I find it difficult to adjust to his physical presence and am shy and ill at ease. It is late at night on the third day after his arrival that I am woken by sounds coming from the kitchen. As the result of Mother's illness I sleep lightly and wake at the slightest noise, for my hearing has become preternaturally sharp. I rise quietly, expecting to see her. Instead I find Father sitting at the kitchen table, a bottle of schnapps before him. He sees me glancing at the half-empty bottle and laughs harshly. I am about to retreat for, ever since the time when, as a small child, I was knocked over by a drunk, the sight of anyone under the influence of alcohol has induced in me a feeling of terror and nausea; but there is a tone of entreaty in Father's voice when he asks me to sit down, and in his eyes, which he raises to mine, I see such desolation that I force myself to overcome my aversion.

During the brief periods when he has been awake, he has been withdrawn and uncommunicative, and now he sits staring before him, occasionally raising the glass and drinking deeply. Apprehensively I address him and ask about the cold in Russia. I am disconcerted by the blank stare with which he responds to my question and sit petrified by his silence.

When he begins to speak, haltingly at first, then more and more rapidly, the emotions that have been suppressed for so long pour out. His eyes are looking inward and horror is leaping from them. He speaks of temperatures averaging thirty to forty degrees of frost, of inadequate equipment and clothing and starvation rations, of fighting in thin leather jackboots and summer uniforms, of blankets and clothing requisitioned from locals and infested with vermin, of waiting without hope for supplies and equipment, of ceaseless partisan attacks, of sickness and frostbite, of the endless shimmering expanse of blinding white, of icy needles of freezing snow, of the fight against exhaustion and fatigue. As he speaks I see those on patrols or sentry duty, their eyes clung about with frosted tears and their bodies overcome by weariness, falling asleep and joining the many frozen corpses under the icy shroud. I hear the howling of the *Katjuscha*, that shuts out the screams of the wounded, the gasps and groans from lumps of mutilated flesh baring their teeth in their last agony; an army of dead, torn bundles, and among them a few survivors stumbling sweating and filthy through fire. I see them with the courage of despair defending what is left to them. Hungry, freezing, eaten by vermin, exhausted and in constant pain they fight, preferring death to captivity in the dreaded Russian prison camps.

Convoys setting out with supplies never reach them. They have seen junker planes burn and explode until blizzards and cruel winds prevent aircraft from flying altogether. At last even the Russians in their fur coats and felt boots begin to feel the effects of the merciless cold, but they are expendable. After every line that is scythed down comes another, an inexhaustible supply of men for the slaughter.

I start when Father suddenly bursts into violent invective against the SS, calling them bastards and arrogant bullies. I have been aware of the tension between the army and the SS, but only now realize the full extent of the antagonism between them. His voice gradually becomes incomprehensible, and suddenly he slumps across the table. But I am still there among the frozen bodies with their half-open glazed eyes, among death and corruption, unable to shake off the horror of what I have just lived through. It has brought home to me fully the obscenity of war, of men intent on mutual extermination, despicable and hateful. What sort of a god is God if he has made people in his own image? During the triumphant early days of the war I admired the grandeur and courage of our soldiers. The exultation of those days is long past. All that is left is hunger, cold, exhaustion, despair, unimaginable suffering and the fight for survival. My thoughts fly to Lutz, who is out there, in the hell that Father has described to me. He is facing an enemy endowed with superhuman qualities of endurance. Despite catastrophic losses and appalling casualties on our side, the supreme commander will not give the order that can save lives.

To Beatrice I cry despairingly, 'Why don't they just refuse to fight?'

Her voice is bitter. 'When you are caught up in a common conflict, dressed up in the same uniform, fed by an unscrupulous propaganda with ideas of noble self-sacrifice, it is glorious to march shoulder to shoulder to your appointment with death.'

'Beatrice! Do you ever speak to Günter like this?'

'How can I? He believes he is fighting for justice, believes that his *Vaterland* is threatened, and is determined to defend it at all costs.' She bows her head and then adds tiredly, 'Anyway, neither he nor any of the others have a choice, have they?'

Since the first retreat of German forces in Russia the atmosphere has subtly changed. In the first two years of the war the wireless continually announced German victories, accompanied by fanfares and martial music. Hitler had made Germany the most powerful nation in the world, and food had remained plentiful. Now a damper has been put on everything. People's faces are apathetic as they wait in queues for their rations. They no longer want peace with honour, they long for peace at any price. Beatrice and I have joined the thousands who live for the moment when the next anxiously awaited letter from the Russian front drops through the letter-box.

Mother met Lutz in the Riesengebirge. She likes him and applauds his decision regarding an official engagement. Neither of us mentions him to Father, mostly on account of his state of health, but Father does hear about him. I never find out from whom. Whoever it is has misinformed him, for he is under the impression that Lutz is married and has only just instigated divorce proceedings, for which he believes me to be responsible.

He confronts me in my room and accuses me of deceitfulness, of taking advantage of Mother's illness to carry on an illicit and clandestine affair with a married man. He tells me that I have betrayed the trust he placed in me, that I have compromised him and dragged our name through the dirt. I flinch under the whiplash of his contempt. His fury mounts because I do not defend myself and finally takes possession of him. His voice, which up to then has been cold and contemptuous, changes to one of rage.

I have always been compliant, have never opposed him. Never in my life have I seen him like this, and all I can do now is to stare at him through a mist, knowing the hopelessness, the uselessness of trying to explain anything at all. Towering menacingly over me, he calls Lutz an unscrupulous rascal without a spark of decency who has taken advantage of an ignorant, stupid girl. 'I shall write to this man myself and tell him that communication between you and him is to cease immediately,' he shouts. 'You are not to write to him or see him again.'

As he turns to leave the room, he catches sight of the framed photograph of Lutz that is standing on my bedside table, picks it up, flings it on the floor and grinds his heel on it. Struck by another thought, he pulls open the drawers of my dressing-table and proceeds to rifle through them. There he finds more photographs and a bundle of letters, which he stuffs into his pocket. After he leaves the room I slowly sink down on my bed and sit still, waiting for the pain and the tumult to ebb. At my feet lies the photo, broken, scattered, trampled underfoot by my father, and I weep for a lost illusion.

Father and I are no longer on speaking terms. He addresses me only when Mother is present, and for her sake both he and I make an effort to appear normal, but Mother senses that there has been a confrontation. When I tell her what has happened she tries to mediate and tells me that I must bear him no ill will, that he is motivated only by his love for me, that my growing independence, the inevitable result of his absence, has created a widening gulf between us. She says that he feels guilty because he cannot be here to look after us at a time when I need a father's guidance. He has no confidence that I will bow to his parental authority, which he is powerless to enforce and expects me to defy: hence his impotent rage. I listen to her but harden my heart against her pleas.

In June the battle around Stalingrad begins to rage. Between September and October the 6th German army penetrates into the centre of Stalingrad. A month later British and American troops, under the leadership of Eisenhower, land in North Africa and the Germans are defeated in Libya. Shortly after this the 6th army in Stalingrad is surrounded by the Russians, and in January it capitulates.

Günter is home. I am with Beatrice when he arrives unexpectedly. I have seen his photo but now that I see him in person I can understand how Beatrice fell in love with him on sight. A slim, square-jawed boy with fine grey eyes beneath straight black brows, tall and finely bred, looking superb in his uniform with the cap set at a rakish angle on his dark hair. They gaze at one another, and I am moved when I see the wonder in their shining eyes; but there is something else I see in the way Günter looks at Beatrice and I shrink from it in horror: it is the fear of one threatened with annihilation.

The morning of yet another day of waiting for the long-overdue letter from Lutz dawns grey and bleak. A fierce wind hurls itself against weeping windowpanes. I switch on the wireless. The news broadcast is preceded by the number one hit of the moment:

> *Es geht alles vorüber,*
> *Es geht alles vorbei,*
> *Auf jeden Dezember folgt wieder ein Mai,*
> *Es geht alles vorüber,*
> *Es geht alles vorbei.*
> *Und zwei die sich lieben, die bleiben sich treu.*

> It will all be over,
> It will all pass away,
> For every December is followed by May,

93

It will all be over,
It will all pass away,
And two people in love will stay faithful
    and true.

For countless lovers, separated by the war, it is 'our song'. For a short space of time I let my thoughts dwell on those across the English Channel, waiting as I am for a sign of life from their dear ones fighting on foreign soil, and wonder what is 'their song'.

Lutz and I have no song that is 'our song'. Not a song but silence was ours during the glorious week we spent together, silence and the peace of the white slopes, the snow-capped mountains. Then, struck by a thought, I walk across to the record-player and select three records from *Friederike*, acquired since the memorable night we spent at the opera. Carefully I stack them on the spindle, turn the lever and sit back to indulge in the voluptuous luxury of poignant nostalgia as I sink into the music, become the music.

The clatter of the letter-box brings me to my feet, and I hurry to collect the mail. Hastily I sort through it and extract the letter bearing the *Feldpost* stamp. The writing on the envelope is that of a stranger. Pierced by a premonitory chill I freeze. When at last I open it a folded page and a second envelope fall out, the latter addressed to me by Lutz. With shaking hands I open it and take in the first sentence at a glance: 'Dearest, I have given this note to a friend, Captain H., with the request to send it to you in the event of my . . . ' The words dance crazily before my eyes. I feel faint and deadly cold but I force myself to read the rest; and I read also Captain H.'s letter, read the words 'unaccounted for then put on the official missing list, transferred on to the missing believed killed list and reported killed in action.' I read them over and over again.

Sounds, words, echo sickeningly in my numb mind,

hammering at the wrapping of lead upon it, trying to enter my consciousness. I want to stop them, to get up and lift the stylus off the record, but all strength has left my trembling limbs. My hands are held down by a great weight; I cannot raise them to my ears to shut out the sound the words; inexorably the voice continues:

> *Warum hast Du mich wachgeküsst,*
> *Hab'nicht gewusst was Liebe ist,*
> *Mein Herz war leicht wie Laub im Wind,*
> *Ich war kein Weib, ich war ein Kind.*

> Why didst thou wake me with a kiss,
> I did not know the meaning of love,
> My heart was light as leaves that fly before
>   the wind,
> No woman yet, I was but a child.

Long after the last strains have faded and died, I make the vast effort needed to propel me towards the record player, to lift off the record and break it in half.

I cannot cry. Throughout the whole of the night I lie dry-eyed, only within me something writhes and cries in bitter torture, twists and turns in my heart without mercy. Scenes of our short meetings pass to and fro in my mind. I live again the brief hours we have spent together, remember every detail from the first encounter to the last goodbye. As clearly as if he were standing before me, I see again the expression in his eyes at the moment of our parting, the quick smile that transformed his strong-boned face and softened his grave eyes, feel the pressure of his hands and lips. If only I could see him just once more, could tell him that I love him. Remembering his generosity and forbearance, I see that I have been selfish and cruel, accepting so much and giving nothing in return. Aching and cold, I lie in an unbearable anguish of remorse. At this moment it is inconceivable that I shall ever love again, for now that

Lutz is dead, I feel that I love him, always have loved him and always will love him.

In the next few weeks I move in a shadowland, cut off from people who walk and talk and laugh in another world, conscious only of the intolerable ache of loss and loneliness that cannot be eased, not even by Mother or Beatrice, who are anxious to comfort and relieve.

11

The Monster Unleashed

Girls are being called up to help in the war effort. I am sitting in a kind of antechamber waiting for my name to be called. When I raise my eyes to look around, I look straight into the hard blue gaze of the supreme commander of the forces, whose life-size picture adorns the wall. I look at it for a long time, and it seems to me that I am not looking at the face of a human being but at the embodiment of a monstrous and pitiless idea. The eyes that once seemed so kind now frighten me. Then my name is called.

Do I want to work on the land as a land army girl or in a factory? It turns out that because of our special circumstances with Mother I am exempt from either. Instead I have to work from noon till 9 p.m. in a *kinderreichen* family. They are indeed rich in children. There are six of them, four boys and two girls, all children for the Führer, their mother tells me proudly; but she cannot cope with them — and neither can I. In addition to looking after them I am required to wash and iron, chop firewood, carry coal from the cellar, shop, cook and clean.

Six weeks later, I go back to the authority to ask for a transfer. The response to my request is a cold stare, but the man in the next cubicle enquires if I can type and do shorthand. For the first time I am grateful to Father for insisting that I attend the course to learn these skills, for the local chamber of commerce urgently needs a shorthand typist, and in this capacity I start work the following day.

As the days lengthen into weeks and months, the darkness is slowly lifting; the agony of grief becomes bearable, and eventually the day comes when I am ashamed because I feel that it is good to be alive, to experience the sheer delight of a swift canter in the crisp morning air and to feel the beat of my heart. And then the bombing starts.

The British air force has carried out air raids on Germany for some time. In one of her letters Aunt Mia reminds us of Heinz's words that in the next war civilians would become targets for bombers. At the beginning of the war the general feeling was that, as with the use of poison gas, this would not happen because of the prospect of retaliatory action. Now we are constantly hearing special announcements informing us that bomber formations have been reported in certain areas of Germany.

Beatrice and I are listening to a concert on the wireless when the music is interrupted by the words, '*Achtung! Achtung!* We are reporting enemy bomber formations on a changing course between Münster and Bremen; various single bomber formations flying east over northern Holland; enemy fighter squadrons in the area of Hanover, Verden, Leipzig and Brandenburg.'

Beatrice seems unusually depressed, and I am relieved to find that she has had a letter from Günter only this morning. So what, I ask, is depressing her? I am becoming neurotically obsessed by the fear that one day she and her grandfather will be arrested by the Gestapo, for they continue to listen to enemy stations. Then they will be taken to a KZ — a *Konzentrationslager*, a concentration camp — which I understand to be an open kind of prison for political prisoners who have defied the government prohibitions.

In reply to my anxious questions, she reluctantly tells me that the British have threatened to raze German cities to the ground, and the targets will not only be military but will include the dwellings of the civilian population.

I look at her aghast. 'You mean that they are actually

saying that, telling us that they will deliberately kill women and children?'

'They say it will put a speedy end to the war and save millions of lives.'

Soon afterwards reports of the first obliteration raids reach us. Uncle August's sister and her family have left Hamburg and their home. They can no longer bear the nights of horror, the sight of the badly injured being shot by the SS, of bodies being hurriedly thrown into the River Elbe. We are horrified, not knowing that the bombing of civilian targets on the largest scale is yet to come, when countless thousands of women and children will be burned to death, for Dresden is still unscathed.

Our bombers retaliate, and I imagine the reports that those across the Channel have about our raids. Despairingly I turn to Mother. 'Which side,' I ask, 'is God on? There are invocations of "God and the right" on both sides; so who, for heaven's sake, is right?'

Her answer comes in a voice so low that I have to strain to hear it; but it is firm. 'Neither. Do you not remember our Lord's command, "Love your enemies, do good to those who hate you, bless those who curse you, pray for those who mistreat you. If someone strikes you on one cheek, turn to him the other also."' She shivers: 'It is evil to kill.'

I think of Lutz, who has fought and has had to kill and has laid down his life; and in my anguish I quote, 'No one has greater love than the one who lays down his life for his friends.' Then I add, 'And those who kill because they have to, because they are caught up in a political quarrel for which they are not responsible, also lay down their lives.'

She bows her head: 'We are all responsible,' and after a pause, 'but you have quoted out of context. Jesus prefaced those words by saying, "My command is this: Love one another as I have loved you."'

Suddenly the announcements of approaching bomber

formations mention Vienna, Salzburg, Graz. When the air raid warning sounds, Beatrice and I go outside and gaze at the long fingers of the searchlights exploring the night sky. The solicitor who lives in the flat below joins us just as a squadron of bombers in tight formation appears and anti-aircraft guns begin to boom. We stay outside until black objects begin to tumble from the sky and cyclones of flame leap up where they drop. Then we hastily retreat into the cellar, which has been transformed into a kind of doss-house by the addition of chairs, pieces of carpet, sleeping bags and various other impedimenta.

The unmarried daughter of one of our neighbours has come home from Vienna, where she worked until the birth of her baby, and she is calmly feeding her small son a kind of muesli. Every time she lifts the spoon he crows with delight, eager to grasp it. My heart contracts. I do not know who the father is but guess that he is probably fighting somewhere, surrounded by a similar inferno to that raging outside. Perhaps he is facing death at this very moment, or maybe she has already received the letter telling her that he was killed in action. I turn my head to look for Mother, and at that moment the foundations of the house shake with the force of an explosion. Instinctively people cover their heads with their hands. Within the split second before the light flickers and goes out I see that Mother is not with us. Grasping my torch I head for the door. Someone is barring my way. 'Stay where you are, that was a direct hit.' But I push him away.

'Mother!' I cry hoarsely, 'Mother!' With noise reverberating all around me I stumble up the cellar steps that seem to sway under me, and wrench open the door that leads into the entrance hall. I smell burning, but the staircase is intact. There is glass underfoot and smoke is drifting through the shattered windows. The bright glow behind them is throwing everything into ghostly relief. The door to our flat is open, and in the bedroom I find Mother on her knees.

I throw my arms around her and implore her to come down, but she is perfectly calm. I cannot hear her reply because the noise of another ear-splitting explosion rends the air. Detonation after detonation rocks the house as I kneel beside her. She is holding me in her arms, and in the ghastly reflection of the conflagration that is raging outside I see her lips moving. I bend closer, putting my ear to them, and she raises her voice: 'Thou shalt not be afraid for any terror by night: nor for the arrow that flieth by day. There shall no evil happen unto thee: neither shall any plague come near thy dwelling. For he shall give his angels charge over thee to keep thee in all thy ways.'

At this moment, with death and destruction all around us, the words that strengthen and comfort her appal me, for surely a God who can look upon this must be a monster of cruelty.

Gently I disengage myself from her embrace and approach the window, which miraculously is still intact. Mother, who has also risen, is opening it. I had not thought of it, but leaving it closed might have meant injury if another explosion were to shatter the glass. I wonder why she had not opened it before. Incendiaries cascade from the sky and the air is alive with the drone and throb of engines. Smoke drifts into the room, and with it comes ash, huge black floating flakes of hell.

The red glow is coming from the centre of the city, but further down our road a house stands in flames. A white-starred plane nose-dives with a horrible scream, and involuntarily I duck. An explosion follows and once more hell erupts.

Then, in a probing finger of light that catches and imprisons it, I see a bomber hanging like a yo-yo on a golden thread. The plane spins madly and drops, dragging behind it a trail of fire. Another plane is caught in the golden flute of the searchlight, flutters madly like a tormented moth and then escapes with the beams wildly darting across each other in their endeavour to relocate it.

I stand and watch, having ceased to care about safety, fascinated by the spectacle of destruction. The monster that has threatened my childhood has been unleashed and is now in total control.

When the all clear sounds, Beatrice and I go outside. Rescue workers are already at the house at the end of the road. Part of it is still standing and a bathtub is dizzily suspended in the air. In horrified disbelief we stare at bodies arranged side by side in the debris on the pavement. Further down a building is blown inside out and a thick pillar of black smoke rises behind it.

As the days pass, we become inured to the wailing of the siren; sometimes we even sleep through it, for it is not always followed by an air raid. At times the planes that approach our area change course, at others they pass over us, having jettisoned their deadly cargo elsewhere. I am amazed to see that the worse conditions become, the more people's attitudes harden, and they increase in their determination to endure hardships and suffering. I remark to Beatrice that the bombing, far from demoralizing people, appears to be having the opposite effect. Even though no one is any longer certain of victory, everyone battles on with grim endurance. Sadly she points out that what we are experiencing is not yet obliteration bombing.

Mother is praying continually, no matter where she is or what she is doing: praying not only for those of our country but for everyone involved in this diabolical war. She has taken upon herself the penitence for the suffering endured by all humanity caught up in it. On foreign soil everywhere our soldiers are dying in their thousands, yet Goebbels still proclaims that our nation is about to witness the proudest victory in history.

July sees the downfall of Mussolini, and in September a special German task force sets him free. Just before Christmas our phone rings. When I lift the receiver, I am surprised to hear the quavery voice of the old admiral asking if I will be kind enough to step over. Filled with foreboding, I hurry across the yard. Beatrice is lying on her bed. Frau Trapp whispers to me that she has been given a sedative. I look at a letter that is lying beside Beatrice and to which she points. 'From Günter?' I ask. She tries to speak but her voice is so choked with tears that I cannot understand what she says. I turn to Frau Trapp. 'Is he . . . ?'

She nods, pressing her handkerchief to her eyes. 'We've just been told.'

Beatrice lifts one of the pages of the letter and points at four words underlined twice: *'I want to live.'* 'His last letter.' Anguish shakes her voice. I kneel down by the bed and take her hands in mine, and so we remain until the sedative takes effect and she falls asleep. As I walk back across the yard, I hear a woman's voice rising shrilly in a familiar song above the rattle of crockery:

> *Es geht alles vorüber,*
> *Es geht alles vorbei. . .*

By the beginning of 1944 Soviet troops have advanced as far as Poland. In the preceding year the British and their allies landed in Sicily and southern Italy, and in June 1944 they land in Normandy. The fight along the coast of northern France has begun.

Air raids have become a problem, for Mother sets out for the nearest church as soon as the siren is heard and, once there, spends hours in prayer. Alone with her in the church, oppressed by the faint odour of incense that contrasts strongly with the acrid smell of burning from outside, I sit resentfully while Mother is kneeling, marvellously still, her self utterly lost in contemplation and prayer.

Sometimes I try to pray, but prayer will not come, for I am sore with revolt — revolt against what is happening all around, revolt against having to spend my time here, revolt against God. Sometimes we are in time to reach the church before the bombing starts; at other times we seem to make our way through a hail of bombs, shrapnel, dust and flying masonry. There is as much danger from falling anti-aircraft shells as from bombs. It is always dark in the church: only the glow of the conflagration outside creates a false illusive sunset. My feelings during these excursions range from abject terror to almost complete apathy.

On one such night, on our way home, we pass what had been until a few hours ago the house of Günter's parents. I gaze at the unbelievable ruin as I start to pick my way through piles of bricks and broken glass but am ordered back by rescue workers who have begun to clear the masonry that has fallen. I confer with Mother: should I tell Beatrice about this now or wait until morning? I shrink from telling her. It is too cruel. Since Günter's death, she has visited his parents regularly. It seems unlikely that those who have sheltered in the cellar are still alive. Mother thinks I ought to tell her tonight.

I slowly climb the stairs to the admiral's flat, debating on how best to break the news to Beatrice. Frau Trapp opens the door. She is in her dressing-gown. 'Beatrice is out,' she says, eyeing me curiously, 'she has gone to see Günter's parents.'

I stare at her stupidly, then push past her and make for Beatrice's room. I open the door and switch on the light. On Beatrice's bed the duvet is neatly folded; on her bed-side table stands a photo of Günter. My eyes take in the details that my mind refuses to register.

Frau Trapp grips my arm: 'What is it, what is the matter?'

I try to speak but my lips refuse to form the words.

'The house,' I stammer, 'the house has been hit.'

'Your house?'

I shake my head. 'Günter's, his parents' house.'

Frau Trapp's face whitens, she looks at me in stunned disbelief, then she turns abruptly and leaves the room. My legs are shaking uncontrollably and I sit down on the bed. When Frau Trapp returns, she has put on a coat but is still wearing her slippers. I point to them and she kicks them off. Pulling Beatrice's fur boots out of the wardrobe, she puts these on instead. Without speaking we rush out into the night.

The area around the ruin is now cordoned off. Rescue workers are working feverishly among piles of bricks and shattered wood, lifting doors, twisted metal, sofas, tables. Somewhere under the rubble, the bent iron and twisted steel lies Beatrice, if not dead then stunned, suffocated or dying in agony.

At the corner of the road firemen are playing water jets on the burning walls of a house. Suddenly with a hiss and crash a ceiling comes down, then slowly the walls crumple and cave in. Beside me Frau Trapp stands staring at a heap of tangled pipes. Tears are streaming down her cheeks, her lips are moving soundlessly and her fingers are slipping along the beads of her rosary. Someone offers us some *'Ersatz'* coffee, which we refuse.

Some of the rescue workers are inserting timber supports, while the others continue to tunnel.

'They are so slow, so slow.' Without being conscious of it I have spoken aloud.

The man beside me explains that they have to work slowly, an over-hasty move can ruin what has been achieved so far, can mean that the whole operation has to start afresh.

'The debris has poured into the cellar,' someone else says. The faces around me are grey with exhaustion and dust.

The man in front of me raises his hand; everyone falls silent, for the rescue workers have ceased to work. One of them is kneeling where an opening has appeared among the twisted girders. *'Könnt ihr mich hören?'* he asks.

Oh, please let them be alive to hear, I pray. A picture of Beatrice flashes through my mind, a picture of her crushed and unable to speak. He repeats his question. Silence! When the men continue to work, those watching are silent, listening intently for any sounds indicating that there might be survivors underneath the wreckage. The silence becomes oppressive. It might be hours yet before anyone is reached.

When Beatrice is brought out on a stretcher, the first light of dawn is trying to break through the haze of dust and smoke. She is covered with a blanket and given a shot of morphine. Her hair is matted with blood and her face is waxen, but her eyes are open and I think I see recognition in them as the men lower the stretcher beside me before pushing it into the ambulance. All the way to the hospital my mind concentrates on one thought, 'Beatrice must live.' I am willing her to live. I clench my hands until the nails bite into my palms.

The young doctor at the hospital is a friend of ours. While he speaks I stare at his coat, see each thread of the stitching on the lapels and begin to count them. Had she lived her legs would have had to be amputated, he says. My eyes are clinging to the stitches as to a lifeline that will save me from falling. Later Frau Trapp comes over and tells us that Günter's parents must have died immediately under the first great fall of masonry.

My early conviction that I must overcome my fears by stoicism has led me as I grow older to the study of the Stoics. So now I turn to the writings of Seneca for help. I tell myself over and over again that I must remember only the joy I have had from Lutz, from Beatrice; that even though I have lost them both, no one can snatch from me what I have had, and it will remain mine for ever. But stoicism fails me. It is as though the bomb that has destroyed Beatrice has also destroyed the barrier that I began to erect after Mother was taken away for the first time and I determined not to give in to self-pity. Then I had deliberately begun to harden myself, resolved that nothing, however terrifying, should see me give way to despair and tears, not realizing that the emotions I was trying to suppress would eventually take revenge, that tears could save me from the ultimate despair.

Beatrice's death has released all the pent-up torrent of my grief. I lie on my bed, shaken by sobs. At last, in the spurious peace of exhaustion, I lie empty of tears, knowing that the pain will return but that now, for a brief spell, there is blessed, mindless calm, emptiness, a state of no thought, of not feeling, that I want to prolong for ever. Mother is sitting by me. She sits quite still, just as she did after the news of Lutz's death had come, speaking no word of pity but sharing my grief, my pain, and her presence is balm. I know she is praying, and I am glad, though I no longer believe that the world in which we live is directed by a loving and compassionate God but feel it is rushing pilotless and rudderless to its doom. A line from Shakespeare is beating a relentless rhythm in my head:

Like flies to wanton boys are we to the gods.
They kill us for their sport.

By now there is no doubt left in my mind that Hitler's regime is evil, and yet many of those whom I know to be in sympathy with it are honest men and women who sincerely believe, as I once did, that Germany is the victim of envy and malice and must be defended by any means and at all costs. There have been rumours from time to time of attempts at opposition, but they all appear to have failed. I hope that now is the time to carry out a coup and am electrified by the announcement one afternoon, on 21 July, that there has been an attempt to assassinate the Führer. The announcement is followed by the information that Colonel Count Stauffenberg and the officers who with him planned and made the attempt have failed and have been executed that same night. Later Hitler himself, in a broadcast to the nation, thanks his maker and divine providence for preserving him to carry on the work. I start when I hear Mother quoting the Psalms, saying 'The words of his mouth were softer than butter, having war in his heart: his words were smoother than oil, and yet be they very swords.'

12
Defeat

On 25 September the *Deutsche Volkssturm* is set up. This campaign to involve even more of the German people in the defence of their *Vaterland* means that able-bodied men aged between sixteen and sixty are to be called up. Children, eager to play soldiers and to show their loyalty to a Führer whom they believe invulnerable, and old men, with thinning hair and bowed shoulders, take up arms. I am convinced that the war will be over soon.

Father is now in charge of civil defence in the Cologne area. I have to go to see him there, and from the moment I arrive I begin to live a nightmare that is dominated by the incessant blood-chilling sound of the sirens that howl and wail disconsolately. Searchlights cross and recross like the foils of giants fencing among the stars, but the anti-aircraft defences are powerless against the continuous stream of enemy aircraft. I now know that the bombing I have seen in Graz is as nothing compared to the inferno raging in this city where nothing appears to be left to be destroyed. At night *Weihnachtsbäume*, marker flares that do indeed look like lighted Christmas trees, as their name suggests, descend anywhere, and people run like rabbits into bunkers that shake continuously under the unceasing onslaught of explosions.

After two days Father sends me home and, feeling that it cannot be any worse there than in Cologne, I decide to go via Berlin and call on Mother's brother Paul and

Father's two brothers Erich and Martin and their families, who have remained in Berlin throughout the war. But I never get to see either, for when I arrive at what was once the station, the drone of aircraft and the blinding Christmas-tree markers that descend crackling loudly drive me into the doorway of one of the few remaining buildings in the street, which happens to be a hotel. I join those who make for the cellar when a violent explosion pulverizes the building above us and is succeeded by the crash of falling masonry.

The horror of what follows is undoubtedly responsible for a kind of amnesia that in later years blots out most of the memory of my visit to Cologne as well as the reason for it. In the cellar there is increasing panic as the oxygen in the confined space in which we huddle decreases rapidly and the dust begins to choke us. Someone from somewhere gets wine into which we dip our handkerchiefs, which we then hold over mouth and nose. I have no recollection of how long we were buried alive. My next memory is of my trying to make my way back to the station. There are fires all around me creating an illusory summer's day as I stumble along in a stupor. A building that I have just passed collapses with a sickening crash; a sheet of flame sends white-hot sparks towards me where I try to make my way through burning wreckage; snakes of black smoke curl around me, attacking my eyes so that I can hardly see. I am driven on by one thought — Graz. I must get back to Graz, which has become a haven offering protection.

There is a train in the station, and just as the inferno starts anew it crawls out into the night.

As it ploughs through the debris of twisted metal and through exploding shells, I see in the light of the conflagration that turns night into day that buildings are disintegrating like piles of toy blocks playfully knocked over by a child. I put my head through the gaping opening of the window and shout. My shouts are drowned by the noise of explosions, and I am compelled to shout louder

110

in an insane desire to make myself heard. At last, when miraculously the train has left Berlin behind and all I can see is a brassy sky smudged with smoke, I collapse and weep. In some rational corner of my mind a voice seems to whisper that I am suffering from shock; yet in later years it is this departure from Berlin that I remember more clearly than anything else surrounding my visit.

The 'holy night' of 1944 is rent by the explosions of countless bombs, for on that Christmas Eve three thousand American aircraft attack thirty-two towns and cities in the biggest operation of the war. Shortly afterwards the Russians start their big campaign, while in the west the Allies are advancing. We hear rumours that the Russians have reached Posen and that Russian tanks are standing by the Oder between Oppeln and Ohlau, names familiar to us who had lived in that area. SS leader Himmler — a man detested by Father, though I am not supposed to know this — becomes supreme commander of the army division Weichsel. After the war is over I learn that it is about this time that the army's chief of staff is trying to warn Foreign Minister von Ribbentrop that the situation is critical. Mother and I are convinced of the imminence of total breakdown and are agonizing about the fate of our relatives east of the Oder and that of Opa in the Riesengebirge. Reports filter through of the shelling of overcrowded cattle trains full of refugees, of the killing of defenceless women and children, the old and infirm, of the nightmare flight of those escaping on foot, stumbling through the snow behind the push-cart on which they have piled a few belongings while behind them their homes are going up in flames.

Light Russian aircraft, unannounced by sirens, appear over Graz, flying very low and dropping small bombs at any and every target. They come in ones and twos. The fighting between Russian and German troops comes nearer and nearer. Villages are captured by Russians and recaptured by Germans. Reports of terrible atrocities reach us.

Girls and women aged between eleven and eighty or more are raped by gangs of Russian soldiers. A farmer who tries to stop a gang from raping his wife and daughters is crucified on the door of his barn while they are being raped by successive gangs. While the Russians push forward from the east, the Americans advance in the west and the British reach Germany from Holland. Fighting in Italy is over and Mussolini has been executed. Dazed, we receive news bulletin after news bulletin. Hitler has taken his own life in the bunker of the Reichskanzlei; his successor, Karl Dönitz, Admiral of the Fleet and supreme commander of the navy, signs the unconditional capitulation of Germany.

On 9 May 1945 we are told that since midnight fighting has ceased on all fronts. We stand with bowed heads and remember the millions who have died. We remember also the words of Goebbels, published in *Das Reich* on 14 November 1943: 'We have burnt our bridges . . . we are forced and resolved to fight to the last . . . we shall enter history as the greatest statesmen or as the greatest criminals.'

13
Flight

With a mixture of apprehension and relief we wait for the arrival of the British who, we are told, are to occupy Graz. Before the war I saw some of Shakespeare's plays performed in German, and in translation I have read books by Jane Austen, Trollope, Galsworthy, Dickens and others that I have found in our bookcase. My picture of England is therefore coloured by what I have read and is somewhat dated. Although we are vastly relieved that we shall not have to live under the terror of a Russian occupation, we are nevertheless apprehensive, for we do not know how the victors will treat us, the vanquished.

One morning, when I raise lids heavy with sleep to see instead of the black-out curtains the blue sky and green trees framed in the open window, my mind drowsily gropes towards the concept of peace, and happily I surrender once more to sleep. Dream and reality merge when Mother enters the room to tell me that she has just heard that the Russians are advancing on Graz. Even while I protest, I squeeze my eyelids shut in an endeavour to recapture the images of my dream that are rapidly losing form and focus. Briefly they rise once more to the surface, waver, then sharpen in outline. As so often when dreaming just before waking, I have had an extraordinarily vivid dream of Russian tanks approaching Graz, of streets rapidly emptying and people waiting huddled, apprehensive and frightened in their homes, listening for the tread of heavy boots and voices raised in a language that sounds barbaric because it is incomprehensible. A prophetic dream? Mother dreamed that Father had been shot, and he had indeed been wounded at the time when she had dreamed this. I recoil in horror from the idea and resolutely dismiss the notion as foolish and fanciful.

I am due to take Graziella, who is at the moment stabled in Graz, down to Hetty, where she is to remain until things have settled down here. As I prepare to mount I hesitate for a moment. Can what Mother has heard be true? I dismiss the thought and decide to turn back immediately after delivering Graziella so that I shall be back in town by early afternoon.

In the town the scent of lilac floats sweetly over fire-blackened ruins. The morning is perfect for a ride into the country. It is going to be a hot day, but as yet the air is pleasant, with a soft breeze dancing in the trees and caressing my face. I revel in the peace and stillness. Away from the ruined buildings one can almost forget destruction and death, forget the last fearful months. Graziella, who has not been sufficiently exercised of late, is restless, flinging up her head and tossing her tail. I talk to her and pat her glossy neck, promising her a spanking trot as soon as we get out into the country. The woods are arrayed in glory, with the straight slim trunks and slender spires of the pines showing black against the glossy luminous green of beech and ash. The lush meadows are ablaze with golden dandelions and buttercups. They stretch upwards to the hills and mountains that tower above them in proud and lonely splendour under the sky of a world once more at peace. The early morning light reflects on each leaf and petal with such brilliance that my eyes are dazzled.

I give Graziella a light touch with the whip and, arching her neck, she is off at a splendid gallop. With the war over and the exciting promise that spring brings year after year of life out of death, of all things made new, my heart lifts, and I begin to build castles in the air. Mother will

114

now get completely well, and Father will come home. We shall build the house on the plot towards Maria Trost that we have already selected. I shall complete my studies and become a surgeon. Life might once again be good. Admittedly there is much uncertainty about the future, and the scars the war has left will remain with us for a long time — perhaps for the rest of our lives; but there is so much still to be enjoyed, and now there *is* a future. On this brilliant May morning, with the the breeze fanning my cheeks, the woodlands in splendour, I am once more in love with life, in love with the future.

At the crossroads I rein in sharply and Graziella rears at the check. Approaching us in the distance is a seemingly endless column of soldiers. We stand in the utter stillness, sunlit and colonnaded with trees. My heart is beating like a drum. Are they Russians? I narrow my eyes in an effort to get a clearer view. Then I recognize the uniforms — or rather what is left of them — and see that I am looking at defeat, the pitiful remnants of what was once a great army, crack soldiers sent out by Hitler to conquer the world in a war that was not of their seeking. They stagger like drunks. The rags that they have wrapped around their heads and their feet show red where the blood has seeped through. Here and there two stumble along trying to support a third whose eyes are sunken in their sockets and look dead. They shuffle and hobble along as fast as their bleeding feet will let them. Their faces, drawn, grey, haggard and utterly weary, are ghastly. The sun is still shining but all the warmth has gone out of it. As they come up to me they point behind them. 'Move! The Russians are right behind us.'

'But,' I argue, 'the English are to occupy Styria.'

They lift their hands in a helpless gesture: 'The Russians are already in Graz.'

So the rumours were right after all. I wheel Graziella round and head back. A cry rises behind me: 'No, not that way, you'll run straight into them.' Giving Graziella

115

a free rein and leaning forward I head for a nearby copse. Once inside it, I follow a narrow track, putting my head close to Graziella's mane to avoid overhanging branches. Graziella swerves as a rabbit scuttles across our path and I take a firmer grip on the reins. Then the track widens, but here the ground is very rough and quite unsuitable for a gallop. I am trying to approach Graz while keeping well away from main roads, but I have been born without any sense of direction and after a short while I am hopelessly lost. Still the thought of Mother having to face the Russians on her own drives me on. Looking ahead I see a wide ditch, and on the other side of it a bank, a formidable obstacle. On either side of me an impenetrable wall of fir trees borders the track. There is nothing for it: we must jump. I give Graziella a steady rein, and whinnying she gathers herself for the leap, rises like a bird and with her mane soaring clears the ditch and the bank. 'Good girl,' I murmur, patting her neck and flanks when she stands trembling on the other side.

The track is still widening, and after a few minutes it occurs to me that we might be approaching a road and that I might get my bearings if I take a brief look along it. Except for the clicking of Graziella's teeth on the bit, the creak of the saddle and the soft thud of her hoofs, all is silent. Cautiously I urge her forward, listening intently. Suddenly the track comes to an end and there is no road — just another track to the right into which I turn. Then I freeze.

We have come to a halt in front of two tanks. Before them stand two Russians, and two more stand on the second. I notice that the gun hatches are open. They must have heard us approaching. With my knees I grip Graziella's heaving sides. 'Go on, Graziella!' She stands terrified, her nostrils dilating, her body quivering. I give her a sharp cut and she rears and paws the air, her eyes rolling wildly. One of the men laughs and grabs hold of the reins. Graziella gives a shrill neigh, pawing the ground and tossing her head. At the same moment I am grabbed from behind and pulled down.

Another man, who appears to be an officer, has emerged from behind the second tank. He barks a command and I am handed over. He hauls me on to the rear deck of the tank and the vehicle lurches off, throwing me off balance, and only by clutching wildly at the turret do I save myself from falling. I am sick with terror and incapable of thought or action. Eventually, after what seems an eternity, we draw up outside a house where a number of Russian vehicles are parked. The officer moves unsteadily towards the door and kicks it open with his boot. Then he motions to one of the soldiers and shouts an order. I am pushed into a downstairs room. Closing the door behind him, the officer advances towards me. I retreat, stumble against a chair, grab it instead and hold it in front of me. He takes hold of it with one hand and, laughing derisively, flings it aside. With my hands held out to fend him off, I stare at the slanting eyes, the prominent cheekbones, the leering mouth. Paralysed with terror I watch him approaching very slowly and deliberately. I am trapped, and suddenly he pounces, pins my hands to my sides and pushes me hard against the wall. I scream and kick as hard as I can, when suddenly the door opens to admit a soldier. The officer wheels round and shouts angrily. An argument follows, then he turns and roughly pushes the grinning soldier, who is showing signs of taking over, through the door. He shuts it behind him and locks it from outside.

The air is heavy with fumes of alcohol. Wildly I look round for some weapon, a way of escape, but my eyes refuse to focus, and objects become distorted and unstable as I fight faintness and nausea. The noise outside has increased and now I become conscious of many voices creating a general uproar, of the revving of engines, and then another blood-chilling sound — the piercing screams of a woman in a room above. With an effort I force my limbs to move and find myself facing the window. At the same time my mind registers the fact that I am imprisoned in a room on the ground floor. It is instinct rather than will-power that propels me towards the window. My hands, weak with shock, fumble with the handle, but the window swings open easily and I climb over the sill and drop to the ground in the vegetable garden at the back of the house.

Adjoining the garden is a cemetery, and behind it a track leads through pine woods into the hills. With my heart racing violently and my throat constricted with fear I run towards it. All the noise is coming from behind me, where the Russians appear to be congregating in the road. I have reached the cemetery when a bullet whizzes past my head. Assuming that the shot has been aimed at me I drop to my knees behind a bush. Any moment now I shall be dragged back to the house. At the thought I spring up and continue to run across the cemetery. Better to be hit by a bullet and killed than to be recaptured.

Bullets continue to whistle through the air, but most of them ricochet off gravestones that are nowhere near me. I have heard people say that the Russians, when drunk, are trigger-happy and shoot into the air. But any moment now my absence must be discovered and the open window will indicate the way I have gone. There is little hope that I shall get away, but I run and crouch and run on again bent double, zigzagging between the gravestones. Though perspiration is trickling down my back, I feel deadly cold, and my mouth is dry with fear.

A stone wall bordering the far side of the cemetery presents a worrying obstacle. It is too high for me to climb; moreover I shall be in full view if I attempt to do so. I look behind me. I can still see the open window, and unbelievably there is no sign of anyone following me. They are still firing in all directions. I have reached the wall when I hear a shout behind me. Frantically I look up and down the wall. Just to my right there is a small gap in the stones. I race towards it. Wriggling furiously I manage to get my

118

head, one shoulder and an arm through, catch hold of the low-hanging branch of a small fir tree and pull with all my strength. After an eternity, scratched and torn and bleeding, I drop down on the other side where the trees are growing close together and crash through the undergrowth like a hunted hare until, dazed and quivering, I collapse with my breath rasping and my lungs bursting.

With my face pressed to the ground, inhaling the sweetish odour of the forest soil, I try to control the grating noise of my breathing that must surely be audible throughout the wood. I am still gasping for breath when I hear the voices of those who have followed me coming closer. Gagged by my handkerchief I flatten myself as much as I can. The sound of voices and of bodies crashing through the undergrowth comes closer, then a stick is thrust close to where I lie paralysed with horror, as I am to do in the nightmares in which for years to come I am to relive this moment over and over again.

For a long time after the voices have faded, I lie motionless, wedged between tree trunks, listening intently; apart from the hum of insects and the drumming of the pulse in my ears all is still. When I am sure that the men must have returned to the house another way, I proceed slowly and cautiously up the hill. Every bush is a Russian soldier; the brambles and boughs catching my jodhpurs and my sleeves are clutching hands; the pulse still hammering loudly in my ears is the sound of pursuing footsteps. The wood is full of eyes and hands, watching, waiting to pounce. I must get as high up as possible: the Russians in their drunken state will hardly feel like mountaineering. But the fear and exertion of running away have exhausted me, have robbed my limbs of strength, and I have to give in. Curled up in a small hollow where herbs and weeds grow in thick profusion, I fall asleep.

I wake shivering with the stale taste of fear in my mouth. I feel weak and very thirsty. I have had nothing to eat or drink since morning. There must be a stream nearby, and I set out to find it.

Clouds have appeared. In the feathery shade of twilight the brightest light has drained from them and they are flushed with a rich afterglow. Swarms of gnats dance round the trees. The wood, which on days when I have walked for pleasure has always been so friendly, is dark and alive and watching me coldly; the cheerful sparkle of the stars has hardened into a cold, frozen and sinister glitter. Now that it is dark, I move along the track, but close to the edge of the wood so that I can disappear quickly if need be. From time to time I stop to listen for the sound of water. Everywhere in these mountains there are hundreds of laughing springs, running down in singing brooks and white-laced waterfalls, but today I cannot find them.

It is not long before tiredness overtakes me once more and, after breaking some branches off a beech tree to use as mattress and coverlet, for it is turning very cold, I lie down under the shelter of a tall fir tree, pillowing my head on my arms. My thoughts rush through my mind as erratically as the ants I feel running over my hands. Where is Mother? What has happened since the Russians arrived in Graz? I know now that it was foolish of me to try to get back. I am powerless to prevent whatever it is that is taking place there, and she will take comfort from the fact that I have escaped. But I cannot stop thinking of her, though I shrink from considering some of the unspeakable horrors that have been perpetrated elsewhere or the consequences of them to someone as sensitive and vulnerable as she is. Then my thoughts turn to Graziella. Where is she now? Can she have escaped? And if she has, where will she head for? Or are the Russians holding her? I imagine her whinnying disconsolately for home and stables.

The crescent moon that has hung in the sky disappears behind the clouds, and I lie embedded in the pitch darkness, feeling utterly forsaken by God and all humanity. After a time I become aware of the intensity of wildlife

120

in the forest; all around me I hear rustling, the stealthy movements of woodland animals, the swish of wings, an owl's hunting cry and the shrieks of some tiny creature hunted as I am. On the point of sleep I am startled by a dead twig snapping with a loud crack. Hours later I fall into a fitful sleep.

I wake as grey dawn is breaking, stand up, bend and stretch to ease my aching limbs and breathe in the dewy scent of the flowers. My clothes are damp with dew, and a pearly morning mist is clinging like spiders' webs to twigs and branches. As I set off once more, I feel that I would give anything for the gift of a sense of direction, for without even the sun to guide me I have no idea whether I am heading east or west, and my only hope of getting as far away from the Russians as possible is to climb higher and higher to where wind-tossed mountain larches stand like the bent figures of old women.

At last I come upon a crystal spring gushing from rocks to water the slopes, leaping merrily from boulder to boulder, and with a glad cry I thrust my hands into the liquid crystal and drink greedily. Mother and I, when walking in the mountains, have often enjoyed the ice-cold water of a mountain stream like this, but never before has it tasted so delicious. When I have drunk my fill I wash my face and, having pulled a small comb that I carry in my jerkin through my tangled hair, I feel ready to face the day. I am terribly hungry but I know that one can easily survive for days without food as long as one has water. I try to persuade myself that I have just eaten a breakfast of rolls with ham and cannot possibly feel hungry. It does not work, but as the day wears on I feel less ravenous.

After stumbling through dense undergrowth, I emerge into a beech wood. Looking upwards to the canopy above me, I am reminded of the vaulted roof of a cathedral, and the luminous brightness and serenity has a calming, soothing effect on me. Eventually the path I follow leads into a dark and rocky ravine, where great boulders and fallen trees make progress difficult. Here and there spears of sunlight strike through branches, dappling the leaves. Once a deer bounds across my path. I look up to where there are no trees except the stunted larches, then scrub and eventually bare scree, and I continue to scramble upwards, sweat streaming down my face, until I stumble on to a little plateau and see the valley spread out far below me with roads meandering palely through it. Among a clump of trees a chimney smokes, and further in the distance a cluster of houses indicates the presence of a small village.

What is happening down there? I can see no movement, no cars, though occasionally a faint sound very much like the revving of an engine reaches me. I scan the mountain panorama but cannot work out where I am. The profound silence is broken only by bird song, the intermittent call of the cuckoo and the faint crowing of a rooster in the far distance. Before me the meadow is alight with colour: cowslips, primroses, ranunculus and buttercups glimmer pure gold, patches of forget-me-nots are blue clouds over the green, marguerites sparkle like stars, there are wood anemones and clusters of deep blue gentians and myriads of other alpine flowers. Presently a group of swifts begins to swoop and dip overhead in the soft blue, cutting through the silent air. Sometimes they pass so close to where I sit motionless that I can almost feel the tips of their wings brushing my cheek. The scene is one of peaceful friendliness, but I could not feel more alone if I were the only human being left in the world. I look again at the birds soaring effortlessly, diving and dipping and circling round me as though trying to comfort me in my loneliness. Down there are men and women working and children playing, but I am cut off from them by my fear.

As the last streaks of daylight begin to fade I decide to climb down and try to find some sort of habitation. The descent is long and tedious, for in my desire to get away I have climbed high. It is quite dark when at last I reach a clearing and see a faint glimmer of light through the trees above a slight incline, and in a few minutes I reach a path leading to the front door of a wooden house. There is no response to my timid knock; a further louder knock remains unanswered, and suddenly feeling desperate, I begin to hammer on the door. I almost fall into the arms of a burly man when it opens and light spills out on to the path. He glowers at me. 'What do you want?'

'Oh please,' I stammer, 'can you sell me some food?' I hold out some money. He looks at it suspiciously: 'Money's no good to us.' Round my neck I wear the gold cross that Mother gave me for my first communion, but it is hidden under my clothes and I am determined not to part with it.

A woman comes up behind the man. 'What are you doing here?' she demands, looking curiously at my riding outfit, torn clothes and scratched face and arms.

'I am running away from the Russians, they caught me down there' — I gesture vaguely downhill — 'but I got away.'

'You'd better get on then,' she says curtly, 'we don't want any Russians here.'

'But that was yesterday,' I protest, 'I've come a long way since then. Please sell me some food, I have had nothing to eat since yesterday morning.' I reach for the doorpost that recedes into blackness.

When I open my eyes I am sitting on a chair and someone, I guess it is the man, is holding my head down to my knees. Then he sits me upright and holds a bottle of *Enzian*, gentian liquor, to my lips. The spirit runs down my throat like fire. I see that I am in a room serving as combined living-room and kitchen. The woman gathers up some crockery from the table and lowers it into the sink, then she disappears into the pantry and comes out with a saucepan. She places it on the top of the big black kitchen range and begins to stir the contents. My stomach is churning so much that I have to restrain myself from getting up, for despite my weakness I want to see what she is doing.

I put my handkerchief to my lips to wipe away the saliva that is beginning to accumulate in the corners of my mouth. At last she sets a steaming bowl before me and immediately I start to eat and burn my mouth. It is *Polenta*, a kind of porridge made of ground maize. The woman, who has once again disappeared into the pantry, now comes out with a jug and from it pours buttermilk on the *Polenta*. Then she fills an earthenware mug with buttermilk and watches me.

Burning my mouth has reminded me that it is advisable to eat slowly after a long fast, and I try to force myself to savour each spoonful. Never before has food tasted so good, and when I have finished scraping out every tiny morsel I say so. Then I tell them my story from the moment of waking in Graz. They are clearly disturbed and question me closely. They in turn tell me about the people roaming the hills. There are men who they think must be prominent Nazis trying to hide, but recently some of those who have called looked like Russians, spoke German with a distinct Russian accent but were wearing German uniforms. I can think of no explanation.

The fact that I blacked out has made them sorry for me, and I am allowed to spend the night in the loft, where I bed down on what is left of last year's hay. When I wake in the morning I feel rested and full of optimism, especially since they have told me that I am heading in the right direction for Carinthia. After washing outside under the pump and eating another bowl of *Polenta* I am ready to leave. When the husband is not looking the woman hands me my folded jerkin and, by putting her finger to her lips, indicates that I am not to comment on the fact that it feels heavy. They point me once more in the direction of Carinthia, which I know is already occupied by the British, and I stride off.

Once out of sight I examine my jerkin and find wrapped in it a loaf of black bread. This is treasure indeed, and I break off small sections that I put into the various pockets of my jodhpurs and shirt. I shall only eat two pieces each day, since I don't know how long it will be before I reach Carinthia. By the time the sun stands high in the sky I have covered a fair distance. When I come to a stream I sit down and eat my first piece of bread and drink the water, and after resting for a while I set off once more.

I am walking through a plantation of well-grown fir trees, when several times I have the feeling of being followed. From time to time I stop to listen, but the sounds I hear might be caused by birds or other small creatures rustling through leaves. By late afternoon, however, I have become convinced that something or someone is following me. I begin to run through the wood with my arm up to guard my face from being hit by branches. At last, out of breath, I stop and lean against a tree; and then I see a shadow moving towards me. I start to run again, dodging between trees, but I am tiring and my pursuer is gaining rapidly on me. I run on blindly and crash against a trunk. Dazed by the blow I stumble and go down on my knees. I am pulled up and stare into a face that I have seen before. It is a handsome face with with a scar from a fencing wound across the left cheek. The expression in the eyes regarding me is cold, cynical and mocking. I remember that the last time I saw this man he was wearing a gold party badge, that he is a fanatical Nazi who, with his wife and two grown-up children, lives in a house not far from us.

'And what are you running away from?' he asks.

'The Russians,' I gasp.

'Well, well now, isn't it lucky that we have met; it really isn't safe for an attractive young girl like you to roam these hills unprotected.' When I don't reply he continues, 'You don't seem to have any luggage.'

I look at him scathingly. 'You don't get far in the mountains with a suitcase.'

'Not a suitcase, but at least a sleeping bag and the

wherewithal to prepare some food. But never mind, I have enough for two.'

I have no option but to walk with him, for if I try to run away he is sure to catch up with me. Walking beside me he asks questions to which I reply as briefly as I can. The shadows grow longer and the sun is dipping towards the mountain peaks when we reach a clearing. Taking the pack off his back and lowering it to the ground, he pronounces the place suitable for camping. I hesitate, but only for a moment, then I sit down and watch him lighting a fire and putting some ham into a frying pan. 'You can share my sleeping bag,' he says without looking up. My heart is beating furiously. He puts the pan on the fire and picks up a small kettle. 'Watch this, won't you, I'm going to get some water.' I move obediently towards the fire and with a forced smile tell him that the ham smells delicious and is making me feel hungry. Delighted, he bends down, and cupping my face in his hands, kisses me long and lingeringly. Then, straightening up reluctantly, he promises to be back very soon. Sick and trembling I watch him until darkness swallows him. Hastily I remove the pan from the fire and retreat from the clearing, slowly at first, for fear of creating a noise, but when I have increased the distance between us sufficiently, I begin to run.

Once again clouds have gathered in the afternoon and the darkness of approaching evening closes in on me. I repeatedly bump into trees and stumble over roots. At length, out of breath, I stop and lean against a tree trunk. Somewhere in the dark bushes a bird is twittering. Up above the tree tops the sky still retains some lingering shreds of soft pink which slowly merge to pearl and finally the plum velvet of night. A phosphorescent glow surrounding a cloud grows progressively lighter, at last revealing the moon, and my surroundings are once more as clearly visible as in daytime. The wood, brought to life by moonlight and my imagination, is frightening, and I am startled by the grotesque shadow of myself that shoots out ahead of me every time I emerge into it. The clouds too are throwing strange shadows over the silvered grass, the branches of the trees cast weird patterns and above them the mountains tower menacingly.

I move quickly, for though I can see clearly now, so will he. He will have to extinguish the fire when he returns and will need time to pack the things he has unpacked before he can follow. Once again I am looking for water, but there is none along the path I follow and I dare not stray from it. I decide that I shall not sleep in order to put as much distance as possible between myself and him. It does not occur to me that he might not bother to follow me. The fact that I am avoiding humans, sleeping exposed to the elements, hungry and thirsty, afraid of people and animals is affecting my perception, endowing existence with a vague, dreamlike quality, with the result that at times I feel as though I am walking on another planet, have left the world I lived in.

From time to time I am forced to stop when the moon disappears behind clouds. Then I jump at the slightest sound and the night is once again alive with the many different sounds produced by various forest creatures. I am getting desperately tired. How much time has passed, I wonder. I try to see the face of my watch but just then a cloud scuds over the moon, followed in quick succession by several others so that for some time I am plunged into darkness. I must have slithered down the trunk against which I was leaning, because the next thing I know is that I am still leaning against it, but now in a sitting position. Rubbing my eyes I wonder how long I have slept: an hour perhaps, or maybe only minutes.

A bird pipes, is still, then another bursts into song and is joined by one after another until the whole glorious symphony culminates in a paean of praise to the dawn, beautiful but somehow intensifying my feeling of having been forsaken. The horizon becomes brighter and trees, starkly outlined against the sky, are burnished with fire that slowly changes to gold as the sun's first rays shed their light on a new day.

Wearily I stagger to my feet. There is not much bread left, and by the time the sun has climbed high I have eaten the last of it. My feet are very sore. Back in the loft, an eternity ago, when I had taken off my boots I had seen blisters on my heels. Now they have burst and the raw flesh is rubbing against the leather through a hole in my sock. It is hardly surprising: my boots are intended for riding and not for mountaineering. Suddenly I see water cascading down the hill and joyfully hasten towards it, but when I get closer it turns out to be scree glinting in the sun. I must find water. Then I remember what Lutz said to me on the eve of his departure from the Riesengebirge: 'I was a thirsty man, wandering in a parched land, and then the miracle happened for I found you, a clear, pure, sparkling mountain stream.' The words rise to the surface of my mind and float round it, adding to the physical torment of my obsession with the thought of water, of mountain brooks leaping over stones, pebbles and jagged rocks into frothing pools, splashing, murmuring and gurgling. The liquid music of running water and the imagined sights and sounds torment me intolerably.

On top of the sheer rock that towers above me I glimpse a pocket of snow, tantalizingly near, yet inaccessible from where I stand. I look for hand- and footholds and decide to try to climb the rock, for the thought of cramming a fistful of snow into my mouth is irresistible. Taking off my boots, for it will be easier to find a hold with bare toes, I begin to explore and find a first foothold. My fingers clutch at a projection, grasp for another, and my foot too manages to find another hold. I claw the slippery rock face, slide and clutch, hold for a second before my foot loses its hold and I fall. My hands and toes are burning, painful, scratched and bruised and my nails broken.

When I pull on my boots I think I hear the lowing of a cow and dream of milk, cool and rich, trickling down my throat, realizing at the same moment that even if there were cows around, they would not be of use to me who cannot milk. I pick clover flowers and suck them, pull off the tops of sorrel, dandelion leaves and herbs and eat them. Wearily I stumble on. Then suddenly, I throw myself on the ground behind some bushes, for a short distance ahead some figures have emerged out of the wood. They are wearing fur hats and greatcoats and they are speaking Russian. I lie motionless, reflecting despairingly that I must have turned back and am now heading into Styria instead of Carinthia. While I lie listening to the incomprehensible sounds, I see the figures in my mind with quivering, over-clear senses and suddenly I know that something is wrong with the appearance of the men I have so briefly glimpsed. Cautiously I raise my head until I can look through the branches. The hats are Russian but the coats are German military issue. I remember the Russians in German uniforms that the couple who sheltered me had spoken about. Why would the Russians want to put on German uniforms? I cannot think of an answer, but whatever it is, their presence here terrifies me, and when at last they move away, I proceed with even greater caution.

By now my tongue seems to fill the whole of my mouth and still there is no water in sight. When night falls I cannot fight off sleep. I dream that I am having an impression of my teeth taken at the dental surgery. My mouth is full of plaster that has hardened and clamps my jaws together. I cannot swallow and am choking. Panic grips me but I cannot scream. When I wake, covered in sweat, I wipe away the loathsome phlegm that has collected in the corners of my mouth.

An angry sun hangs in the brazen vault, and looming black clouds are massing ominously in the distance. The light is dimming fast and suddenly all is plunged into the blackness of night. A fierce wind drives wild clouds across the dark sky, and every now and then the trees are lit luridly by the strange pallid light of an uneasy moon. The birds too have ceased to sing and the stillness is leaden. It is broken by the mutter of thunder. At last the storm breaks. Boughs tossing tormentedly whip my body, strike like a whiplash across my face, and I cry out in pain. A vivid flare of lightning is followed by a roar of thunder so tremendous that the echo crashes from mountain to mountain, deepening as it descends to the hills like the echo of a gigantic gong from on high. I am caught in a fantastic world where flashes of light reveal a terrible and ghostly scene. As always when a storm is trapped in a valley, it continues for a long time with undiminished fury, while I crouch and shiver. When the rain starts I lie down flat and open my mouth for the longed-for liquid, letting it fall on my swollen tongue, but immediately I start to choke. Eventually I manage to swallow without choking and feel refreshed.

It rains all night. Bright forks of lightning flash ceaselessly, followed by the long, tumultuous roll of thunder. Water is beginning to run down my hair and clothes in rivulets, for no foliage, however thick, can afford shelter from the torrent. Overcome by exhaustion I sleep, only to wake some time later feeling frozen and weak. No need to look for water. I lift my arm and suck my sleeve. To get the circulation going I try to run but have no strength left. I doze throughout the day. The rain has stopped in the morning and the wind is drying my clothes, but by nightfall it begins to rain again. The fierce wind and the rain driven by the wind sluice my face, and my clothes feel like an icy armour. The cold is now deep inside me, has frozen my heart and mind. I am shaking, my teeth chattering under the freezing lash of wind and rain. I continue to doze fitfully, from time to time convulsed by frightful rigors.

At daybreak I am alternately burning with heat and shivering with cold. I do not want to but know I must go on. Drunkenly I rise to my feet and stumble on, wavering from side to side. Foaming cataracts cascade from the

mountains and the air is full of the sound of rushing water.
Food is what I need to get my strength back. I scrape at a
tree trunk with my finger-nails and cram the bark into my
mouth but have difficulty swallowing. I force myself to eat
as much as possible of it and then begin to gag. From then
on I lose all count of time, struggle on and collapse, lying
prone for a long time. When night falls, a mist has risen.
Suffused with moonlight it flows above the ground like a
ghostly river. All sounds are muffled; droplets condense,
tremble and fall with a faint plop.

In the morning I am completely enclosed by a wall of
mist. When it lifts I see rising above the tree tops the
double arc of a rainbow, glowing with iridescent lambency.
A symbol of hope? I try to force my mind to focus on what
I must do, but it refuses and goes off at a tangent, and I
pass into a world of unreality. Hopelessly I stare at the
drops of water flashing in the sunlight with the fire of rare
diamonds. I am feeling too ill to move. I don't know where
I am, but have by now become convinced that at some time
I have doubled back and am once again in Styria. Incomplete thoughts and images are continually passing through
my brain, until I fall into a state of total exhaustion. I am
overcome by a feeling that is akin to peace.

Death has become infinitely desirable: complete oblivion
without nightmares, without any dreams. Suddenly I have
the presentiment of a presence so close that it fills me with
warmth. Then very clearly I see Mother in her usual attitude of prayer as she kneels on the floor of her room, her
hands raised, her beautiful face transfigured, and I know
that she is praying for me. She turns her head and looks
at me, an infinitely tender expression in her large eyes.
Instinctively I lift my arms to be enfolded in hers. My
head drops forward and nestles in the soft hollow between
her neck and shoulder, and totally relaxed and happy I fall
asleep.

When I open my eyes, the sun is low in the sky and
the evening fragrant and still. It is a long time since I

have prayed and now I fold my hands as I used to do in childhood. I cannot pray in words, for I am too weak to formulate them. My prayer is a wordless cry out of darkness for help. I try to sit up but the motion makes my head spin and I sink back wondering vaguely why I cannot move without pain. After two more tries I am on my feet. Leaning against the tree trunk, I push off like a swimmer and stagger drunkenly forward, aware only of the need to drag my aching body towards the edge of the wood. There below me stretches the ribbon of a road. Beneath my feet, the ground falls sharply away. I lie down to rest and then slide on my back to the edge of the road, where I lie, eyes closed, aware of disintegration, of my body floating apparently separated from my mind. After a long time, the silence is broken by the sound of an engine. The noise grows steadily louder and then abruptly stops. I am dimly aware of the opening and shutting of a door, footsteps and someone bending over me. The next instant I am picked up in a fireman's lift. My face presses against cloth that smells of what I am later to identify as a mixture of army-issue soap and virginia tobacco. Then all is darkness.

14
Reunion

For a time I live in a world of pain in which it is impossible to think of past, present or future. When, after long days of illness, of semi-consciousness, I begin to recover, I am told that I am fortunate to be alive, that during the nights of the storm, when drenched and freezing I fell asleep, I should have died from exposure, from hypothermia. My survival is regarded as miraculous. I ponder on this, ponder on my vision of Mother praying for me. Was I hallucinating, in delirium? One thing is certain: throughout my ordeal I have been supported by protective love — hers and possibly that of a higher power. Now I lie on cool white sheets, covered by an eiderdown. Through the window I watch the rain that has no power to drench and the wind that can no longer lash me. I am given food: it is impossible to describe the savour of the first spoonfuls of broth, or later of the mouthfuls of bread. There are no adjectives that can adequately evoke it.

What is uppermost in my mind now is my concern for Mother. After my discharge from hospital I go to the Schloss Hotel in Velden, where I have spent happy holidays, where Lutz recuperated just before we met and where we had planned to sail on the lake and to dance on the terrace after the war was over, and I marvel at the coincidence that has brought me there once more.

The Schloss, originally built as a nobleman's castle in 1603, had long been converted to a hotel that had been a favourite with royalty, politicians, film stars and other celebrities. Queen Mary, the King of Siam, Gustav Adolf IV of Sweden, King Olaf V of Norway and the Prince of Wales are among those who have passed under the old baroque archway into the extensive park where now English officers relax on the lawns. They lounge in the public rooms where once sat Somerset Maugham and Bing Crosby, play tennis, row, sail and swim in the lake, for the Schloss is now a convalescent centre for English officers.

When I have recovered sufficiently to earn my keep, I begin to work in the kitchen, cutting sandwiches and making myself useful in a variety of ways. My persistent enquiries regarding Graz and its occupation at length produce results. I am introduced to Teddy, who, I am told, has repeatedly been to Graz with the British commandant designate to talk to the Russians about their withdrawal from the British zone. Teddy, young, ginger-haired, with candid blue eyes and a shy smile that goes straight to the heart, promises to look up Mother next time he is in Graz. My command of English is basic. In Germany I was taught English for one year. In Austria I learnt French, Italian and Latin. Now, surrounded by men speaking English and helped by books and a dictionary that have been lent to me, my English improves rapidly, especially since my anxiety about Mother makes me eager to learn, in order to converse with Teddy. I read anything I can lay my hands on, from Hardy to Wodehouse, newspapers, magazines — in short, whatever I can borrow. Steadily I add new words and expressions to my somewhat quaint vocabulary.

The days pass, while impatiently I wait for news of Teddy's next trip to Graz. At last, two weeks after my introduction to him, Teddy sets out. To pass the time I settle down with the dictionary and Dickens' *Great Expectations*. The fact that I have read this and many of the other books in translation is of great help to me in my reading and study of the language, but I am quite unable to concentrate. Will Teddy find Mother? And how will he find her? I have given him a letter to take to her and I try to imagine her joy when she receives it. But what if terrible things have happened to her? What if she is back in a mental hospital or even dead? What if Teddy cannot contact her, is not given the opportunity to do so? Ceaselessly the questions and the doubts race through my mind as restlessly I pace about the room. I am glad when I am called to the kitchen to cut sandwiches, but in my agitation I cut my finger twice and am sent off.

Teddy has not been able to give me a firm date for when he will return. I go to bed at midnight but I am unable to sleep. Five o'clock finds me walking in the lake-cooled morning air. A light morning breeze sends tiny ripples over the smooth surface of the lake and a few boats sway slumbrously in a mist of light. The peaks of the Karawanken Mountains stand out in diamond clarity above the blue shadow of the foothills. Like majestic, shining sentinels, they look serenely on my agitation. By lunchtime I am prepared for the worst, and when Teddy bursts into the room late in the afternoon I am near collapse. Seeing the agonized question in my eyes, he takes my hands and holding them firmly repeats several times, 'She is all right, quite all right.' Then he hands me Mother's letter. She too has been miraculously protected, has been confident that I would be safe. Teddy has brought money and clothes and soon, he says, I will be able to return to her.

Now that I am reassured about Mother, I begin to enjoy my involuntary holiday. Teddy and I meet often. He is unfailingly kind and courteous and tells me of his home, his parents, his hopes that he will soon be able to go to England on leave. One day we talk about the war. The effort of speaking in English about a subject so sensitive is great, and our conversation is punctuated by small, meditative silences. I try to explain to him the situation in Germany before Hitler came to power and am surprised when he mentions the harsh conditions of the treaty of

Versailles which resulted in the unemployment, inflation and economic crises of which I am speaking. I ask him whether many people in his country recognize this. 'Some, not many.'

My thoughts fly back to the night when Beatrice and I stood gazing up at the long-fingered searchlights that were probing the night sky in their search for the white-starred planes that were bringing death and destruction, and I marvel that so short a time after the holocaust I am sitting beside the former enemy in peaceful surroundings with both of us speaking without rancour about the terrible time just past. I am about to put my thoughts into words when Teddy forestalls me by telling me that I am the first German with whom he has exchanged more than a few casual words and that I do not at all conform to the generally prevailing idea of what Germans are like.

'And yet, I would say that I am fairly typical of Germans of my age.'

'Are you?' He smiles, 'Then I think I shall like the others too.'

Presently he asks me about my flight from the Russians. When I describe my encounter with the small group of Russians in German uniform and tell him how puzzled I still am about them, and the others like them that the people who sheltered me for one night had talked about, I see that his eyes become troubled. I ask him if he knows anything that would explain the mystery. He is silent for so long that I feel uncomfortable and am about to change the subject when he interrupts me by saying that the people I had seen had in all probability been Cossacks, Georgians, Ukrainians or other anti-Soviet minorities, who had been fighting with the Germans and who were hiding in the hills. It is only then that I remember what Father had been telling me about the Ukrainians and understand.

'But why are they hiding now? They must know that sooner or later they will be taken prisoner by the British.'

'They don't want to be repatriated.'

'Naturally, but they would not be, would they?'

After another silence he says in a voice that is barely audible, 'We have agreed to hand them over, have already handed some of them over.'

I stare at him open mouthed, then lower my eyes, for what is there to say? Once again I realize that, though the war is over, the repercussions will continue for some time, perhaps for years. Later, back in Graz, I learn that of the fifty thousand Cossacks who had surrendered in Austria some had been held in Graz, where they were loaded into trucks at Graz station and taken via Hungary and Rumania back to the Soviet Union. I hear about terrible scenes, despair and suicides, and remember again the day when I had lain trembling in the forest, thinking of myself as hunted while looking at men who themselves were hunted and condemned to certain death.

We are now in high summer and still the Russians have not left Styria. Teddy makes several more trips to Graz and each time brings news of Mother. The house has been requisitioned by Russian officers. One of them, a major, has taken on the role of Mother's protector. Mother is living in the little box-room next to the kitchen and has to cook for him. This means that she is not short of food, for he generously allows her to eat the left-overs. The lights in the house are on day and night, for some of the Russians equate these modern conveniences with culture. Most of the soldiers in Graz come from Asiatic Russia, and they are behaving very much like small children with new toys. One of them, so Mother has told Teddy, had marched into the lavatory on arrival, pulled the chain and then washed in the pan. Teddy has seen many of them wearing up to ten watches on their arms. He says there are pigeons perching on our Steinway piano. He does not tell me then what I learn after my return from Carinthia. Friends who later describe these Russians as looking like the hordes of Genghis Khan, tell me how, inflamed by alcohol, they had looted furiously and publicly raped children, girls and woman of any age and committed the most terrible atrocities. The major, they tell me, had been a member of the so-called 'quality' troops, and Mother was fortunate indeed to have had him billeted on her. Mother later describes him as a gentleman who had thanked her when he left and kissed her hand.

The days are hot, and at night I go to a deserted little bay, take off my clothes and slip into the still, warm water of the lake, feeling it slide silkily and caressingly along my naked body. When I tire of swimming, I lie on my back and gaze at the peaks of the Karawanken gleaming in the moonlight that transfigures everything, so that my body when I climb out of the lake seems ethereal. Moonlight trembles on the limpid water, and in the distance the lights of the Schloss Hotel wink like misty jewels. In my mind I hear the echo of Lutz's voice, 'We shall sail on the lake and dance on the terrace of the Schloss Hotel.'

'Where are you now, Lutz?' Without realizing it, I have spoken aloud. For an instant the words tremble in the still air, then sink into emptiness and silence. The brief interlude that was Lutz and happiness is light years away, floating in memory as insubstantially as the mist above the shining sheet of water.

At length, despairing of the Russians' ever leaving Graz and despite Mother's repeated requests not to do so, I make up my mind to return. When I am preparing for departure, they leave. They have waited for the harvest which, along with other things, they take with them. The cars that set out along the road to Vienna are piled high with furniture and clothing and, among other curious objects, lavatory pans. From Vienna they broadcast to the people of Styria, thanking them for their most generous gifts!

After what seems like an absence of years, I arrive back in Graz on the heels of the British occupation forces. I am delighted to find Mother looking well. A great weight seems to have been lifted off her. For the next few days we

138

talk and talk, while scrubbing and polishing to remove the dirt left behind by the Russians, for Mother had been banished to the kitchen and had not been allowed to touch any of the rooms. Whether intentionally or unintentionally, the major has left some food behind, including coffee beans, sugar, flour and eggs, and for a few days we feast on coffee and cakes. When the supply runs out I am thankful for the days of hunger, thirst and want. They provide the contrast to all the good things that are once more mine — water, shelter from the elements and whatever food is available, be it ever so little, all of which has become infinitely precious, and I know that as long as I live I shall not forget the days of deprivation.

Soon after I return, Teddy calls several times before going on leave to England. He and Mother are of course already acquainted and now he no longer needs to bring an interpreter for I am quite capable of filling the post. Both Mother and I regard him as our benefactor, but there are those who cut us dead because we receive an Englishman, an ex-enemy, into our home. Others who now disown Hitler, whom before they had proudly acknowledged as an Austrian, now regard us as *Reichsdeutsche* who have invaded Austria with Hitler. Not so our friends, who are greeting me joyfully.

In the last year of the war I had made friends with a young war widow who lives not far from us in the Liebiggasse. Her husband, a doctor, was killed in Russia, and she and a number of young doctors and students now meet frequently in her small flat, for her parents own several cafés and through them she can get food which she generously shares with us.

15
Frank

Annelies, better known by her nickname 'Schnucki', is elegant, pretty and vivacious, the archetypal Austrian with an unlimited capacity for laughter, fun, enjoyment and happiness. On 10 September 1945, a beautiful autumn evening, she appears in my room, where I am on my knees polishing the floor, and informs me that I am needed urgently as interpreter. Her flat is the venue for a party organized by some doctors from our hospital for officers of the Royal Army Medical Corps, all but one of them doctors as well. They have given a great deal of help to the local hospital, and it is in recognition of this that the party has been arranged for them. I don't want to go, and explain to Schnucki that though I would like to help out as interpreter, our position is precarious enough already and that I shall certainly be branded as *Engländerliebchen* — an English soldier's tart — when people in the neighbourhood find out that, in addition to receiving an Englishman here, I have been to a party with English officers. Eventually I give in when Mother, in her unbounded gratitude to Teddy and the English who have saved my life, joins forces with Schnucki to persuade me to go.

The first person I see as I enter is a slim young man with an enormous handlebar moustache. Hastily I retreat into the hall where Schnucki is opening the door to her sister Gretl and splutter, 'Goodness, what a monstrous moustache.'

'Go on,' Schnucki laughs, 'that's Frank, he's a darling.'

'How do you know? You've only just met him, haven't you?'

'Oh well, you can just tell by looking at him,' and taking me by the arm she propels me towards him and introduces us.

I try to concentrate on the part of his face not covered by the moustache. Long lashes curl over green-gold eyes that are full of light, and the infectious smile that greets me has carved lines of humour and benevolence in his thin face. I am disturbed by no premonition, no presentiment, no consciousness that this is a fateful encounter, but he, as he will tell me over and over again in years to come, recognizes at that moment, in the beat of a second, that he loves me inevitably and instantaneously then and for ever. The hand he extends in greeting is long and thin but strong, with an amazingly firm grip that makes me wince. His laughing eyes look at me with such warmth that I am completely disarmed and respond joyously, and for the rest of the evening I allow myself to be monopolized by him. When, just before curfew at 11 p.m., I say goodnight, he and his friend Eric, a major, invite me to the opera. I say that I have a prior engagement and decline, though it is hard to refuse, seeing the eagerness, the pleading and the clear sincerity in his eyes.

In the morning Schnucki calls. She is partnering Eric and wants me to come. I remonstrate with her. Does she not realize what will happen if we are seen in public with English officers? We shall be stigmatized and despised by our own people and the English alike. With a grand gesture she consigns them all to perdition. What does she care about a lot of hypocrites? Then she tells me that Eric is a Jew. He is the one who should shun us, isn't he? It would be mean indeed of us to refuse to be seen in public with him when he does not mind fraternizing with us, in spite of the official order prohibiting the occupying troops from mixing with the locals.

I give in once more, but when Eric and Frank, very smart in their dress uniforms, stop the jeep in front of the opera house, we find that Frank, who has obtained the tickets, has made a mistake: they are for the following evening. In the end we attend a symphony concert where we do not have even the comfort of dimmed lights during the performance and thus are the target of half-envious, half-contemptuous looks throughout. So when Schnucki begs me to come to the opera the following day I put up a very weak fight, for I feel that we have already burned our boats.

After the performance we go back to Schnucki's flat for a drink and realize that we are too late to leave in time for the curfew. Schnucki is delighted, for now we can have a small party. She hurries to sort out some dance records while Frank and I are sent into the kitchen to cut up sandwiches — a job at which, she tells me, I should be expert. We dance until 5 a.m., when the curfew ends, and then tiptoe down the three flights of stairs from Schnucki's flat, with Schnucki giggling helplessly at the thought of what the neighbours would say if they could see us now, while I try to stifle her giggles by holding my hand over her mouth.

After seeing Frank and Eric round the corner to where they have parked the jeep, I turn to look back at Schnucki. 'I think,' she says dreamily, 'I think I've fallen in love.' Amused I watch her waltzing up the stairs, waving a chiffon scarf and humming a love song. Schnucki, I feel, must be the personification of the 'Merry Widow'. But then, she had known her husband for only a very short time before they were married and was widowed a few weeks later. Nevertheless, I wonder which of our two escorts she was thinking of when she made her announcement. She had told me that Eric wanted to take her to the opera, and I had assumed that she wanted me to partner his friend, but she was constantly eulogizing Frank, telling me what an absolute darling he was, how it made her happy just to look at him. So perhaps it is Frank with whom she is falling in love. I am startled by my reaction to the thought. I don't like it but don't know why. I admit to myself that I have become fond of him. He positively radiates gaiety, warmth, buoyancy and vibrant life, and possesses great charm; whenever he enters a room the atmosphere changes noticeably and becomes more exciting. Eric says of him that he can make any party a success by just being there. Am I jealous? Probably; but not because I am in love, simply because so far I have thought that I alone have had his attention. In the end I dismiss the whole idea as fanciful.

Mother is awake when I get in and I apologize and explain. We sit talking companionably for a while before turning in for what is left of the night, and I rejoice again at the difference in her. She is looking well and, apart from the fact that we have not heard from Father for several months, nothing seems to worry her and she expects to hear from him any day now. In this she is proved right, for a few days later we receive a letter in which he assures us that he is well and that he will send for us as soon as things regarding his future are sorted out.

Since June the Allies have had supreme governmental power in Germany and have set up a control council. Germany has been divided into four zones of occupation. At meetings in Potsdam, large areas of Germany are awarded by the American, British and Soviet heads of government to Poland pending the conclusion of a peace treaty. As a result the local population is expelled. Aunt Mia, who had transferred large sums of capital to Switzerland years ago, had tried to persuade Grandpapa, his wife, her brother and sister and their families to join her when she left Germany before the advance of the Russians, but without success. She and Uncle August are in West Germany and are trying to trace the others. We have news neither of Opa, his wife and daughter, nor of my uncles and aunts in Berlin.

Despite pointing fingers, whispering voices and unfriendly eyes, Schnucki and I continue to meet Eric and Frank. I know now that Schnucki is in love with Eric and am sorry for her, for I can see that Eric, though very fond of her, is trying to keep their relationship on a purely friendly basis. I spend my days drifting between pleasurable recollection and anticipation, for I have come to enjoy Frank's companionship to such an extent that I miss him when he is unable to call. Though as aliens we are forbidden officially to fraternize, most of the officers and soldiers have become friendly with the local population and I am greeted warmly by the commanding officer of Frank's unit when we meet at a concert.

By now I have received several threatening anonymous letters. These, I know, come from former Nazis who, even though they have thrown away their membership badges and are denying that they have ever been members of the party, resent the fact that 'German girls and women should prostitute themselves with the enemy'. These letters worry me less than the obvious contempt shown by certain British officers for girls who associate with members of the occupying forces even though they themselves are quite ready to take advantage of them.

In the foyer of the opera house I am introduced to the commanding officer of another unit. He compliments me on my English. I thank him for the compliment but add that my vocabulary is still rather limited and mention a phrase that I have heard used by some soldiers that day. I am startled by the expression on the faces surrounding me and notice that Frank's face has turned crimson.

'No decent person, certainly no lady, would use those words.' The colonel's voice is glacial as he contemptuously turns away from me.

He is arrested by Frank, whose blush has faded leaving his face deadly white, saying quietly, 'Even if you spoke German as well as this *lady* speaks English, sir, you could

144

still in ignorance of their meaning use words not in common use in polite society.' And, saluting smartly, he takes my arm and guides me towards the door.

That night I lie awake, tortured by the memory of the incident which has left me shaken and deeply humiliated. In Carinthia I have heard people speak of girls and women, often with families who were hungry, ready to sell themselves for food, of others who did so for cigarettes and chocolates, while the soldiers, far from home and family and weary after long months of fighting, were anxious to exchange anything and everything for what they considered love. Only a few days previously I had overheard an English major laughingly declare that Austrian girls do not know the meaning of morals. Over and over again I relive what has occurred, and the recollection of it makes me squirm and grow hot with indignation and shame. Bitterly I reproach myself. How foolish and self-indulgent I have been and how disloyal to those who have died in the war. To enjoy the company of the former enemy, to laugh, dance and go out with him must be wrong, even wicked. Tomorrow, I resolve, I shall tell Frank that I cannot see him again.

I have rehearsed a little speech in which I tell him of the difficulties, the pointlessness of continuing our meetings and my determination to end them. Only when we have returned from our walk and the jeep stops outside our house do I summon up the courage to deliver it. Then, anxious not to prolong the agony, I jump out and run up the steps, from where I watch the jeep careering at breakneck speed down the road and out of sight.

Having done what I have persuaded myself is the only thing to do, I expect to feel relieved, released from my feelings of guilt and shame. Instead I feel restless and miserable and spend half the night tossing and turning. When at last I drop off, I dream of Frank, walk and talk with him and wake up confused and unrested.

During the day I work hard and in the evening try to lose myself in a book. Mother, sitting opposite me darning stockings, looks up after a while and asks, 'Are you all right?'

'Of course, why do you ask?'

'I wondered because you have been looking at the same page for at least twenty minutes.'

'Just thinking about what I have been reading,' I say brightly while turning the page that I have not read because, instead of words, I have seen Frank's face, the deep hurt in his eyes when I told him I was not going to see him again. The image fills me with an aching tenderness and an awareness of his kindness, gentleness and innate goodness. The memory of his physical being, the texture of his hair, the laughter lines etched along his eyes and mouth, the modelling of his head — all these things make me long to be near him, to hear his voice, to watch the way he walks. Suddenly, with a shock of innermost recognition, I know that I am in love, most unsuitably in love; and I know too that though I have sent him away, it has been too late. And with this untimely conviction of love comes the realization that ahead of me stretch long days of regret, remorse, longing and useless grief.

I tell myself that nevertheless what I have done has been right, for nothing has changed and the reasons for my decision are still there. But they no longer seem to matter — we might at least have had a few weeks, perhaps even months, together. That night, heavy-hearted, dejected, feeling utterly bereaved and desolately lonely, I lie sleepless. Hour by hour I relive our meetings, the things we have done together, the words he has said to me. I know now that I never felt for Lutz what I feel for Frank. Lutz gave me warmth, understanding and tenderness. What I had thought of as love was kindled by admiration and distilled from a mixture of gratitude and adolescent worship. Lutz, with love's clairvoyance, had divined this and made no demands, had been prepared to wait for me to grow up. When I heard of his death I had believed that I loved him and part of me had died with him while part of him remained with me, for there is gain even in apparent loss. For a short time his life had been joined to mine and the love and laughter we had shared were henceforth mine. My love for Frank is different in every way. It is the love of a young woman for a young man. There is a depth of feeling in it, such as I have never known before. But oh, how useless are these speculations now that I'll never see him again.

The following evening Schnucki calls and enquires about Frank. I am non-committal and tell her that I have no idea when I shall see him again. She looks concerned, then asks if I am ill. I cannot talk to her or anyone and eagerly snatch at the excuse, telling her that I feel very unwell and am, in fact, about to go to bed. When she leaves she looks thoughtful.

The following day, Sunday, I surprise Mother by saying that I shall go to church with her in Maria Trost. In the tram I am guilt stricken, for though it is most unlikely that I shall see Frank, since the church is quite a way from the house in Maria Trost where he is stationed, I have offered to go with her only because it would bring me nearer to him.

It is years since I have been to a service with Mother. I kneel down beside her, longing for peace and overcome by the deep longing for Frank that sweeps over me intolerably. In the quiet candlelit darkness peace slowly begins to enfold me, only to flee when the service starts, for the preacher's words, 'I have not come to bring you peace but a sword,' strike not only at my present situation, but bring to my mind the horrors of war. The whole ceremony — the genuflecting, bowing and crossing — seems, to my anguished mind, to be an act of propitiation, a vain attempt to placate an angry and vengeful God. Instead of listening to the sermon I find myself thinking about Frank. Even if I had not sent him away, I tell myself, how do I know that he cared for me? Perhaps he, like all the others, wanted only a good time. Even if he did care for me, he will get over it and meet another girl. Gay, friendly, unselfconscious and universally liked, he will have no difficulty in finding someone else. I torture myself by imagining him with a girl, laughing and dancing with her. When the service is over and I return with Mother I feel more heavy-hearted than when we set out.

In the evening the phone rings and I have to restrain myself from running to answer. It is Schnucki. 'How are you, feeling any better?'

I try to keep the disappointment out of my voice. 'A little.'

'Look, there is something I want to show you. Do come over, I promise it'll cheer you up.'

I hesitate. I am in no mood to talk, but the evening stretches ahead interminably and I agree.

Climbing up the stairs to her flat on the top floor I am overcome by painful nostalgia as I remember the evening when I first met Frank. The pain that grips me is so strong that I have to wait before pushing the bell in order to compose myself. Schnucki opens the door and gestures towards the sitting room. 'Go in, won't you, I'll be with you in a minute,' and disappears into the kitchen.

The next moment I am face to face with Frank, see the surprise in his eyes change to joy and am locked in his arms. Removed from time and place, with his arms so tightly around me that I can hardly breathe, the struggle that I have passed through is forgotten and I am utterly and completely happy. We cling to each other, laughing and crying, unable to separate, loving each other beyond words, understanding each other perfectly, lost in each other with exquisite joy. No need for him to plead 'Don't ever send me away again,' no need for me to promise 'Never.' And when, clasping my hands in his, he repeats the beautiful words spoken by Ruth to Naomi, they hold for me a new, deep and wonderful meaning.

Intreat me not to leave thee or to return from
following after thee; for whither thou goest, I will
go: and where thou lodgest I will lodge: thy people
shall be my people, and thy God my God: Where
thou diest, will I die and there will I be buried:
The Lord do so to me and more also, if ought but
death part thee and me.

The knowledge of the absolute rightness of each for the
other is both sweet and bitter, for the future is uncertain
and as yet the pain of parting has only been postponed.
Frank has boundless faith, is certain that the ban on
marriages between aliens will soon be lifted; he is not afraid
and has no doubts because he is certain that we are meant
for one another, are perfect together and shall be together
for ever. I listen to him, my face pressed against the
rough khaki of his uniform, rapturously inhaling the now-
familiar smell of soap and tobacco that seems to cling to all
British uniforms, determined that from now on I shall live
only for the present moment, without plan or forethought.
All my doubts and worries are things of the past and I
am transfigured by the ecstasy of self-surrender in an
exultation that is boundless and flooded with wonderful
and buoyant life. At last, when in the exhaustion that
follows deep emotion we sit quietly, content to hold hands
and smile, Schnucki emerges, her smile as smug as that
of the proverbial cat that has stolen the cream and highly
delighted by the success she has achieved as *deus ex
machina*. After much hugging and kissing we leave her
to go back to my house.

Mother, who has grown very fond of Frank during the
past weeks, is happy when we tell her of our unofficial
engagement, and we celebrate quietly with a bottle of
wine. After she has departed to the little box-room next to
the kitchen, where the bed she used to sleep in during the
Russian occupation still stands, we feed the kitchen range
with my old school books to keep ourselves warm until the

curfew ends, the military police finish patrolling the streets and Frank can catch the first tram back to Maria Trost.

In the weeks that follow we meet every day. I do not think of the future. The future must take care of itself; the only thing that matters is the present when we are together. Not being together is a sad waste of time when we impatiently look forward to being together again.

The evenings are beginning to draw in, yet they are still fragrant with warm, heady scents. Motes of dust and swarms of gnats dance in a shimmering golden mist. In the gardens blooms flame extravagantly in drunken exuberance and, with starlight imbuing each flower with miraculous lambency, we are reluctant to turn in at night. On sunny mornings, when jewelled spiders' webs reflect the early light, we set off to walk along the mountain ridges, at one with the air and the sunshine. When we are tired out, hot and breathless, we drop on to the soft carpet of pine needles and watch the blue-green branches sway in the wind, listen to the sweet notes of birdsong cascading through sunlight and melting into the wonderful, serene silence. Bathed in light and radiance and utterly filled with love, I become aware once again of the glory of God.

I had thought that I had discarded what I had considered to be an outworn belief in a God who did not exist. Now, through my love for Frank, I am once more reaching out towards him. I search, question and listen. And when, like the bride in the Song of Solomon, I sigh, 'I sought him, but found him not; I called him, but he gave no answer,' Frank takes me in his arms and says, 'Don't worry if you can't find him; he will find you and then you will know without the slightest doubt that you are loved by him.'

Winter comes, but I walk through rain, slush and snow totally oblivious of the cold; for that night in Schnucki's flat I stepped out of winter right into the heart of spring and since then have been ablaze with the fire and splendour of our love. It fills my whole being with an intensity of joy and rapture that is almost unbearable. I never dreamed

150

that it could be possible to be so happy. Wherever I am, I see his face, his eyes that are full of light, the lines crinkling around them when he smiles, the corners of his lips curling upwards — every loved feature; and I glory in the knowledge that I belong to him utterly and completely to the end of time. I look at the grey clouds, the pavements streaming with rain, and my heart sings with the writer of the Song of Solomon: ' . . . the winter has passed, the rain is over and gone, the flowers appear in the land, the time of singing is come.' And I feel the need to pour out upon all around me some of the bliss, the wonderful happiness, that fills my heart.

Just before Christmas, Frank is due to go on a skiing course. We plan a party and invite Teddy who has just returned from England. I am in the kitchen, fetching some plates, when he appears in the doorway. 'Are you in love with him?' he asks, motioning with his head towards Frank, who is talking to Eric and Schnucki. Taken aback by the rudeness of the question so uncharacteristic of Teddy, I stiffen; but the haughty rebuke that rises to my lips remains unspoken when I see the expression in his eyes, and instead I simply nod. He turns and leaves the room abruptly. I do not see Teddy again and my heart aches, for I shall never forget his kindness to Mother and me.

Frank is on his skiing course in the hills behind Judenburg and every few days he escapes in the evening and we meet clandestinely for an hour or so, for we cannot bear to be away from each other. The famous moustache, grown for a bet, has had to go. He shaved it off after arriving at the bottom of a ski slope to find icicles hanging from it. According to Eric he looked like an amiable walrus.

We spend Christmas Eve quietly at home, but on New Year's Eve we are invited to another unit where kilted pipers pipe in the haggis and we dance 'The Dashing White Sergeant', 'Strip the Willow', 'The Gay Gordons' and other dances that enchant me. When the bells ring out the old year and at the last stroke of midnight all the windows are thrown open with glad cries of the traditional toast *'Prosit Neu Jahr'* and the clinking of glasses joins the music of the bells, Frank and I step into the garden. The bells are quiet, the windows are closed once again and in the place where we stand all is still but for the soft thud of a slip of snow from a laden branch. In the arc of the sky the pale yellow moon breaking through the frost-rimed tree tops casts blue shadows on the deep snow that covers the ground. Here, away from the noise of the party, we wish each other a happy New Year and pray that this, the first new year of peace, will see the lifting of the ban on marriages between aliens and fulfil our passionate desire to become one in body as we are in spirit. A few hours later we attend the New Year's service in Graz Cathedral with the chorus and soloists from the opera house singing Franz Schubert's *Mass in A flat Major*.

When primroses are in bud and violets raise their heads in sunny sheltered spots, their scent filling the heart with longing and all nature is wooing, we decide to become officially engaged. Time is passing ever more swiftly, for the day of Frank's demobilization has been fixed for May. The primroses and violets fade before we have had time to take our fill of their beauty, and when they are succeeded by bluebells lying like azure pools in every hollow, and winding like rivulets through every wood, I sorrow.

The currency that can obtain almost anything these days is the cigarette, and Frank pays for a broad golden band with two hundred cigarettes. It is melted down by the jeweller and fashioned into the two rings that are to become our wedding rings but that serve as engagement rings for the time being. Frank's fellow officers have accepted the fact that we are serious and treat me with respect.

At parties our eyes meet across a room full of people with

a delight so great that it takes our breath away. Schnucki watching us sighs, 'You two just radiate happiness,' and then adds musingly, 'What a pity that all this is so ephemeral.' When I look at her in consternation she explains: 'You only have to look at couples who have been married for a while to see that they have either become indifferent or that they squabble and go to look for someone else. I suppose that after two people have been together for a year or two there is no more mystery, the intimacy of the marriage bed is bound to lead to loss of excitement and in the end those that stay together do so merely for convention's sake.' I stare at her aghast, appalled at such cynicism. I cannot conceive how a love like ours, triumphant and inviolable, could ever fade or tarnish. Admittedly our youth must fade but our love will be lit eternally and grow with the giving — though it seems almost impossible that it could grow further, for even now I sometimes feel that it is too great to be contained.

Through our love I am slowly finding my way back to God, for Frank has a deep and abiding faith in the love of God and in the life to come. While I want to believe in an afterlife, for I cannot bear the thought of a time when we can no longer be together, I refuse to think of us as two immaterial souls. I want him as he is now. I love him so completely, his mind, his soul and body, the way he smiles, walks, talks. I want to touch and be touched, to feel the clear sincerity of his gaze, to bury my face in his hair and smell the clean freshness of him. And so I push the thought of death resolutely away. While in Velden I came across some words written by William Penn that I found comforting when thinking of those I had lost in the war and wrote them down. Now I read them again:

They that love beyond the world cannot be
separated by death. Death cannot kill what never
dies. . . If absence be not death, neither is theirs.

> Death is but crossing the world, as friends do the
> seas; they live in one another still.

Yet the idea of death terrifies me and the thought of
separation is insupportable.

On a glorious morning in spring I stand in the tram
on my way to Maria Trost to meet Frank. The thought
of being with him within a few minutes transforms the
world around me; even the clanging of the trolley pole,
which sends blue sparks shooting into the air until they
die in the dewy hedgerows, is music. I am filled with such
ecstasy that I feel myself becoming pure flame and surreptitiously glance at the other passengers, convinced that
what I feel must be obvious to all. Yet I see only apathy
in the eyes that stare at their surroundings and am filled
with deep pity for all people leading drab lives, looking
glum, indifferent, bored or worried, prosaically plodding
on, quite unaware of the miracle that has happened to us
and of the music that permeates us every hour of the day
and night since we found each other.

One after another Frank's fellow officers are demobbed.
Eric leaves and Schnucki is inconsolable. Frank and I are
sad, for we have come to love him and miss him sorely.
Some time ago Frank's batman went home and has since
been replaced by Frank M., who is devoted to us and
becomes a friend.

One afternoon, while we are on our way to see friends of
mine, we bump into a young woman whom we have often
seen at mess dances with a young captain. Her appearance comes as a shock. She begs us to come to her flat
for a drink. There she pours out her story to us. She
lost both father and fiancé in the early days of the war
and her mother in an air raid, and from that time on has
lived alone. Lonely, hungry not only for food but also for
affection, warmth and sympathy, she became easy prey to
the handsome young captain whom she met and who gave

her the attention she yearned for. Inevitably she fell in love with him. Conscious of the obstacles to a permanent relationship and the imminent danger of a sudden departure, the affair on her side was tense and deeply emotional, but she was unable to resist her feelings, to control her emotion, and recklessly followed her impulses. Dizzy, drunk, happy and sad she gave into them as she would never have dreamed of doing in normal circumstances. For her, a woman living alone, it was highly compromising to receive an English officer night after night — as well I know from the reactions of our neighbours to my relationship with Frank, even though we are chaperoned by Mother. After he left, she found that she was carrying his child. She did not tell him, choosing rather to wait to hear from him; but she waited in vain. Then she began to write to him, and receiving no reply wrote to his mother, whose address she found on an envelope that he had once used for a scribbled message to her. The letter that she has now received briefly informs her that her son is married, that it has been wrong of him not to have told her of the fact and that she hopes she will get over the shock. We sit and listen, and my empathy is so strong that I have to fight the tears; but we are powerless to comfort. She assures us that being able to tell someone of her plight has been of help, and sadly we leave.

Food is scarce, and one by one Mother has bartered many treasures for flour, fat and other necessities. On her latest visit to the farm, the farmer who has given her some flour in exchange for our dining-room sideboard has boasted that the cows in his shed will soon have Persian carpets to lie on. Frank fishes for trout and is so successful that we have never yet been hungry. I love to watch him fishing with the absorption of a small boy. The water swirling round his thigh-high boots emerald green and white crashes against the rocks and is spewed out again in cascades of foam. While he casts I watch the slow rhythm and listen to the gentle sound of the line on the water or lie stretched out lazily by the riverside. The sky above is a brilliant blue with high white clouds sailing across it. On one occasion I am gripped by excitement when he plays a large trout and jump up and down on the bank. Suddenly I lose my foothold on the wet grass, slip and fall into the ice-cold water. Frank rushes to my aid and one happy trout escapes. Frank carries me dripping wet across the meadow to a small farmhouse where I sit by the kitchen range, wrapped in his battledress jacket and an old blanket while my clothes dry. Meanwhile Frank is plied with *Slibowitz* liquor. When we get back to the jeep, where we have left several wet khaki handkerchiefs flying from the windows to dry, we find some curious cows, which have come to inspect the vehicle, busily engaged in eating them.

We are now in May and our separation is imminent. In the evenings we sit at home by the window and listen to the croaking of the many frogs that live in the static water tank, which was installed in front of our house during the war in the place where the tennis courts used to be. With the heat of the day distilled into a warm afterglow, the fragrance of lilac and jasmine that grows all along the roads floats through the open windows in golden waves. We are poignantly aware of every precious moment of those last few days, when even the croaking of the frogs sounds sweet.

Since Christmas a couple have been quartered in our home. They were homeless and now sleep in Mother's bedroom, where they have installed a small cooking stove. They are not fastidious, and I recoil from using the bathroom, where there is always a rim of grease around the basin that they use for their pots and pans. Since we are the only ones in the house who have had people billeted on them by the local authority, we guess that it has been done because we are *Reichsdeutsche*. Mother does not object: she feels sorry for the poor people who have lost their home and gladly puts up with the inconvenience. Besides, very soon now, we ourselves will leave, for Frank has found lodgings for us in Maria Trost. He is afraid of what might happen once he has gone and we no longer have his protection. Our furniture will be stored by Schnucki's parents while we wait for Father to send for us.

In his next letter Father informs us that he has been appointed chief of police and is once more in Cologne. He himself is living in digs but is looking for accommodation outside Cologne for us all, and as soon as he has found something suitable he will send for us. He has also been successful in locating his parents in a refugee camp in East Germany. He writes of the old people's nightmare flight, when with others from their mountain village they had left the place where they had lived all their lives. Most of their neighbours had piled as many of their belongings as they could on whatever means of transport they could obtain. Opa and Oma left behind them everything they owned because they were too weak to push or carry anything through the snow.

Opa, who for years had talked of not being in this world for much longer, has survived the incredible hardships and sufferings of the flight and the refugee camps, while all around him many others, both young and old, have died of typhoid, tuberculosis, starvation or just hopelessness. We guess that he has survived because he stubbornly refuses to die anywhere but among his beloved mountains and because he tenaciously clings to the belief that he will return to them. His dream is to remain a dream. A few years later, at the age of ninety-six, he dies in the camp. In that time Father makes every effort to bring him to the West, but Opa refuses to move any further from his home.

The last day has come. It has a dreamlike quality; we are trying to live each moment while endeavouring to make each moment last for ever. Frank is due to leave first thing the following morning. For the last evening the unit has arranged a special dance to say goodbye. 'Salerno', the jeep we have come to regard as ours, rattles along below the giant candelabras of the chestnut trees towards the mountain we intend to climb.

After an hour's climb, we emerge from a wood where sun-drenched firs release the scent I love and green-breasted finches and blue-headed tits flit from branch to branch into bright sunlight, while high above the sweep of pine trees a buzzard rises majestically and soars into the blue. The very air is throbbing with spring and the bird cries are urgent and vibrant. At last, hot and breathless, we arrive on the sunlit summit. In the distance the mountains are amethyst and the valleys overwhelmingly lovely, with clouds flitting in sun-chased shadows across them. The silence is broken only by the faint tinkling of cowbells and of falling water far below us. We are steeped in beauty, in solitude, in air containing the heat of the sun and the cold of the snow, so pure it enters mind and soul and fills them with immortal longings. Yet one phrase hammers insistently and remorselessly in my head: *the last time, the last time*.

On the way down, taking a slightly different route, we pull up sharply at a picture of heart-rending loveliness, of 'sunlit snowdrifts flung upon gnarled trees'. Below us spreads a miraculous orchard. Holding hands, we run down the slope into the fragrant, foaming, frothing sea and, intoxicated by so much loveliness, begin to waltz through the trees in a shower of silken petals that drift down indolently where the breeze flirts through the heavy drooping blooms, scenting the air with delicious sweetness.

The last golden light lies still in the folds of the hills, and shadows grow longer and darker when we get back to the house in Maria Trost where we now live. Mother thinks that I ought to rest for at least an hour before going to the dance, but I cannot bear the thought of losing one single precious minute. Besides, I crave physical tiredness. It will be welcome once Frank has gone, for it might bring merciful oblivion to shut out the pain of parting.

We approach the officers' mess as the sunset turns rose and flames above the pine trees. The clink of glasses, music, chattering voices and sounds of merriment greet us. The party is in full swing and is obviously going to be a huge success. Officers in dress uniform and girls in long flowing dresses throng the garden and mill about in the house. Couples laugh and jostle each other on the dance floor. As we enter the band strikes up with 'For he's a jolly good fellow', and all at once we are surrounded by laughing, singing well-wishers. Spirits are high, excitement rises as with drink the party becomes more and more animated, reaches fever pitch.

We move on to the packed dance floor to join the couples who are swaying cheek to cheek, circle and glide to the music. I close my eyes to shut out the giddy movements of the dancers. Once when I open them I see Major R. dancing past with a girl whose long blond hair falls in a shining wing across her face, partly concealing it. He is the only officer I do not like. He is handsome and self-assured but wholly cynical and without regard for anyone. Women are conveniences to be used and discarded when his appetite is sated, but he attracts and fascinates them. When he dances past the next time, I recognize his partner as the daughter of an old aristocratic family living nearby. They dance with their hands entwined round each other's neck and she is gazing up at him through half-closed swimming eyes. His eyes, one eyebrow cocked mockingly, are impudent, his smile sardonic; then seeing me watching him, he winks. Hastily I look away to escape his bold glance of direct appraisal. I remember him once stating coldly that there can be no fellowship between conqueror and conquered.

It is very hot. Drops of moisture gleam on the flushed faces of the officers, and the batmen threading their way in and out of the dancers with drinks are perspiring freely. I catch sight of Frank M., Frank's batman, precariously balancing a tray of drinks while curiously peering into the face of the girl with the long blond hair. The noise and chatter all around us seems to drive time relentlessly forwards, and tired of being jolted and bumped by gyrating bodies, I long to escape from the noisy gregariousness. The atmosphere is becoming more and more feverish as the tempo of the music quickens and with it the dancing, the talking, the loving. So little time left, so little time.

The pain that grips me is so deep that I stop in the middle of the floor. Without a word Frank takes my arm and leads me past small tables littered with glasses, past the flushed faces and shining eyes, through talk and laughter and the fumes of tobacco into the sweetly scented garden. Between the trees a couple moves, the girl's bare shoulders showing white; then they return to the house and we are alone in the moonlight, which outshines the many lanterns that are suspended from branches and shrubs and wraps all in mystery and silver enchantment. For a long time we walk silently to and fro with the sound of music from the house seeming to come from another world, until the velvet of the spangled sky grows lighter, turning to soft pearl even while we look. 'Night's candles . . . are . . . burnt out,' I whisper.

Frank takes my face in his hands and whispers his reply, but his words are drowned by a roll of drums from behind us that is followed by the first bars of the national anthem. The dance has ended. 'I'll be back; I'll either be back or will send for you as soon as humanly possible, and I'll move heaven and earth to make sure it will be soon.' I smile but I cannot speak.

I have made up my mind to smile right up to the last moment. I must not admit to even a shadow of pain. For his sake I must be brave, I must not cry. When we walk into the room, everyone has left — everyone except Frank's batman Frank M. 'I've got all your stuff ready, sir.' Frank nods.

'How much longer have I got?'

'One hour, sir.'

When he has left, Frank walks across to the gramophone, selects a pile of records and places them on the turntable. The motor whirrs and we stand silently waiting for the record to drop and the needle to enter the groove. As record after record drops, we dance through the dawn.

Now that the moment is almost at hand the fight against tears that well up relentlessly becomes intolerable, but the necessity of keeping up an appearance of self-possession comes to my aid when the driver arrives with the jeep. For the last time I look at the features that have become so intimately familiar by sight and touch, at this man who has become as necessary to my being as the air I breathe. The driver is clearing his throat and Frank M. is standing by. We both look down at our clasped hands and the two gold bands inscribed with our names and know that the marriage that in law has been denied us has nevertheless taken place, that we are united in a love that is binding us to each other just as surely as if we had repeated the words of the marriage service before the registrar or priest. The engine roars into life. Tenderly Frank takes my hands and for the last time touches them with his lips. '*Jetzt, nur und für immer,*' he whispers, a promise of loyalty throughout time. In a tension that is physical pain, I see him leap into the jeep. With a mounting roar of the engine it turns the corner out of the drive and is gone. The scent of lilac in the early morning dew is heavy, and I know that for as long as I live the scent of lilac will take me back to this moment.

16
Farewells and Departures

The fatigue that I thought would come after our day's climb and the night spent dancing does not bring sleep. I have been living so intensely that now I have tumbled from the heights I am seized by an intolerable restlessness. I shower and change and, after assuring Mother that I am all right, set out for a walk.

Maria Trost is full of soldiers and officers, who remind me of Frank with their uniforms, their caps tilted jauntily over one ear, their walk and their talk. I feel the need to be near them, to hear them speak English. I feel that if I could talk to them it would help to fill the terrible void that his going has left.

The day is grey and a fine drizzle is beginning to soak through my blouse. For nine months I have regarded everything and everyone around me with the eyes of love. Now everything has turned dark and bleak, and I am drained and lost and empty because part of me has gone.

I turn back, and when I reach the house I go straight upstairs to our room. Mother is out and I am glad of that, for my longing for Frank overwhelms me so completely that I fling myself on the bed, burying my face in the pillows, frightened that my sobbing will be heard by the other members of the household. I had thought that I had plumbed the depths of hell during the war, but this is worse. I am haunted by the memory of the past hours, his voice, the look in his eyes, the feel of his cheek against mine.

When night falls, I sit by the open window. The night air is heavy and unstirring. Over and over again I relive the poignant moment of our parting, see Frank's face, his tender, anxious face, and the grief and pain become insupportable. 'O God, help me,' I cry, and then I remember what Frank has told me in one of our long discussions concerning the existence of a loving God. 'If you know that you matter supremely to another human being, it will help you to recognize that you matter supremely to God.' I know that not only does Frank matter supremely to me but that I matter supremely to him. There can be no doubt about this. He has told me so over and over again and proved it by kindness, tenderness, thoughtfulness, and the courtesy and protection with which he has surrounded me. I think of all the qualities that I admire in him — his acute sensitivity of mind and imagination, his generosity, his fine intellect, his delightful sense of humour and above all his humility, born of his deep abiding faith. And with this thought I fall into a deep and dreamless sleep.

When I wake, I see Mother sitting quietly at the table. She smiles, 'Youth has at last asserted itself and you've had a good long sleep.'

I yawn and stretch; and then memory comes flooding back and, giving in to the compulsion to talk of Frank, I begin to speak of our climb, tell her about the buzzard, about the dance, about the way the garden was decorated with paper lanterns, about the band specially hired for the occasion, about everything but the way I feel. She listens quietly as she has always done, ever since I was a little girl, whenever I have felt the need to talk, either from happiness or sorrow.

Frank had said goodbye to her when he collected me to take me to the dance and he had told her his itinerary. 'I expect he is in Villach now,' she says quietly.

I nod dumbly. When I look up and see the loving concern in her eyes, I cry out, 'Oh, Mother, I do miss him so!' And then I sob in her arms as I have not done since I was a small child.

I have always marvelled at Mother's spiritual unity with the living Christ who is so real to her and seems so remote to me, and now more than ever I envy her this mystical fellowship. Both she and Frank have a gift for praying that seems unique and they are continually in communion with the source of their being. In my agony of bereavement I try to pray, but when I close my eyes I see only the face of which each feature has become so inexpressibly dear. The pain, the arid ache, does not ease as the days pass. For nine months we have spent part of nearly every day together, woken every morning to the exquisite delight of knowing that in a matter of hours we would be basking in the warmth and delight of each other's presence, be able to touch, to caress, to smile, to share our innermost thoughts. A mere nine months, yet they enshrine a whole lifetime. The beauty of those days and the memory of them cannot avail against the deep yearning and the bitter loneliness that I feel now. Jealously I guard anything that reminds me of him: not only what he has given me but the things I find after he has left — a uniform button, a box of Craven A cigarettes, a khaki handkerchief and our records, which I play. They are the silly, sentimental tunes to which we have so often danced. Having been nurtured on the music of the great composers I have never cared much for popular music but have known that sounds, like scents, can bring back memories, stir up acute aching for what is past by recreating emotions associated with certain events.

I have never listened to 'Lili Marlene' without seeing Anna and Hans-Georg embracing under the lamp-post in front of the barracks, and there are a few songs that are rooted in events that have deeply affected my life. Friederike's song will always bring back the memory of the day when I learned that Lutz was dead, the moment that had turned me from a girl into a woman. So now, when I listen to the words of the popular song 'Yours till the stars lose their glory', I see us once again standing outside the officers' mess in Maria Trost under the snow-laden fir trees on an evening when Frank is on mess duty, when a large bank of cloud shifts and all of a sudden a thousand points of light leap out. While both of us are gazing up at them, Frank, holding me tightly, sings those words that into old age will tug at my heart whenever I hear them. There is one other that has now become 'our song' — the song entitled 'I'll be with you in apple-blossom time'. It recreates for me the last enchanted afternoon in the orchard where thrushes and blackbirds competed ecstatically and we waltzed to their music through the blossom.

These are precious memories, but I don't want to live on memories for I want Frank, want him to be more than a wonderful and tender memory.

The next day, with a grin so wide it threatens to split his face, Frank M. brings me Frank's first letter, sent from Villach. I know that there will not be another one written from Austria, for it is written just before he leaves the country for good. He writes about going for a walk that he wishes he had not taken because everything he sees reminds him of me. He looks at the hills, a trout stream where someone is fishing, and he passes a pond where the frogs croak as they do outside our house. The hurt he feels is unbearable. What is even more unbearable is the thought of my being left behind. He is praying for me and tells me that he will continue to do so daily. He is sure that God will look after me and in his mercy and love bring us together again. There are ten wonderful pages and I read them over and over again until I have every word by heart.

Frank M. is wonderful. The house where we now live is just a few steps away from the officers' mess and I see him every day. Frank has asked his batman to look after me — and look after me he does. After receiving Frank's letter I sit down to write to the address he has given me, and eagerly look forward to his next letter, which will come from England.

Mother and I have received news that transport for *Reichsdeutsche* is now available and we must leave the country. We are allowed to take only one very small case containing the absolute essentials with us. Mother's eyes are moist, for we are leaving behind us not only all our possessions but the place that was home to us, where we have spent more years than anywhere else and that for both of us holds many memories both happy and sad. We are leaving, too, the country of Father's forebears, a country we love. With us on the platform stand our Austrian friends who have come to bid us farewell.

When our train arrives, we are surprised and dismayed to see that it consists of cattle trucks. They are crowded already and become more crowded, so that in the end we are unable to sit on the hard, dirty floor. The passengers consist of a remarkable assortment of humanity from every walk of life. As the trucks rumble slowly along, stopping for long periods at practically every station we come to, we begin to realize the demands that this journey will make on our endurance, for we are not permitted to leave the trucks when they are stationary. Packed tightly, standing shoulder to shoulder, it is impossible to relax, let alone sleep, and the journey soon becomes torture as we are rocked and flung about, jolted back and forth and from side to side, each time the train changes speed or direction or on the many occasions when, for no apparent reason, it halts abruptly.

In Bavaria we are at last permitted to get out to find some water to drink and to wash in, and to ease our aching limbs by walking up and down the platform. As we proceed north from München towards Frankfurt, we see some similar trucks, carrying displaced persons of many nationalities, some of them in the most deplorable condition, very ill or dying. Like us, who are classed as *Reichsdeutsche*, these ethnic Germans, *Volksdeutsche*, have been expelled from Czechoslovakia and Transylvania or, like my grandparents, from Silesia and other areas ceded to Poland. More than a million of them have died; Poles and Czechs have committed deeds of unspeakable sadism in revenge for what they have suffered.

Before leaving Graz we bartered some of our remaining silver and china for food but had not expected the journey to take so long. We have taken mostly bread with us, for we have been told that bread is at a premium in Germany. Mother shares her bread with all around her, but I retain half a loaf in the small satchel slung over my shoulder for a possible emergency and have reason to be thankful for this later on.

As our journey continues, I feel my throat becoming dry and raw. This adds to the already intolerable discomforts of the journey, and by the time we reach the Palatinate I am running a temperature. When we stop I fight my way to the open door of the truck, but once again we are not permitted out, for a long line of German prisoners of war is struggling along the platform, staggering, panting and trembling. Ranged either side stand French soldiers, once of whom is wielding a horsewhip with which he belabours the ragged figures, shouting, *'Vite, vite, les cochons!'*

The war is over but man's inhumanity to man continues. When in the summer of 1945 I had learned of the dropping of the atom bombs, first on Hiroshima and then on Nagasaki, I was filled with such horror that I vowed I would never have children. It seems inconceivable that scientists use their inventive genius for the creation of ever more maniacal and diabolical weapons specifically designed to annihilate humanity. Is it really easier to deter enemy attacks by the invention of more and more deadly weapons than by developing friendship, trust and co-operation? Must suspicion, envy and hate remain for ever? And hate begets hate. Frank says that in the kingdom of God there will be neither Jews nor Gentiles, there will no longer be nations but only persons, and they will be brothers and sisters. Will it ever come?

I am grateful for Mother's physical powers of endurance and try to keep from her the fact that I am unwell, but pass the last interminable hours of the journey in a semi-conscious state, sliding in and out of fantastic dreams. Father has been notified of our departure from Austria and I know that he will have initiated enquiries immediately and will be at Cologne station to meet us. We are eagerly looking forward to our reunion as well as to hot water, soap, a clean bed and fresh clothing.

We arrive in the late afternoon when the twin towers of the cathedral opposite the station point into a sky that is tinged red with the fading glow of the setting sun. I am reminded of another glow that was the reflection of raging fires in this city the last time I was here. There is no sign of Father. Exhausted and at the limit of endurance, we sink to the ground and wait.

The sight of the dereliction, the piles of debris and the squalor appal Mother. Even though I knew what to expect, the contrast between Graz and Cologne is so great that I shudder. Mother is gazing at the cathedral and the damage caused by fourteen direct hits. 'A thousand years of history,' she murmurs, shaking her head.

A woman whom I have noticed talking to some of the people who stand or sit around is now approaching us. 'Are you looking for accommodation?' she asks, but I shake my head and she turns away dejectedly.

Why is Father not here? My throat is hurting abominably. I stand up painfully and pace up and down, but my legs give way. It is getting dark, and I tell Mother that I shall ask the woman who is still hanging around where we can stay the night. But she objects: we must wait for Father. Only when I tell her that I am ill, cannot possibly wait any longer, does she consent to leave the station.

The woman's thin face brightens when I ask her if she can get us a room. 'Have you any food?' she asks eagerly. I pull the half loaf of bread out of my satchel and she snatches at it greedily. 'I'll get you a bed.' We stumble after her as she makes her way through the desert of destruction and finally descend into a cellar below one of the skeleton buildings. Stupefied with fatigue, I fall at once into the bed she indicates and which Mother shares with me. We sleep fitfully and awake to a grey dawn. We have not eaten since Mother gave away all she had left to our fellow passengers and, having bought our night's rest with the bread I had saved, we breakfast on a cup of water before going back to the station where I intend to leave Mother while I go in search of Father.

I have no difficulty in finding my way. Something has obviously gone wrong, I tell myself: either Father has not been informed of our imminent arrival or there has been a mistake regarding the date. I look at the Hohenzollern bridge lying like some prehistoric amphibian partly submerged in the Rhine, at the faces marked by penury and hunger of those hurrying past, and am grateful that Frank has no knowledge of either the journey or our present predicament. When I am nearing the police headquarters, I am surprised and delighted to see coming towards me an old acquaintance whom we have not seen for years, a Captain S. from Silesia. I greet him with pleasure but notice that he seems ill at ease and, after I tell him about our arrival on the previous day and our concern because Father was not at the station to meet us, he asks me to come to his room with him. His request alarms me, for I cannot understand why he cannot tell me here and now where Father is. It is not until we sit down and I am gratefully sipping a cup of *ersatz* coffee that I learn that he had no idea that we were coming.

By now I am certain that something terrible has happened to Father, am expecting to hear that he is dead. When Captain S. tells me that Father has been arrested, I am stunned. Father, who has suffered through-out the Nazi period because he has never been a member of the party that he opposed in its early days along with all that it stood for, is now arrested by the Allies. It doesn't make sense. 'Why?' I ask incredulously and am told that no one knows why. He was arrested in his lodgings and since then nothing more has been heard. Captain S. speaks of post-war dangers, of denunciations, intimidation, revenge for real or imagined grievances; but I am not listening.

How am I going to tell Mother, and what are we to do without money, food or shelter in this place where people whose spirit has been stripped of all that is human crouch like rats in the cellars of bombed-out ruins? Even in the short time I have been here, I have seen that they are past the stage where they cling to one another for com-fort. Alone and lonely each of them fights for one thing only: survival.

The captain is still speaking. He suggests that we pick up Mother and drive out to Father's lodging to find out if we can stay there. Even though I am grateful to him for his support I feel angry and indignant that nothing has been done about Father's arrest, and the anger upholds me in my weakness, fills me with resolution. It is obvious that none of his staff have made any efforts either to try to find out why he has been arrested or to initiate procedures for his release. Now that we are here I shall soon get him released, get reparation for this outrage.

On our way back in the car I comment on the stone-age existence most of the people are leading. 'Better than last summer,' the captain says laconically, and he briefly mentions the stench of putrefying bodies, rats in the cel-lars, sewage leaking from fractured pipes into the drinking water, typhoid fever and dysentery from which thousands died each day.

Mother is relieved when she sees us and very pleased when she recognizes Captain S. but is obviously puzzled that it is not Father who has come with me. On the way

I have thought of all sorts of explanations that would post-pone the moment when she has to learn the truth, but decide that it is wrong to conceal what has happened and I tell her exactly what I have been told, adding only that there has been some mistake which might even now have been discovered and that I am sure that Father will be restored to us within a very short time. After I finish speaking she sits quietly, her eyes closed. The captain too is silent, lost in thought and concentrating on the road that is full of craters.

After a time Mother asks after the captain's family. We know that a few years after we had left Silesia he had married and had since then lived with his wife and family in Gleiwitz and later still in East Prussia. I see a shadow pass over his face, and for the first time I notice what in my preoccupation with our problems I had failed to see: that he looks old and worn.

In a voice devoid of all emotion, he tells us of the escape of his wife and two children from the advancing Russians, when they with thousands of others had walked for miles, leaving behind them everything, haunted by the fear of being overtaken by the enemy. While he speaks, I am reliving once again the fear I experienced when running through the graveyard, dodging between the stones; but what he describes is worse, much worse, for those who were running away were fleeing in the bitter cold and many of them were old, sick and weak and they died along the way. His wife and children managed to get as far as Dresden and there, during the raid that obliterated most of the city, they too died. Many years later, on the fortieth anniversary of the war, I am reminded of the captain's account when I read a British report and listen on the radio to the voices of survivors recalling that night when 300,000 dead had to be disposed of by burning with flame-throwers.

I sit with my arm around Mother's shoulder, and my thoughts fly to Opa who, at the age of ninety-two, has been expelled from his home and has joined the columns of refugees. Then my thoughts return to Father, who has looked forward to a new life, an era of freedom and democracy, and who is now interned for something of which he is innocent; and I reflect bitterly that the Allies' powers of arrest and their methods seem little different from those of the Gestapo.

Father's room is already occupied by someone else, and his landlady is unable to help us either with information or advice. His belongings have been packed into two large cardboard boxes which she tells us we can take with us. We return to the captain's room, where we stay while he goes out to see what can be done for us. As soon as the door closes on him, Mother is on her knees praying while I take out Frank's letter. Though I know every word by heart, the sight of his writing is comfort for a brief moment until my thoughts return to our problems and my stomach reminds me that I have eaten nothing for the last forty-eight hours and that despite my sore throat I feel hungry.

It is not until evening, when Mother and I have drunk so much water that we feel like sponges, that the captain returns and invites us to a feast of turnip soup, bread and jam and *ersatz* coffee for which he triumphantly produces both sugar and milk. More welcome even than the food is the news that he has found a room for us in Siegburg — a triumph indeed and one that has been achieved, I suspect, by pulling a few strings. More than that, I have a job. Before leaving us he had asked for my qualifications, and as from tomorrow I shall work as an interpreter.

Fortified by food and good news, we set off once more for Siegburg, and now even my throat feels better. Though there is no glass in the windows, the house where we are to live is almost undamaged. Our room is in a flat on the first floor. It is minute, furnished with a single bed, a cupboard, a wash-stand with a chipped enamel bowl, and one chair. Our landlady, a taciturn, middle-aged woman, whom I later learn has lost both husband and son in the war, informs us that rent has to be paid in advance and that this has already been done by the captain. We cannot thank him enough for what he has done for us, and he leaves with a smile on his worn face. Mother and I fall into each other's arms with tears streaming down our faces; but when we draw apart I burst out laughing at Mother's unexpected remark that we look like scarecrows. Far too exhausted to worry about how we look, we creep under the one blanket that lies on the bed and instantly fall asleep.

In the weeks that follow I work hard, for I am not only interpreting but have to type reports and occasionally take down letters in shorthand, transcribe and translate them. Once again I am grateful to Father for his insistence on my taking the typing and shorthand course, because these skills have helped to procure my job, which provides us with shelter and whatever food can be purchased with money. It serves also as an anodyne during the long months of waiting — waiting for news of Father, for a letter from Frank.

PART THREE

Darkness and Despair

Cologne, 1946-47

17

The Long Wait

On the day of our arrival in Siegburg, I had scribbled a hasty note to Frank, telling him of our new address. I confidently expected to hear from him at the latest within the month. Immediately afterwards I had begun enquiries regarding Father's arrest. I was passed on from person to person, all of them politely indifferent, all promising that enquiries would be made and that I would be informed. But I never heard anything further.

It is now two months later. I still have no news from Frank but have just learned that Father is in an internment camp at Recklinghausen.

Mother hastily makes up a small food parcel, even though it will leave us without anything to eat for the next few days. I take this and a letter to Recklinghausen. The guard at the entrance to the camp looks at me stonily. No, I cannot see anyone, he cannot give me any information, cannot tell me whether Father is there, cannot take my parcel. Only after I have pleaded with him for a long time, perhaps affected by my distress or just in order to get rid of me, does he reluctantly take the letter that Father is never to receive. I walk round the tall wire fence for several hours in the hope of catching a glimpse of Father, of anyone, but see no one. A thunderstorm accompanied by torrential rain at last drives me back to the station.

In Cologne a grey-faced woman, her eyes ringed black like a panda's, is crawling among the sodden rubble of mud-spattered ruins. She mutters to herself and looks half-crazed. I imagine her looking in the heaps of debris that might have been her home for something of sentimental value when she comes up with a handful of nettles. This, I think sadly, is what we would have had to eat if the guard had taken my small parcel.

As I step over the deep hollows in the road that hold filmed, stagnant water, I think of Mother, and fear constricts my throat. She has always been very slender but now she looks transparent. Diseases are rampant; there are thousands of cases of tuberculosis, and those who suffer from the disease have little hope of recovery, for there are only a few hospital beds available in the whole area. I remember too that Grandmama died of tuberculosis.

This then is the peace we have all longed for. Instead of fighting for survival from bombs, from the approaching enemy, we are now fighting for survival from starvation. Returning soldiers find wives and children who are strangers, find that concern over food and fuel takes priority over anything else, that all they associated with home and order has crumbled like the houses that were once their homes. Others coming back, wounded, maimed and abject, find their wives, their fiancées, their daughters associating with the former enemy. I have heard some of them say that they wished they had never returned, that death would have been preferable to what they have found on their return; and many thousands of others never do return, are never heard of again. I think of them and all the others who have gone forth courageously, inspired by noble emotions, and have fought and died bravely and have achieved only this: ruin and destruction, chaos and disaster.

When I get to the Alleestrasse in Siegburg and look up at the sightless window sockets of our room, I imagine that a letter is lying on the bare table, the letter for which I have longed and waited for two long months. How foolish I had been to imagine on that far-off sunny day in May, when

178

Frank M. handed me Frank's first letter, that from then on letters would regularly fly to and fro between us. At times the last months in Austria seem like a golden dream, an oasis of sunshine and happiness. The walks in the mountains, the sunlit valleys, the bright river with the swallows dipping where Frank fished, the music listened to at concerts and at the opera — all these things are memories so sweet of a past that now seems totally unreal, and the sense that it has all been a dream grows ever stronger. Surrounded by squalor I thirst for beauty as the parched thirst for water.

I realize now how festive life was when, cherished so sweetly by Frank, I enjoyed the half-envious yet warm friendship of Schnucki and others, lived in a comfortable home in an atmosphere that, despite post-war austerity, was pervaded by a sense of leisure. The light-heartedness, the mood of those days stands in stark contrast to the abject misery that permeates Cologne, where it is impossible to imagine people living in lovely homes, looking on beauty, going to concerts or to the opera. And I remember riding forth when the war had ended, hoping for a bright future, a hope that was strangled at birth. Was every renascence of hope to be extinguished like this? Each time I had thought that we could at last put the terror of war behind us and make a new start, it had reared like an evil monster, casting its ghastly shadow, so that, like the psalmist, I was once more thrown into the 'parched places of the wilderness'.

Each morning I wake thinking that this must be the day when I shall receive Frank's letter, and each evening I fight darkness and despondency. Then I close my eyes and imagine his beautifully-shaped head, the fair hair curling at the temples, the strong chin, the light dancing in his gold-green eyes, his strong slim hands that can be so tender — I have often marvelled how anyone can be so strong and yet so immensely tender. Oh, how desperately I want and need him, need his reassurance, his gaiety that can transform people by a look, a word, strike sparks out of them, make them come alive, transform life itself. When he enters a room, faces light up with surprise, joy and delight. If he were to walk in now, his eyes laughing. . . He has asked me never to lose faith, sure that the day will come when we shall be together again. I must hold on to that certainty or drown. But his long silence is inexplicable and sometimes I fear that he is dead, has met with some fatal accident. If this is the case, I shall never ever love anyone else, for he has absorbed all my powers of loving. But there are also moments, precious though rare, when I am able to pray and, though there appears to be no tangible answer to my prayers, I feel reassured that our love will triumph. I become aware of Frank's presence and, though physically we are separated by many miles and the cruel waters of the Channel, he is with me, holding my hand.

By now I have written innumerable letters, spent hours waiting for interviews and talked to many who, I have been told, are influential and might be instrumental in bringing about Father's release. The replies I receive from them are invariably the same. 'We are sorry but there is nothing we can tell you,' or 'We are afraid we cannot help you.' I feel as if I am battering my head against a brick wall.

Our diet consists mainly of turnips. To vary it, we look for edible fungi and berries. We are, however, not the only ones looking for these delicacies and so we try to get up very early in the morning in order to be the first in the woods. Even dandelion leaves, chickweed, acorns and beechnuts are difficult to find because everyone is collecting them.

Food is available on the black market — and not only food but luxury goods, but only to those who can pay the inflated prices that the big-time profiteers, the *Grosschieber*, demand. They are unscrupulous criminals, making fortunes. Most of them are stateless East Europeans, who now enjoy free rations and other privileges. We stay away from them and in any case have no money and nothing with which to barter. We in the British zone are worse off than those in other zones. An often-repeated slogan states that 'the Russians have the corn, the French the wine, the Americans the scenery and the British the ruins.' I could get spirits and cigarettes from British soldiers, who are happy to sell some of their weekly issue, and could perhaps trade those for food, but I am not very good at that sort of thing and Mother thinks it is wrong.

From time to time a supply of bread becomes available and Mother, who has been queuing with many others, triumphantly returns home with a whole loaf. I immediately fall to, tear off big pieces and, regardless of the consequences, of which I am well aware, greedily devour them. While I am munching, Mother talks of people jumping the queue, of others trying to elbow her out of the way, and I reflect on how thin is the veneer of what we refer to as civilization. When I was small, being civilized meant curtseying when shaking hands with grown-ups, saying 'please' and 'thank you', not pushing ahead of others.

'Always think of others first,' Mother had admonished.

'Eat like a civilized being,' Father had commanded when I held my knife and fork incorrectly.

I smile bitterly. In order to survive one has to be inconsiderate, elbow out of the way the skeletons that fight for food, push ahead of others. To the starving, table manners are as inconsequential as to a new-born babe.

I am deeply touched when I learn of the letter from the publisher Victor Gollancz to *The Times* at the time of his visit to Germany. 'If Mr Attlee would only come out here,' he writes, 'and see for himself, it is inconceivable that he could maintain the ban on private food parcels . . . when I see the swollen bodies and living skeletons in hospitals . . . then I think not of Germans, but of men and women.' This from a Jew who, as I now know, has every reason to hate us.

When I had first heard reports of atrocities committed in concentration camps, I had been outraged at what I considered to be allegations on the part of our ex-enemies which could not possibly be true. In the face of incontrovertible evidence, my mind still refused to believe that any human being, least of all members of my own people, could be capable of such bestiality. Later, in England, when I was questioned on this and I tried to explain that I had not known what was happening in the concentration camps, my statement was received with incredulity. In the end, and this is undoubtedly cowardice on my part, I closed my mind to anything that reminded me of what had happened in these camps because the thought of it filled me with such horror and revulsion that I became physically ill, unable to sleep or eat.

18

News at Last

In the morning, after a restless night spent tossing in pain, I look with distaste at our breakfast of turnips. My stomach is bulging like a balloon and there are knives twisting in my abdomen, for the bread is baked only partially with flour, the greater percentage of its contents being sawdust. When I set out to work I feel that even death must be preferable to the existence we are leading. At the end of the street I meet the postman, who hands me a large bundle tied together with some kind of string. I stare at the well-known writing on the topmost envelope. 'Frank,' I whisper unbelievingly, and clutching the bundle tightly I stand undecided. Surely on this day of days, just for once, I can stay home! But this morning I am wanted most particularly to interpret during an important meeting. The struggle between conscience and the overwhelming need to know what is contained in the letters I am holding is brief, for at this moment I am joined by a colleague, and together we proceed towards our destination.

The fact that I seem to be very much off colour has not gone unnoticed, and after the meeting I am given permission to leave work early. By this time I am bubbling over with joy but manage to hide it, for they may change their mind if they see me suddenly cheerful.

When I get home Mother, instead of asking me for the reason for my early return, pulls me excitedly into the room, where on the table stands an open parcel. 'Look,' she cries, 'look at this and this and this!' and each time she pulls out a packet and holds it up for my inspection. 'Coffee, sugar, flour, dried milk, dried egg powder, cod-liver oil capsules,' and laughing at my wide-eyed amazement she explains, 'It's a parcel from Canada.'

'But who. . . ?' And then I remember that Frank's mother lives in Canada.

Mother holds up an envelope. 'There's a letter too — will you translate it?'

'Yes, of course, but look!' I hold out my bundle of letters, but she is not looking at them. Instead she is pointing to the label of the packing, 'Gift parcel'. I laugh, for the German word *Gift* means 'poison', and happily explain. Then at last she notices my bundle, and after embracing me joyfully she quietly slips out and leaves me alone with my letters, letters full of tenderness, warmth and love. The first one is dated the day of his arrival in England and since then he has been writing daily even though he has only recently received my address.

When Mother returns I have just started to reread the first letter. While I am reading excerpts to her she brews coffee, which we sip slowly and reverently. Later we mix flour, dried egg and milk together and, after breaking three cod-liver oil capsules on the hotplate of the little stove that Captain S. has procured for us, we spread the mixture over it. Despite the fishy taste, the little pancakes are delicious and we lick our fingers appreciatively.

Frank's letters are now arriving fairly regularly. There are days when I receive none and others when three or four come together. In August a letter arrives that startles me because of its formality but I soon realize that it has been written for a special purpose. Frank informs me that it is now possible for German fiancées to come to England to marry British ex-service personnel and asks me to take the letter to the nearest military government officer and apply for a permit to visit England for two months, during which time we can be married. I lose no time in doing this, and my application for a visa is filed.

As the result of my application Frank is asked for a statutory declaration in which, before a commissioner for oaths, he has to declare 'solemnly' and 'sincerely' that he desires to marry me as soon as possible, that he is a single man and has never been married, that he has arranged accommodation for me and is able to support me from the date of my arrival and afterwards as his wife. It seems as though I shall have the visa within a matter of weeks. My euphoria soon wanes as late summer passes into autumn and I hear no more about a visa. Adding to the gloom is the fact that all my endeavours regarding Father's release remain fruitless.

A fierce wind charges through the unglazed window of our room and invalidates the little warmth that our small stove is capable of emitting. Mother has looked through the boxes that contain Father's clothes and has managed to cut down one of his jackets for me. After taking the buttons, braid and insignia off his uniform coat, she declares with satisfaction that it will be a wonderfully warm coat for her. We also use this and other items from his box as extra covers on the bed. Shoes are a problem, but there are Father's riding boots, which she says we can wear with paper insoles and many pairs of socks. When I object and say that we shall look ridiculous, she tells me that we are fortunate indeed, for there are many who have no coats or footwear, and she has seen children still going barefoot. She has piled up a small store of wood in one corner of the room, and there is hardly room to turn now, with Father's two boxes, the wood and a few briquettes of ash and clay, purchased at an outrageous price.

The snow comes earlier than expected. It begins to blow in flurries before the wind, and great drifts of it soon pile up against the ruins, with several inches falling within hours. Icicles hang from the roofs and the water in the bucket in our room is frozen solid. An icy wind moves over the land, clouds hang livid and low, and in the woods branches are bowed under the heavy load. It becomes impossible to gather wood from under the heavy blanket of snow. On the rare occasions when the sun comes out, it hangs crimson in freezing mist. The surface thaws, only to be frozen to a solid sheet when night comes, and the icy air smites our faces with the sharpness of needles. All Germany is in the grip of what is described as the severest winter in decades. We have no light, for coal has run out and there is no gas or electricity. The newspapers in the window and the snow lying against them exclude daylight, with the result that we live in semi-darkness during the day. As soon as it gets dark outside, we crawl into bed, heaping as many of Father's clothes on top of us as we can, and huddle close together for warmth. When we speak, clouds of steam rise from our lips and I watch them, expecting them to turn to ice.

In the cellars people freeze to death and everywhere birds and beasts cower benumbed and starving. Many die. We look like rag-bags as we trudge wearily through the snow and ice, with the endless east wind cutting through us like a knife. I am reminded of Father's account of winter in Russia and try to console myself that this is as nothing compared to the hardships and privations that he and so many thousands had to endure. At least we are free from vermin and partisan attacks. Our endless diet of turnips and the occasional loaf of sawdust bread, and the struggle against disease, starvation and the deadly cold would certainly have proved too much but for the knowledge that another gift parcel from Canada is on the way.

I am sustained most of all by Frank's letters and poems. Their music sets my heart singing, helps to appease the ever-present pangs of hunger and to lighten the profound passive gloom that surrounds us. Touching, sincere and infinitely tender, they are my lifeline.

Though the snow adds to the already unbearable hardships of the population, it levels the ground, softens the gaping wounds left by bombs and throws a merciful blanket over shattered trees, derelict houses, piles of rubble, the whole dark miasma. Only the crosses that mark the places where humans lie buried stand out sinister and black above the white shroud. The stars, usually so beautiful and comforting, look down on them, shivering icily and millions of light years away.

At last I have news of Father. He has been moved to the American Zone. I have heard reports of the internment camps in the American Zone, have heard them described as notorious. There are rumours of beatings, rape and starvation, and my heart fails me. There is little hope that I shall be any more successful with the Americans than I have been with the British military authorities, but I am resolved to try anything. Father has now been interned for nine months, and we still do not know why he has been arrested. Frank expects me to get the visa any time now, but as long as Father remains interned, I dare not even hope.

After long deliberations I have applied for a post as censor with the British in Bonn. I was motivated in this not so much by the better pay as by the fact that I would get a midday meal at the department, half of which I intend to take home for Mother if I should be offered the post. After filling out an exhaustive questionnaire, I am relentlessly grilled by several people. An English test is then followed by another oral interview. *If* I am appointed I shall start work on 1 March 1947.

On the day when I set out on my journey to Frankfurt to enquire about Father, conditions are still arctic and blizzards rage. The train is several hours late, as always incredibly crowded, and of course unlit and unheated. I know that most of the passengers who carry suitcases or rucksacks are on the way back from a black market. There is an air-raid bunker at Cologne railway station where one can get most things, though I have never been there. The train arrives in Frankfurt with a ten-hour delay. The whole

187

atmosphere of the journey and in particular my interview with the US officer who assures me that he is powerless to do anything for me, that the lowest rank in US army intelligence carries more clout than an army general and that there is no chance of my seeing anyone in intelligence is one of unreality, demoralizing and nightmarish. When I arrive back in Cologne I am convinced that I shall never see either Father or Frank again. It is useless to remind myself that I am one among thousands who are waiting to be reunited with loved ones, useless too to take refuge in memories, for they only increase the intolerable longing, the pent-up emotions.

Mother, wearing Father's greatcoat and large boots that make running difficult, has been chased by a wild boar in Siegburg's main street. She escaped by running into the open front door of a house. Like us the wild animals are starving, and deer have been coming into town quite often in search of food. In Berlin wolves have appeared in the woods, and the bitter cold continues. Trains are still arriving with refugees, some of whom have frozen to death on the way. Our living conditions, appalling though they are, are comfortable when compared with those that others have to endure, yet only Frank's and Mother's courage, deeply rooted in their faith, saves me from despair.

Frank has gone through the harrowing experience of many young men returning to civilian life after six years in the army. He has written over a hundred letters of application for jobs and never lost heart. For a short time he worked in a government office but found the work monotonous and undemanding and so he continued to search for another job. Just before Christmas he found what he had been looking for — an opportunity to live out his Christian ideals by working for a Christian organization, the YMCA. He has never written much about his own problems but is always full of solicitude for ours. Before the war he obtained a scholarship to the university in Toronto, Canada, where his mother, brother and sister are living. His mother left England after the death of Frank's father. At the time of his father's death, Frank was seventeen. His father was a well-known Methodist preacher; Frank had loved him deeply and had at that time decided to offer himself for ordination. The war had prevented him from taking up his scholarship and, though he assures me that it is not on account of me that he has decided to stay in England, I suspect the fact that he will not have to take me so far from my parents has something to do with his decision. He has also decided to look for a job rather than to study for ordination because he needs to support me as his wife. I have from time to time felt guilty when thinking about all this but know that our need to be together is too great for things to be otherwise. Now I rejoice that he has found what he was looking for.

My inability to do anything for Father depresses me more and more, and often despair holds me in its grip. I want Frank, want to hear his voice, to feel his touch, to shut out the misery that surrounds me. I picture him in his room as he writes to me, describing every minute of his day, every detail about the people he meets, and yet there are times when I feel that I must have become a memory to him, an image in his mind summoned from the past with the help of the photograph of me that he keeps by him just as I keep his by me. I long to hear his voice that can transform the most banal words into music. If only we could speak on the phone, how incredibly, how wonderfully happy it would make me.

I have obtained the job in Bonn and for a few days have been making the rather strenuous daily journey there, where, slithering and sliding on snow and ice, I make my way to the offices of the British Censorship Department, but as soon as I begin work I know that changing my job has been a mistake. To earn our bread by reading the innermost thoughts intended only for those to whom they are addressed is distasteful to me, but I am compelled to continue until I find something else.

The unexpected sight of the first frail snowdrop, drooping on a pale, slender stalk, fills me with longing and a strange conviction that soon, very soon, things are going to change. This conviction has been growing steadily since my prolonged interrogation by a stern-looking man who had questioned me closely prior to my appointment as censor regarding Father's internment and my application for a visa to England. Here at last was someone who asked questions concerning all the circumstances of Father's arrest, someone who actually wanted to hear about his past and, forgetting my interrogator's forbidding appearance and with a total disregard of the fact that what I was saying might prejudice my chances of getting the post I had applied for, I gave vent to all the pent-up feelings of outrage at the injustice of his arrest, my treatment at the hands of those to whom I had applied for help and the fact that we had never been told why he had been arrested. After nearly a year, to the best of my knowledge, Father had had no hearing and had not been told the reason for his arrest. My interviewer had listened unmoved, making no comment, and had concluded the interview with the terse statement that I would hear from him. I had gone away convinced that my application would be rejected and, when I was nevertheless appointed, I searched my mind, trying to remember whether there had been any sympathy in the penetrating gaze of the eyes that had studied me so intently; but I could recall only disinterest and indifference. Yet, however hard I try, I cannot suppress this illogical conviction that things are about to change for us.

A few weeks later I wake after a particularly vivid dream in which my visa is delivered by a courier. I have so often dreamed of receiving the letter containing my visa from our postman that this new twist makes me smile. The letters I have to censor that day are particularly harrowing, and I leave Bonn determined to go and ask whether there is any chance that I can get my old job back.

When I get home, Mother hands me an envelope that

she says was delivered by a uniformed motorcycle rider. My heart lurches and I sit down abruptly. 'Aren't you going to open it?' Mother asks, looking puzzled. With trembling hands I take the knife she hands me and slide it under the flap, but when I hold in my hands what I have been waiting for for so many months, I feel numb. There is no sense of elation. This is real, I am not dreaming, in a moment it will come, I tell myself, the wonderful happiness that in dreams I have anticipated so many times will surely come. Mother's worried expression and her anxious questions rouse me and I hand her the paper. She looks at it searchingly. 'But this is your visa, isn't it?' I nod. Then from a long way off I hear my voice, 'It's useless as long as Father remains interned.'

The next day we are notified of Father's release. For a few more hours the sense of anticlimax, which I cannot understand and which frightens me, persists. At last it is replaced by impatience, for the waiting is not over. Accompanying the visa is a small slip that states that 'fiancées in the British Zone who have been granted Exit Permits and visas to the U.K. are required to contact by letter or phone the Foreign Relations Section/British Red Cross, 35 Weser Strasse, Vlotho, Tel.: Rhine Army 2491, where instructions will be given for their onward journey to Cuxhaven.' When I ring them, I am told that I shall receive written instructions in due time.

Father is home! We are as shocked at his appearance as he is at ours. He is so emaciated that the collar round his neck is several sizes too big. What is worse is the look of bitterness in his eyes, the deep lines of suffering engraved in a face that is the colour of old parchment. He has never been very demonstrative; now he alternates between a state of almost total withdrawal and one of emotional agitation. Only once does he speak of the conditions during his imprisonment, and he seems less upset by the appalling treatment he received at the hands of those holding him prisoner than by the behaviour of fellow prisoners who, deprived of all their personal belongings, starving and sick, fought over potato peel and rotten vegetables, which they devoured voraciously, and who did not shrink from stealing from one another. He tells of his struggle with his conscience, and of how easy it would have been to give in and to become less than human. When he was notified of his impending release, the only explanation he was given for his arrest and internment was that his was a case of mistaken identity.

Cowardly, I shrink from telling him of my impending marriage to an Englishman for which in his absence Mother has already given the written consent required by the authorities. Though he has always been an ardent anglophile, I feel sure that, embittered by his recent experiences, he will oppose the marriage, and I tremble when I remember the day when he found out about my relationship with Lutz.

While I am away at work, Mother, who is aware of my fear and has been waiting for the right moment, talks to him about Frank. That evening I am surprised and greatly relieved when Father tells me that, after Mother's account of Frank's care for us and her description of his fine character, his integrity, his warmth and his compassion, he feels that he cannot withhold his consent to the marriage, even though he is distressed to hear that my departure is imminent. I hand him a letter that Frank had written to him some time ago, and shortly afterwards he shows me his reply, written in impeccable English, in which he expresses his regret at not being able to provide me with a dowry, his grief at losing me after so short a reunion, but also his gladness that, released from starvation and penury, I will be restored to full health and happiness in Frank's loving care. Though distressed that he and Mother will be unable to be present at their only child's wedding, he hopes that the restrictions that at present prevent them from coming to England will soon be lifted and promises that they would then visit us, for he is anxious to make Frank's personal acquaintance.

The letter, which reflects his present, highly emotional state, touches me deeply and increases the feeling of guilt at leaving them to hardship and insecurity while I escape to happiness. I feel easier when Father receives confirmation that he will shortly be reinstated as chief of police. In the meantime I wait impatiently for a letter from Frank, confirming that he knows that I have received the visa and that Father is home. At last I get Frank's jubilant letter. He has immediately paid the eight pounds required for my fare from Cuxhaven to Tilbury to the Friends' Committee for Refugees and Aliens and tells me of the special licence we shall need, the hotel where the reception is to be held, the wedding dress I am to wear. All this is punctuated by outbursts of rapturous joy that reduce me to tears. I had thought in terms of a quiet wedding without any fuss but, realizing that he is going to endless trouble and has already involved his dearest friends, one of whom has recently been married and whose wife, Molly, has generously offered to lend me her wedding dress and provide the dresses for the bridesmaids, I happily enter into the discussion of his preparations.

The snow and ice that has for so long held the country in its grip has begun to melt, revealing once again the devastation, the abomination it has so mercifully concealed. Nevertheless the thaw seems to be the outward symbol of hope deferred, even though spring is still a long way off. It is a cold thaw, followed by gales, sleet and floods. Rivers burst their banks and overflow and the east wind continues to blow. Instead of slipping on ice, we now slip in mud, for the roads have become quagmires and nature continues the wreckage of war.

Father chafes under the conditions in which we have to live. In a gesture of generosity that seems out of character, Frau S. offers him the couch in her sitting room for him to sleep on. Mother feels that she can put up with anything now that he has been restored to us and I have got the visa; moreover, as she often remarks, the war has shown us all too clearly the truth of the parable of the rich fool, and I am in wholehearted agreement, for all I want and need is Frank's love, a treasure incorruptible by rust or moths.

My clothes have been washed and brushed and mended for my journey and my case is packed. On 28 March, a telegram arrives from Vlotho and the ten words it contains — *Bitte ersten April Cuxhaven sein* — *Irene Cholmondeley, British Red Cross* — transform a day of wind, cold and sleet into one of sunshine and warmth. Father, who is aware of how hazardous the journey will be for me, is resolved to accompany me to Cuxhaven. I do not remind him of our journey from Austria or my trip to Frankfurt.

The train, when it arrives, has, as always, people standing on the steps and buffers and sitting on the roof, and generally draped all over it like bunches of grapes. Since it is impossible to get inside through doors, people climb on to the coupling and through the unglazed windows. Father puts down my case, lifts me up and pushes me head first into an apparent gap between heads, where for a moment I lie horizontally, supported by those on whose backs and shoulders I have landed. There are loud cries of protest, but I am lowered to my feet and remain tightly wedged in the same position until we arrive in Hamburg. I have no idea where Father and my case are.

When the train begins to move I turn my head sharply and for one second see the pale oval of Mother's face disappearing from view. I had said goodbye, had embraced and kissed her while we were waiting for the train to arrive, but I had been over-excited. It is only now that I realize the full implication of this parting and reproach myself with being selfish and callously insensitive and am overwhelmed with grief.

In Hamburg, where we have a long wait, I am reunited

with Father and my case. While we are waiting, I talk to him and for the first time dare to raise the subject of Hitler and the Nazi regime. Why had there not been any opposition, I ask him, especially from the church. The church, he says, had opposed the programme for euthanasia and the hostility to the Jews, and he names Niemöller and Bonhoeffer.

'But,' I protest, 'as far as I remember there was no open opposition by any group or groups.'

He sighs, there had been many who, like him, had been anxious to avert the danger of war, had tried to persuade others to join with them to create a more powerful, more effective force against Hitler and his regime. But Hitler, by going to war successfully, had paralysed any attempts at opposition. 'All of us, who had individually fought the system in the years before he came to power,' he continues, 'and had hoped to build up a powerful resistance, became powerless once the war started.' He takes out his handkerchief and wipes the beads of perspiration from his forehead, and instantly I reproach myself. Knowing how precariously his emotions are balanced I ought to keep off anything that is likely to upset him, especially now, when I am leaving him and Mother, am virtually deserting them, and hastily I change the subject.

We arrive in Cuxhaven totally exhausted, and Father takes leave of me at the camp where I have been told I must remain for examination before embarking on a former troop transporter, the *Empire Hallidale*. I give him messages for Mother but cannot convey to him what I feel about leaving them. A mist dims my eyes and I find it hard to control my voice. Father's eyes are brilliant with tears which he does not allow himself to shed. After embracing me tightly, he turns abruptly and strides off. That evening, as I lie on a lumpy mattress, I think of him and Mother, both so painfully thin, mere shadows of their former selves, and pray that they will be happy together.

Though the conditions in the camp are primitive, there

are showers, and after months spent washing from head to toe from a small enamel bowl on which I often had to break the ice, I glory in being able to shower. I now live entirely in the future, impatiently waiting for the wonderful moment when I shall disembark and step straight into Frank's arms.

When the time comes for me and others who are travelling with me to be examined, I am asked to remove my clothes and march naked through a corridor into several rooms where I am examined by a succession of young male doctors. Though there are female nurses with them, I am filled with shame, rage and humiliation when I am obliged first to stand and then lie nude and helpless before men who examine me for eczema, lice and, last of all, VD. At the time of the examination, I am ignorant of the horrible types of VD, among them a particularly virulent syphilis, that are rampant among the occupying forces and the girls who associate with them. In the last room I am sprayed from head to foot with what I assume to be DDT. Tears of helpless anger blind my eyes, and only the thought of Frank waiting across the water makes me submit to the indignity of being treated as a pariah.

We finally embark on 5 April and are to spend two nights at sea. I have travelled by road, rail and air but never by sea and have a horrible feeling that I am not a good sailor. I have often been car sick, and this threatens to be a rough crossing. During the first night I sleep soundly through the storm and am taken aback when I see that I am the only one who sits down to breakfast. A smiling steward hands me a bowl of prunes, and as I set it down it careers wildly across the heaving table. I manage to catch it in time, and holding the bowl tightly pressed to my chest with one hand, I feed with the other. Though the floor below me continues to heave and I am beginning to feel as if I am having breakfast on a roller-coaster, I cannot resist the delicacies that the amused and incredulous steward puts into my hand. After the prunes I consume bacon, sausage and fried bread, which he has considerately cut up for me, and finish with toast, butter, marmalade and coffee; then I sit back replete and feeling guilty. If only I could have shared this banquet with Mother and Father! Then I remember the instructions I have been given to prevent sea-sickness: 'Go up on deck and put your face in the wind.'

I stand up, holding on to the table, but find walking with the boat tilting first one way and then another incredibly difficult. I am also beginning to feel somewhat odd but manage eventually to fight my way out on to the open deck, staggering drunkenly from side to side. It is a mad thing to do, for the force of the wind is horrific, but the crew are far too busy to bother and there is no one else to stop me. Clinging with both hands to the rail, I look down at the boiling, seething water. Great waves come riding towards the boat, curl upwards and for a moment seem poised to hurl themselves at my head, then crash sickeningly against the side of the boat, rocking it like a nutshell. I fight with all my might to hold on until the spent foam leaves the floor and my feet, then I reel towards the door and pitch through it. Terrified and shaken, I gaze through the window that is encrusted with salt froth at a towering wall of water looming above the deck, certain that when it falls, it will crush the boat; but the vessel climbs the wall and lurches down the other side.

All day long the raging sea continues to toss the helpless *Empire Hallidale* up and down, surging, rushing and roaring. I am beginning to feel very ill indeed. To see the waves building up, the ship poised high and then descending drunkenly into valleys and pits is probably worse than just feeling it climb up and lurch down, and the high scream of the wind is terrifying. But I remain above, resolved not to join those who lie prostrate and groaning on their bunks, for I feel that the fetid air alone will make me vomit, and though I feel sick to death I am determined not to part with the food I have

197

so enjoyed. The storm continues to rage unabated, and by the end of the day I am convinced that I shall be dead by the time we reach land — if ever we do reach it.

When night falls, I am forced to go and lie on my bunk, and as soon as I lie down and close my eyes, I feel better. I have dipped my handkerchief in eau de cologne that one of the other passengers has offered. I now hold it to my nose and think of Frank, who like me will be lying awake. In less than twelve hours we shall be together. Sleep does not come easily, and when it does come it is fitful with sudden wakings full of panic, hopes and fears.

Finally I wake to the realization that the sea has ceased to rage and that the engines appear to have stopped, and I conclude that we must have docked. I gaze through the porthole and see forbidding and alien-looking buildings, the buildings of Tilbury docks. I take a quick bath in sea water and dress quickly, but when I arrive on deck I am told that it will be some time before we can disembark, so I go down once more.

Now that the emotional and mental agonies of the last months should be a thing of the past and the moment is near when our passionate desire to be together for always is to be fulfilled, my courage fails me. I know that I have changed. In the camp, when I showered, some of the girls had teased me because my ribs were showing. What if Frank finds me so changed that he does not recognize me, or discovers that he does not love me after all? Impossible, I tell myself: has he not in more than three hundred letters spoken of his great love for me. Other fears assail me: what if he has not been notified of the correct date, is not here? People will know from my accent that I am German, a national of the country that has plunged them into war. There is a satirical song that the English are singing, 'Don't let's be beastly to the Hun'. If it expresses the national feeling, then they must hate us terribly. I clasp my hands tightly in my lap and notice that they are cold and damp. Will leaving my own country, losing my own nationality and taking on that of my husband mean loss of identity, mutilation of personality?

For the first time I face up to the reality of life in a foreign country. In Austria our life together was one long, glorious holiday. Now we shall have to settle down to the business of everyday living, to mundane, sometimes uncongenial tasks. Will there be an anticlimax, especially after these past months, when expectation has been raised to fever pitch? In one brief moment I foresee dangers in the years to come when as an alien I shall live in an alien land. I remember one of the nuns at the convent where for a time I went to school who had explained to us the meaning of the word 'xenophobia'. 'The instinctive dislike of strangers, those of other nations, other races — you will find it wherever you go in the world,' she had said. I shall have a greater need of Frank's love and understanding than is necessary in marriages between partners of the same nationality. And what of him? He will have to bear the burden of being married to a woman whose country has only recently been at war with his. What if the power and wonder of our love gives way under the strains, if he tires of the demands I make on him to support and reassure me and to cope with my depression and self-distrust?

Suddenly I jump. Over the loudspeaker a voice announces that all passengers should have disembarked by now. The message is repeated. I rush up the steps on to the gangway, eagerly scanning the faces of the few who still stand waiting . . . and then I see him, see the look of bewilderment on the loved face give way to radiant recognition as he strides eagerly towards me. Then I know that I have come home. I am swept up and held so closely that I gasp for breath. His heart is pounding against my rib cage as he kisses my eyes, forehead, lips and hair, traces each feature with trembling fingers. The terror, the fear, the aching loneliness that have been ours during the months of separation are gone in a flash; and I know that as long as we are together, I need fear nothing, for he will keep me from all harm.

PART FOUR

Seeking and Finding

England, 1947 onwards

19

Homecoming

Now that the final consummation of our union is so close there are moments when the strain of waiting becomes unendurable, when it seems that the few words spoken by us and a priest are superfluous. Our relationship, which has been tested, hallowed and glorified by our spiritual and mental affinity seems to need nothing more. The permissive society in which my children are to become adults and my grandchildren grow up is still some way off. We belong to an era that let love grow in all its beauty and innocence. In old age I remember Frank's loving restraint and look with pity on those for whom instant sexual gratification has become a necessity.

Our wedding takes place five days after my arrival in England. The evening before sees a joyful reunion with Eric, who has come from Manchester for the event. Throughout the ceremony and at the reception I am an onlooker, hearing the speeches, the congratulations and seeing the smiling faces from a long way off. In spirit I am with Mother and Father in their tiny room in Cologne. Their meal will probably consist once again of turnips, and they can scarcely remember the taste of the types of food that we are enjoying.

I fall in love with the softly undulating countryside, the woods and glades, the long stretches of empty beach, the rose-red earth and the churches and cottages of north Devon where we spend the first two weeks of our married life. The young spring bracken is just beginning to unfurl and hawthorn trees look vividly green in the sunshine between sea and sky. The space, beauty and tranquillity are a delightful surprise, for I had made for myself a strange picture of England as a bleak, grey country, overhung by a pall of industrial smoke. I am delighted to find reality completely different from what I had imagined.

The harsh winter has given way to an enchanting spring, and in surprise I exclaim, 'And they say it always rains in England!' Frank tells me that the claim is much exaggerated but admits that this is an unusually good year. Smiling lovingly he adds, 'Specially to welcome you, my darling, my country has arrayed itself in all its glory.'

London too, commonly referred to at home as 'England's laundry' because of its reputation of being continually wrapped in a blanket of fog, is a surprise. After the peace of Devon, the roar of traffic, the smells and the heat imprisoned in between houses seem oppressive, but even the dust and glare of the city cannot dim the bright blue sky. One of Frank's friends has found a bed-sitting room in a basement flat in Notting Hill Gate for us, and I settle down to the business of housekeeping. Sometimes when Frank is at work and there seems to be nothing to do, for our room is quickly cleaned, I am overwhelmed by a longing for space, for the mountains. I want to push back the concrete that shuts me in. Then I close my eyes and inwardly gaze at peak upon peak, scarred with rock or clothed in woods, climb the summits and stand with nothing but sky overhead and listen to the silence. Though I say nothing, Frank senses my need and takes me to Hyde Park or Kensington Gardens and, whenever he can, right out of London. Hyde Park, with its orators mounted on boxes, holding forth on anything and everything, including politics, surrounded by an audience that is amused or heckles, is a revelation to me, as I have been brought up under a totalitarian system.

I avidly read anything that comes to hand and listen

carefully to the pronunciation of BBC newscasters. My first shopping trip fills me with terror, but the shop assistants are friendly and helpful when they realize that I am not English. Sometimes they even ask if I am Scottish or American, and then I am badly tempted, but after my first tremulous admission that I am German does not result in my being evicted from the shop, I take courage.

In the autumn, to our great joy, Frank is transferred to Devon. Our joy is tempered by the difficulty of finding a home, for our means are limited. Frank earns £27 a month, so most of what we see on offer is way beyond what we can afford. Eventually, however, we find a furnished cottage that we are able to rent for £1.7s.6d. per week. The cottage is minute and damp, with an outside toilet and no bathroom.

We do not think of ourselves as poor but as immeasurably rich, and I look back over the years and see sunlit memory pictures of sheer bliss in the glory and wonder of our togetherness. The summer lingers on, perfect and enchanting, as we live and laugh and love in a world apart from others.

Our first Christmas together, so joyfully anticipated during our long separation, is overshadowed by the memory of the trauma of two miscarriages. I am still weak and feeling sad, depressed and homesick. Though Father has not been with us for many years at Christmas, I have never known a Christmas without Mother. Nostalgic thoughts of Christmases past crowd in upon me, memories of the tall fir tree, the warm room filled with the fragrance of fir and marzipan, the sound of the old German carols that I play on the piano. I remember the cold, crisp air as we walked through moonlight in a blaze of stars to Midnight Mass, which contrasts with the wet and grey Christmas Eve here. I think longingly of Austria where even in winter the sky is brilliant blue, the sparkling frost clothes all things in brightness and light and the distant mountains look down in stillness with the calm of eternity. There on

Christmas Eve the air is so still that the whole world seems to be listening expectantly for the miracle that we celebrate each year, but here carousing people pass our windows in noisy groups. In my state of deep depression, I forget the last Christmas when Mother and I sat shivering in a cold room without even a candle to lighten the darkness, when I had longed so desperately to be with Frank. To the poignant anguish and torment of the loss of our second baby is added the insidious fear that is secretly torturing me, that I might be unable to bear a child. Frank is wonderfully patient with me and at last manages to persuade me of his own conviction that before long we shall have the baby I so desperately want.

At the end of January I am returning from Exeter to Crediton when I hear of Gandhi's assassination. That same day, I receive a letter from my parents telling me that all Germany is convinced that another war is imminent. I stare at the letter in my hand and shiver. Will people never realize that war is bestial and degrading, a blasphemy against life? I have now seen war damage in England, have read books written by British soldiers and British civilians about their war experiences and compared them with my own. They have been as horrified at civilians being killed by Germans as I have been about the slaughter of women, children, the old and the unfit by the British, the Czechs, the Poles and the Russians. I am reminded of the words of Beatrice's grandfather. 'Nothing has been learned from the cataclysms of history.'

The retreat of winter and the lengthening days bring new hope and, when spring is scattering flowers through the land, I realize that I am once again pregnant. As the weeks pass my health improves, becomes vigorous and remains unimpaired. I seem to have an abundance of vitality and revel in the glow of physical well-being, am filled with a deep and wonderful serenity, with an overwhelming exultation that at last I am bearing successfully the child

206

of the husband I adore. The first time I feel the new life quickening within me with a flutter like that of a butterfly, I am filled with such wonder that I spontaneously send forth a prayer of praise.

Our son, Philip, is born in December, ten days after Frank's birthday. I lie in a mist of spent pain, feeling more dead than alive, but one look at him revives me wonderfully. He is perfect: the bone structure of the face and the shape of the head with a strong outward curve above the nape of the neck are exactly like Frank's. Looking down at the fluffy top of his head cradled in my arms I am filled with happiness, pride and love, and then experience a moment of panic. Have I brought him into a world that is inhuman, a world where horror lies in wait for him? As I look down, the minute, tightly curled fist uncurls like the petals of a flower and with amazing strength clutches my finger. Then fear gives way to a feeling of wonder and exquisite joy. Everything about him fills us with wonder, and when, after a strand of my hair has brushed his face, he wrinkles his tiny nose and sneezes, we laugh out loud with delight.

Mother has at last been granted a visa and arrives when Philip is four months old. I am intensely moved when I see her lift him from his cot and kiss first the small clenched fist and then the top of his fuzzy head. Crowing with delight he punches her nose, and she looks up, her eyes starry with happiness. I know how much she wanted to give Father the son he had longed for and she tells me how proudly he had marched in with our telegram to tell her that they had a grandson. Philip is a happy, contented baby, and we wake in the mornings to his murmurs and chuckles and listen in drowsy contentment while he plays with his fingers and toes.

Before Philip's birth we had moved into a flat in a row of wooden buildings that had been used as offices during the war but had since been converted. Though I had looked eagerly forward to mother's visit, I had also been slightly apprehensive because of our limited accommodation, but she has settled down perfectly happily and declares that the bed-settee is extremely comfortable and that she is delighted with our immediate surroundings. In the grounds are pergolas from which tumble in their season laburnum, wisteria and pink rambler roses in luxuriant and untidy profusion, and at weekends while Frank and I play tennis, Mother sits down in dappled shade under a leafy canopy beside the pram in which Philip, his small toes curling and uncurling, watches the pattern of light where sunbeams pierce the shifting leaves and reaches out to catch them.

During the week Mother and I go for walks with the pram through woods and fields, along hedges starred with wild roses, flowering brambles and yellow broom, and when we are tired we rest in meadows of clover full of drowsy bees, looking across fields of rich red soil at cottages and farms and church towers.

After Mother leaves, Frank takes us in the car whenever he has to go anywhere near the coast, and whenever possible he takes us to Budleigh Salterton, where I swim while Philip in his carry-cot happily chews the large pebbles that I place in it. I look over the tops of the waves, at the gleam of wet pebbles, above me to where the gulls dip and swerve, and I see his head in the white sun-hat outlined against the bright blue sky with its fleecy network of clouds. A fat, placid cherub with hair like spun gold and round eyes that are the colour of periwinkles, he is unique, the centre of our universe, a miracle of God.

In late summer the sun that has turned his small limbs golden is still hot, and brings from the hedgerows the scents of blackberries and late-blossoming gorse. The summer has been beautiful and, even in October, when there are light frosts at night, the sun still shines warmly during the day and in the mornings frosty mists drift like smoke in the early sunshine. We love living in Devon, and when

Frank is moved to Nottingham the following year, we are sad.

At the end of the year I take Philip to Germany to see my parents. Frank is to join us for Christmas. I rejoice to see everywhere renewed hope and energy. Men and women work hard at rebuilding, at creating order out of chaos. In their faces, instead of the desperate hopelessness I remember, I see growing pleasure and pride in their work, and this despite the fact that the tensions between East and West create an awareness of danger and lead many to fear that another war is inevitable.

My parents' flat in Düsseldorf, where they now live, seems palatial with its many spacious rooms and long corridors, and it is furnished with what we had to leave behind in Austria. I am shocked to learn that Mother illegally crossed the border into Austria with a mountain guide to arrange for the furniture to be transported to Germany. She paid for the transport by selling needles, fountain pens and various other small items that were still unobtainable in Austria except on the black market. I feel angry with Father for sending her into danger and, though she makes light of the various hazards she encountered, I know that she will have shrunk from the whole enterprise and that the selling part of it must have been especially distasteful to her.

Though I am happy to be with my parents, I miss Frank terribly, and the small strip of water that divides us fills me with horror now that there is constant talk of war between the superpowers. Would I be able to get back to England in the event of a sudden outbreak of hostilities? I have recurrent nightmares in which I see again the curving lines of fire of anti-aircraft guns and the searchlights criss-crossing, hear the explosions, the wailing sirens, the staccato burst of anti-aircraft guns as with Philip in my arms I try to run through a sea of flames, unable to reach the boat that can take us back to England. When I wake, drenched in perspiration, I can still hear the screams of nose-diving bombers, the ear-splitting violence of explosions. When at last they cease to reverberate, the words Frank quoted to me in Austria echo in my heart: 'Where thou lodgest I will lodge, thy people shall be my people . . . ' For henceforth my home is where he is, despite the fact that I shall never be totally accepted by his people as one of them and for the rest of my life I am to be conscious of this. It is to breed in me a morbid fear, for my sensitivity shrinks from the judgment I see in people's eyes as soon as they know of my nationality. Even though I am British by marriage, and even after I have lived in England for longer than in any other country, there is still this sense of exclusion, of being driven into the wilderness of isolation, especially when trying to take part in discussions concerning internal political issues.

Yet the country that has become mine by marriage has already claimed me. I love it not only because I love Frank but also because I love its people and am enchanted by its beauty. Despite this, I shall also always remain one with those with whom I shared and suffered the hardships of war, fear, bereavement, grief, deprivation and shame.

Just before Christmas, on Philip's first birthday, Frank joins us; and for the first time since leaving England, in his close embrace, I sleep peacefully through the night.

20

The Intolerable Yearning

My search for faith continues. Because I love Frank, I want to believe as he does. I know that I must take the first step in trust towards faith yet am reluctant, for I am fearful of what might be the consequence of total commitment. Frank is gentle and patient. He has never urged me to become an Anglican or to attend church, but at Philip's baptism I am, at my request, received into the Anglican Church. Because I have been brought up in a family with divided allegiances, I want us to be united.

Now that we are one flesh and share rare intimacy, I am disturbed by a yearning that assails me at times, a heart-rending ache, a thirsting for something that I cannot understand and cry out against. Though we are everything to each other, I am still conscious of an essential aloneness and isolation of self. At last I talk to Frank about this, haltingly at first, searching for the right words because I am afraid he might misunderstand and think that he is to blame for what I feel. But he understands immediately and tries to explain. Together we read the words of the psalmist: 'Like as the hart desireth the water-brooks: so longeth my soul after thee, O God.' And then he quotes Augustine's words, 'Our hearts are restless till they find rest in thee.' Is that what it is — a yearning for what is unattainable, for something that is yet to come? But I do not want to think of the hereafter. What I have here is too wonderful. I know that the time must come when everything that is now precious and intimate will have to pass, but I cannot imagine it, for lovemaking is an important part of our relationship. Frank believes in an afterlife, believes in a reunion with loved ones and assures me that, though the corporeal will have to perish, we shall still exist, still know one another. But the absence of his body, and with it of senses and emotion, appals me, and I am frightened by the idea of pure spirituality, pure intelligence.

When Philip is three years old, our daughter, Leslie, is born. Nine months later the children and I go ahead of Frank to Germany. My parents have now moved from Düsseldorf to Essen. They have also bought a house in the country in Linz, on the Rhine. It is a beautiful house, set in extensive grounds high up above Linz, surrounded by hills and woods. Father has named it *Haus Rübezahl*, after Opa's house in the Riesengebirge.

During the week Father stays in the flat in Essen and only comes to Linz at weekends. As always when I am away from Frank, I am insecure. I am all the more fearful now, for on 17 June of this year in the German Democratic Republic the Russians turned their tank guns on demonstrating workers. Out here in the country I am a little nervous at night. I ask Mother if she is afraid to be by herself during the week. She shakes her head and smiles, and I remember her faith that throughout the terrors of the war years was her rock, her strength and her shelter as it was mine during my childhood. When Frank comes, I ask him, 'What is faith?' He tells me that it cannot be apprehended by rational thought. 'And what is faith?' he quotes, and he gives answers from the letters that were written to believers in the young Christian church. 'Faith gives substance to our hopes and makes us certain of realities we do not see.' 'We walk by faith, not by sight.'

To me God still seems infinitely remote; Christ is not real to me as he is to Frank and Mother, both of whom have a relationship with him as their Saviour, someone who is very much alive and present in their lives. When I pray, I pray to someone who lived centuries ago, not someone who is here now and who wants me to speak to him, who will listen and respond. I want what they have, and there are moments when it seems that I am very close to what I have come to think of as a break-through, when I feel lifted out of the mundane, everyday world. Sometimes this happens when I am listening to music, when I see the sun rise behind towering moun-tains, during an exquisitely beautiful experience when the spirit is revealed through the senses and soars, struggling for freedom, trying to escape from its physical bondage. For an infinitesimal moment the spirit has cognition of something that cannot be expressed; yet always the experi-ence is followed by an intolerable yearning that cannot be assuaged. Can sensual experience, I ask myself again, lead to communion with God, give foreknowledge of that which is to come? Does the soul, for a second in and out of time, know the unknowable, become conscious of the absolute? Somewhere I have read that the more the soul sees of God, the more it desires him. Can it be that the more human love approaches the divine, the more it desires to draw close to God?

Mother loves living in the country, but it surprises me to see my once-so-elegant mother arrayed like a peasant, wielding a hoe. I had become used to seeing her dressed in all kinds of strange garments in Cologne but now, when conditions are more normal and Father once again holds a position of some status in the community, I expected her to take an interest in clothes. Father certainly does, and he even asks me to use my influence to get her to take care of herself. He has keenly felt the loss of property and of all his assets after the war. I notice that it is his genera-tion that works feverishly to become reestablished, that complains most and seems excessively preoccupied with appearances and material comforts. I notice, too, that the carefully coiffured women sitting in the shiny new cafés, eating elaborate confections, are mostly middle-aged, and I wonder if they are compensating for the deprivations of wartime and the immediate post-war years. The old are the ones I pity. They are so tired, shaken and hurt. Nearly all of them have lost someone they loved. Many have lost their homes. They also appear to have lost hope and faith and seem to be waiting resignedly for the end of their lives.

When I broach the subject of clothes with Mother, she shakes her head and smiles sadly. 'You have seen the misery in which people lived after the war. There are millions all over the world living just like that. How can I, who am aware of this, spend money on expensive clothes and live in luxury?' I notice, too, that though she is anxious that we should have the best of everything, she herself eats most frugally and only of vegetables and fruit from the orchard. For a fleeting moment I wonder whether Father has bought this house in the depths of the country because she is neglecting her appearance, but I dismiss the thought as unworthy. Nevertheless, it seems strange that he should wish to spend the week alone in the flat in town and only come to Linz at weekends. I cannot imagine my ever agreeing to this kind of life, especially after our enforced separation before moving to Nottingham.

When we leave, I look back to where Mother is standing waving a last goodbye, a brave smile on her gentle, worn face lifting the corners of her mouth and crinkling her kind eyes. She is wearing a grey tunic and a skirt that comes down to her ankles. Her hair, now a dull brown, is once again parted in the centre and drawn back into a chignon. She stands with her hand on the gate, looking small because her shoulders are bowed. My heart contracts, for suddenly I remember the vivacious young woman she once was — with dancing eyes and hair that shone with golden lights, her hands full of roses, her slim figure dressed all in white. I recall the poise of her head, her graceful walk, the dignity of her upright, slender figure. She has faded like the roses; the happiness she enjoyed as a young married woman was struck short by disaster; and now I too have deserted her. I feel resentful towards Father for leaving her alone here, but she loves living in the country; and after all, I tell myself, she can go to join him in town any time. I wave once more, and then the car in which Father is taking us to the station drives off, and I snuggle up to Frank, who puts Leslie on my lap.

I look at our children. Even now it is sometimes hard to believe that they are mine, mine and Frank's, the result of our love. They sparkle with health. The pink of their cheeks under the warm golden tan, the blue of their eyes and the gold of their hair make them look like the pictures of cherubs that I used to stick on my Christmas presents when I was a child. I laugh with joy and delight, kiss them and receive in return their warm, dewy kisses. Then I forget the solitary figure in the beautiful garden.

21
Nightmare

Soon after we return, Philip, who has measles and is running a high temperature, has a fit. The doctor who comes examines him briefly. His reply to my anxious question is terse: 'Convulsions.' He hands me a prescription and departs. To me convulsions mean epilepsy. Frank is away and will not return until the next day.

All night I lie sleepless with Philip beside me in our double bed. I listen to his breathing and am aware of his every movement. Disconnected thoughts drift through my mind, memories of what I once read and heard in Austria. 'The Nazis are going to control life, create a race of supermen. . . People who are mentally unstable, those showing signs of genetic abnormality, the unfit for life, will be sterilized. . . Hitler is creating a master race. . . Is there any history of mental illness in your family? . . . Any schizophrenia? . . . Epilepsy?' I shudder with revulsion: I am a criminal, my blood is tainted, and I have married and had children. Now Philip has epilepsy and perhaps Leslie too will develop it. Just as a pebble dropped on water disappears yet leaves its mark in ever-widening circles, so Hitler, now eight years dead, is still casting his shadow over my life, our lives.

Frantic with worry, I am near collapse when Frank comes home. He holds me close while I tell him of my fears implanted so long ago that have lain dormant until now, fears that are to haunt me for years to come. For though he explains that febrile convulsions are common in small children, I am only partially reassured and often, when I lie awake in the small hours of the night, my mind starts its run on the treadmill of fear and guilt. Could Frank be wrong and my blood be tainted after all? Or perhaps he only wants to reassure me, is being kind and loving while he himself is aware of the truth. If sleep eventually comes it is the sleep of exhaustion and it is accompanied by dreams in which both children writhe in agonizing convulsions, and I wake to mental turmoil and more exhaustion.

Not long after this, on a morning so beautiful that I send up a spontaneous thank-you to God — I still leave prayers to Frank, feeling my prayers to be somewhat perfunctory except at times like this when gratitude swells my heart — I hear the postman's knock and run to the door.

I have to pay for the letter that he hands to me, for it has not been stamped. With a puzzled frown I look at the envelope, addressed in capital letters that sprawl drunkenly in all directions. It seems to contain nothing, it is so light and thin. When I open it I find a snapshot of the children, nothing else. I stare at the two faces smiling up at me, then slowly I turn the photo over. The words that leap up at me awake old fears, evoke images of padded cells, high cots, the haunted eyes of a terrified woman, brittle and inhuman, her high heels beating a frantic tattoo in her staccato run of mania along the long dark corridors of fear. Again and again I read the words that are written on the back. 'Please, please come and take me away from here.'

Glad of our newly-installed phone, I ring the operator and ask first for the Linz number and then the one at Essen. No reply from either. I write an express letter to Father, then send a telegram. By nightfall, after several more unsuccessful attempts to contact Father, I am in a state of violent agitation. Restlessly I pace the room, then I go upstairs to look at the children. Leslie lies totally relaxed, her arms flung over her head, long lashes curling on rosy cheeks, lips parted. Philip, as always surrounded by his Dinky toys, has somehow twisted the bedclothes into a rope and is lying with his feet on the pillow. Today the sight of them cannot soothe me.

There is no reply to my telegram, and four days later I decide to leave Philip, who is recovering from tonsillitis, in Frank's care while I go to Germany, taking Leslie with me. I am ready to go when a letter from Father arrives with the brief statement that he has divorced Mother and has remarried. A postscript informs me that Mother has been taken ill again and is in the mental hospital in Andernach.

Philip calls me from upstairs to remind me of my promise to read a story to him before I leave. I pick up the book that is lying on his bed and begin to read the words on the printed page, while the words I have just read in Father's letter echo in my mind. 'I have divorced your mother and am remarried.' I tell myself that I am having a nightmare. In a little while I shall wake and know that it is not true. When Frank comes back with our neighbour, who will stay with Philip while he takes us to the station, I hand him the letter. He is stunned. In the car he tells me that he will immediately make enquiries regarding the possibility of a visa for Mother. I listen and nod but am incapable of rational thought.

The morning after my arrival in Linz I set out for Andernach. Leslie is young enough not to be affected by what I fear I shall find and so I take her with me, hoping that it will do Mother good to see her. Leslie is enchanted with the trains. From the window beside her seat she can see the boats and barges on the Rhine and she exclaims with delight when she sees a slender tug pulling a string of barges. I try to respond, but my heart is heavy and I am afraid. How will I find Mother? I remember the blind unfocused stare that did not recognize me, remember the times when I felt alienated and frightened by her behaviour, and now I wish that I had not brought Leslie with me. Even on a gloriously sunny day, the mental hospital looks forbidding, as grey and colourless as a steel engraving. It is an eyesore in an otherwise beautiful land-scape.

I have not had time to inform the authorities there of my coming, and I have difficulty in finding the way in. Once inside the warren of rooms, cells and offices, I am assailed by the familiar compounded smell of hospital food, disinfectant and human suffering, and the odours awaken memories of all the other times when I have had to visit Mother.

After a prolonged wait in an office and my repeated declaration that, having come all the way from England to see my mother, I shall not stir until I have seen her, I am eventually shown into a ward. Apprehensively I look around me at the women condemned to a bleak existence in these grim surroundings and see their faces light up with brilliant pleasure at the sight of the tiny toddler with her smiling blue eyes and halo of bright golden curls. The nurse leads us towards a niche by the window where sits a small bent figure, hands folded in her lap, head drooping to one side: Mother.

'A visitor for you!' The nurse's voice holds the peculiar artificial brightness I know so well.

'Mother,' I say quietly, my heartbeat quickening and love and compassion catching at my throat. Slowly she raises her head. Her face is lifeless, immobile. Suffering has compressed her lips to a thin line. Then her eyes focus on Leslie, who has innocently trotted up to her and is lifting her arms to be picked up. 'Omi,' she croons, and relief spreads through me as I see the dull eyes brighten with joy. A great sob shakes her as she presses Leslie close to her heart. The next moment I am kneeling by her with tears streaming down my face while Leslie is happily pulling out the pins that fasten Mother's chignon.

By the time I have composed myself, a small audience has gathered. The nurse, to whom I appeal for privacy, at length ushers us into a small room where we are undisturbed. Bit by bit I piece together the story from Mother's disconnected and sometimes incoherent account. Father had begun to stay away at weekends and, after he had been absent for several weekends in succession, she had become alarmed and had travelled to Essen to find out what was keeping him away, afraid that he must be ill. On arrival at the flat she was told by a caretaker, who was new, that Father had moved when he got married. Mother, convinced that the man was confused, had asked for and obtained Father's new address and had called there. The door was opened by a maid, who on hearing her name led her into a room that was so crowded with flowers it resembled a florist's shop. A woman then appeared who announced that she was Mrs R. Shortly afterwards Father arrived and confirmed what Mother had been told by the caretaker. Her eyes wild with pain, Mother looks at me and says, 'And then I was here.'

I question her gently. Had she not received any communications from lawyers or the court? She only shakes her head. Then I remember, and rage overwhelms me, that Mother leaves all official mail addressed to her for Father to deal with. She has always done so, and Father is well aware of the fact. He must have counted on this and so known that the divorce suit would be undefended by her. How despicable, how utterly contemptible to act like this, and in my anger I include the woman who has been Father's accomplice, wittingly or no. And who brought Mother here? If he has done so, it must have been with the connivance of a doctor. With her past history it was probably quite easy to persuade a doctor that she was insane, especially since she must have been in a state of acute shock.

I think of Father as I have always known him, a man of probity and high principles, and shudder. Mother begs me to take her with me straight away, and in her agony of mind she raises her hands imploringly. She is receiving shock treatment and is terrified of it. Trembling uncontrollably, she describes her own fearful struggles each time she is forced to undergo treatment. Her fear is all the more terrible because she once witnessed another patient being pinned down by several nurses while the anaesthetic was being administered, the black box set up and its apparatus attached to the head. She had watched the horrible convulsions while the strong current of electricity flowed through it, had seen the patient after treatment with frothing saliva bubbling through the gag, snorting and grunting, robbed, she sobs, of every shred of human dignity, of humanity itself.

Her horror makes my flesh creep. When I gently try to explain that it might take time to get her discharged, her despair and anguish is such that I come close to breaking down myself. She sinks on her knees beside me, and clasping mine she tells me that if she has to go down to the theatre just once more, she will surely die. Leslie is looking bewildered and is holding on to me. Afraid that she is sensing our distress, I pick her up and promise Mother that I shall be back directly after I have spoken to the director. He, however, is unavailable, and only when I insist that I must see someone in charge and shall not leave until I have done so am I shown into the room of a senior consultant.

He listens to me while turning over the pages in Mother's file. I notice that it is a thick file and that most of the reports and other documents are from the clinic in Graz. When I explain that I want to take Mother with me, he looks up. 'And where will she go?' It is only then that I realize that Mother no longer has a home, unless Father lets her go on living in Linz. After what has happened I doubt that he will permit her to do so, nor can I imagine Mother wanting to go on living there.

The doctor, aware of my dilemma, smiles patronizingly. 'You see, it is not quite as simple as you seem to think. Moreover, in her present condition it would be quite unsafe for her to live on her own, and if' — he raises his eyebrows — 'the worst were to happen, we would be held responsible.'

'Mother would never commit suicide.' Stung by his attitude of superiority I add, 'The question of her having to live on her own does not arise, for I am taking her with me to England.'

I realize the foolishness of my statement even before he asks, 'You have a visa for her?' His attitude softens a little when he sees my distress. 'You see, your father. . . '

Angrily I interrupt. 'My father has absolutely no right, no say in this matter.'

'Very well. I would, however, advise you to see your father and find out if arrangements can be made that, in the circumstances, would make a discharge possible.' I shudder involuntarily and he shrugs, 'I am sorry, but you must surely see that at present it is quite impossible for us to discharge her.' As I get up my knees give way and I have to hold on to the back of the chair. The thought of what I shall have to tell Mother and her reaction to it make me feel faint.

I find her still on her knees and, kneeling down beside her, I cradle her head on my shoulder and try to explain the situation as gently as I can. I begin by telling her of one arrangement I was able to make with the doctor, that the shock treatment will be discontinued. She understands that I cannot take her with me without a visa and that we shall have to wait until we get one, so she bows her head in submission. Prayer has calmed her, and when Leslie begins to whimper, she takes her in her arms and gently stroking the silken curls murmurs, 'Poor little cherub, take her away from this horrible place.'

'Don't despair,' I beg. 'It may take a little while for me to make all the necessary arrangements, but I shall come. You know that, don't you?'

After embracing her once more, I go. When I turn to look back she is kneeling again. The ache that tears at my throat makes me want to cry out. When the gates close behind me, shutting in the misery and distress from which for centuries humans have turned with superstitious aversion, I am once again ashamed of my own relief at leaving. Those I have left behind are no longer chained and in danger of choking to death by being forcibly fed, but are they really much better off now than they used to be? Will the time ever come when mental disorders will be viewed with the same sympathy as physical illness? I understand the fearful reaction that people can have, for that is what I experience when I see the other patients; yet knowing my own Mother, I realize that the mentally ill are not on the other side of some great divide, but people just like us. After all, there is no difference between someone with heart disease or cancer and someone who is mentally ill, and yet the former are looked upon with compassion but those with any kind of mental disorder are regarded with horror and often loathing.

The following morning I am on my way to Essen. I have considered the doctor's advice and decided that if there is the slightest chance that Mother can be released until I can get a visa for her, perhaps to a convalescent home, I must see Father, however painful and distasteful it will be, for I have no money to pay for her. As the train nears Essen I tell myself that I must overcome my feelings of revulsion for her sake. I phoned Father from Linz the previous night and left a message informing him of the time of our arrival. Once at the station I look for him.

I have no idea where we shall have our meeting but guess that it will be in the lounge of a hotel near the station. Outside the station I am approached by a chauffeur who enquires if I am Frau Baker. He leads us to a gleaming Mercedes — not Father's, I notice. Leslie has already climbed through the door that is held open for us, and reluctantly I follow. I don't want to ask the man why Father has not come personally and assume that we are being taken to our meeting place.

To my dismay I realize when the car draws up at its destination that we are to meet in his new home. I am to be spared nothing, for he introduces me to his new wife. I look at a full face, into bold, slightly prominent blue eyes that seem to be mocking me. She is wearing a low-cut dress that reveals a great deal of ample bosom. Her sensuality and worldliness are the total antithesis of Mother's spirituality and unworldliness. I can see that she dominates Father. Skilfully they convey to me the fact that she is wealthy, but it is not difficult for me to see that she does not have the cultural background to suit. I suspect that she has married Father for the status that marriage to him gives her. My immediate inclination is to turn and run, and only the memory of Mother's anguished face keeps me from doing so.

When at last Father and I are alone and have discussed the matter, I reflect that I could have achieved as much by writing a letter and been spared the humiliation of having to meet the woman I detest, for he firmly states that it is in Mother's best interests for her to remain where she is and that it would be most unwise to discontinue treatment. In time, after she has been declared cured, he will consider what is best for her, though he very much doubts that a cure is possible. Since the divorce has been undefended, he is not obliged to support her. On hearing that I intend to take her to England as soon as we have a visa for her, he counsels against this and predicts dire consequences for my marriage if I carry out my intention.

22

Difficult Decisions

I arrive home utterly drained by emotion. Frank, sensing my deep distress, my fathomless fatigue, holds me strongly without speaking; from his embrace I draw comfort and new strength. When I have recovered sufficiently to talk about my visit, he listens patiently without interrupting. I discuss with him Father's warning about the consequences that Mother's living with us permanently could have on our marriage, the effect of her illness on me as a child and any possible effects on our children. There is also the practical problem of living space. Though our bedroom is spacious, Philip's is small and Leslie's a mere box-room. We shall have to squeeze Leslie's cot into Philip's room, and her room will only just take an adult-size bed.

Frank has no misgivings whatsoever and is certain that we shall manage. A few days later I receive a letter from Father. He writes: 'I can only assume that you are not aware of the full implications of your intention to take your mother into your home, though I doubt that the director of the institution will be prepared to take the responsibility for her discharge. He may, of course, be tempted by the thought that this is a convenient way of getting rid of someone who is incurable. Has it occurred to you that you may die before your mother? What is to happen to her then? Frank's future wife will most certainly put her into an asylum. And what about your children?' There are six pages filled with warnings about the consequences of my contemplated action.

By the same post comes a letter from a mental health clinic in Andernach signed by a Dr F. He informs me that Mother was admitted by order of the court, that hers is a mental disease that results in considerable changes of personality, an inability to reason and consequently the refusal to accept the fact of her illness. 'Unfortunately,' he writes, 'it is in the nature of the disease to deteriorate progressively, though there may be the occasional remission. Since the beginning of her illness goes back many years, it has already resulted in certain character defects, such as unpleasant eccentricities, the deliberate misinterpretation of existing circumstances, negative behaviour towards others, forgetfulness and an inability to discriminate. In view of your mother's psychosis, I doubt that you will be able to obtain a visa for her. If you do, she will have to be collected and accompanied on the way. Furthermore, you must be prepared for the possibility that she will have to enter a clinic in England.'

I show Frank both letters and, after he has read them, look at him uncertainly. 'You know she is really sick; she is hearing voices and thinks . . . ' He interrupts, ' . . . that they are heavenly voices; and so, according to the pundits, she must be abnormal, suffering from hallucinations, delusions, religious mania. She has also had a vision, hasn't she? What does that indicate? That she is psychotic, schizophrenic, neurastenic? There have been others throughout the ages who have heard voices, have had visions and have written about them. According to Dr F., all the mystics must have been mad.'

His words come as a revelation. They are opening a door of escape — escape from the nightmare of guilt and fear that has tormented me since Philip's convulsion made me face up to the possibility of hereditary flaws that, according to the Nazi lies with which I have grown up, are punishable by sterilization. 'If,' Frank continues, 'gentleness, kindness, compassion and sensitivity are madness, what then is sanity? Is what we have seen in the war sanity?'

I feel as though a great weight has been lifted from me. His supreme confidence that, once she is with us, she will soon be well, that it is love — ours and the children's — that will heal her, gives me confidence. Worries concerning finance are brushed aside by him with the words, 'We have never been in actual want, have we?' I have to admit that this is true. 'Well then,' he tilts my chin and smiles into my eyes, 'stop worrying and have faith.'

The doctor's letter is accompanied by a report in which Mother is once more described as suffering from 'severe depression, headaches, nightmares, states of fear and anxiety, inability to relate to others, indifference to others and self, disturbances of memory and recall'. We can think of a reason for each, the last being obviously the result of electroconvulsive therapy. We go to bed that night discussing the possibility of moving to a larger house in a year or two, and until then Frank is convinced that we shall make out very well.

While we are waiting for the visa for Mother, I think of her alone, trapped in a living grave, upheld only by the thought that I have promised to come for her. In spirit I am continually with her in her prison cell or out in the dreary common-room with others who are sick and bereft of hope. I am aware of her loneliness, her discomfort, her agony, and the smells and the sounds that surround her. I imagine her listening to footsteps approaching along the corridor, filled alternately with terror lest they are coming to give her more of the dreaded electroconvulsive therapy and hope that I have come at last to take her away. A hope that is continually roused only to be stifled is contributing to the slow disintegration of her personality.

At last we learn that Mother has been granted entry to

England on a temporary permit that expires on Christmas Eve. She can therefore be released into my custody. She is escorted to the Hook of Holland, and Frank travels to Harwich and brings her home.

When Mother arrives, a shrinking, tragic figure, I am once again seized by the fierce, primitive and ugly anger that courses like poison through my veins against those two who have inflicted such pain and suffering on her. As I look at her grey face, I remember the days when she was serene and beautiful and adored by the man who has now so shamefully betrayed her and has deprived her even of her home. I torment my unhappy spirit with pictures of the laughing voluptuous creature who has taken possession of what has been familiar to me since childhood.

The weeks immediately following her arrival are difficult, and I often wonder if Frank, who continues to believe that all will be well, is right. We pray that the still-open and agonizing wounds will heal, that the anguish will fade and that she will be made whole again by love. Slowly she begins to emerge from her nightmare. Her face, which has been frozen into a mask of pain and suffering, relaxes, becomes mobile; her gentle smile returns. Her love for the children and theirs for her are the most important factors in her recovery. Soon both Philip and Leslie chatter to her in perfect German, for as the result of her partial loss of memory and difficulty of recall she speaks only German to them and us. Frank is proved right in other ways too, for, despite our cramped living conditions, we not only manage but are soon beginning to feel the advantages of her presence, and I see that good has come out of evil just as he predicted. Though she never ceases to love and miss Father, she is no longer lonely because she is feeling wanted and needed.

Father has written to me several times but I ignore his letters. I want never to see him again, never to have anything to do with him. Frank tries to intercede for him but I remain adamant. 'All this talk of the Bible,' I tell him one evening, 'about not judging that ye may not be judged leaves me unmoved.' I go on to describe the woman and compare her voluptuousness with Mother's saintliness. He points out that living with a saint could be difficult. This startles me. To imagine Mother and Father, at their age, in a relationship as intimate as ours is difficult; but the thought of physical intimacy between Father and his new wife is revolting. Frank continues to plead for Father, who, he says, is entitled to news of us. He is sure that Father still loves me and the children. I fiercely deny this, for I believe that if he loved us he never would have acted in the abominable way he has. Obstinately rebellious, I remain unyielding in his arms. He, though not condoning Father's action in any way, reminds me of the effect of Father's injuries, of the long years of separation during the war, of finding himself imprisoned without explanation or cause. He speaks of Mother's striving for spiritual perfection, her increasing asceticism and her withdrawal into a prayer life that must have made him feel excluded since he did not feel able to share in it. He almost succeeds in making me feel sorry for Father, but then I remember Mother's tormented eyes and know that my hatred is irremediable.

Long after Frank has gone to sleep, I lie awake, nursing my anger and almost resentful at Frank's attempt to exonerate Father. I hate him, I hate them both, him and the woman, until with a shock that leaves me ice cold I realize that only a short while ago I had vowed to fight hatred with all my might, hatred that is at the root of so much suffering, hatred that causes wars. The discovery makes me feel despicable, small and shabby. I remember Frank's words when he was speaking about people's disobedience to God, who can only work through his creatures. He had said, 'Hate cannot drive out hate, only love can do that.' I realize too that this hatred, this recurrent bitterness, is already encroaching on and beginning to destroy contentment and happiness. But what can relieve me of it, of the gusts of anger that continually sweep over me, the feelings of outrage and personal injury?

I look at Frank, lying asleep beside me, his face dimly outlined in the faint light of the street lamp that shines through a gap in the curtain. In repose as in waking his face has a happy serenity. He looks very young and absurdly vulnerable. In a few years' time Philip will look exactly like this. He is breathing softly, completely relaxed. Thinking back over our conversation I wonder if there will ever be a time when, dulled by age, I shall no longer thrill to the sight and touch of him or when, coarsened by age, I shall no longer be desirable.

Before falling asleep he has as usual prayed for both of us, and I have listened and joined in the 'Amen'. I have been content for him to pray, for in my present state of mind I have thought that it would be hypocritical of me to pray. Now involuntarily I fold my hands. 'God,' I falter, 'if you can hear me, please take away this hatred that is consuming me.' After a little while my eyes close and I sleep.

In the morning I write a few brief lines to Father and give the letter to Frank to post. His eyes light up and wordlessly he embraces me and holds me close.

We continue our efforts to secure a permanent visa for Mother and at last receive the following letter from the Home Office: 'Sir, with reference to your interview with an officer of this department about your mother-in-law, I am directed by the Secretary of State to say that careful consideration has been given to your representation and, in view of your assurance of maintenance and accommodation and that at no time will your mother-in-law become a charge on public funds, he has decided not to raise objection to her remaining in this country for residence in your household. Her passport is returned endorsed as follows: "The condition attached to the grant of leave to land is hereby varied so as to require departure from the United Kingdom not later than such date as may be specified by the Secretary of State." The endorsement in the passport must be shown at once to the local Police Registration Officer.'

23

Sunshine and Showers

In the years that follow, thanks to Mother's and Frank's unfailing support, I am able to obtain a teaching qualification, language degrees and a higher degree by thesis. In the meantime Frank accepts the post of divisional secretary for the North-West Division of the YMCA, covering Cumberland, Westmoreland and North Lancashire. The post includes accommodation in a spacious old house in Kendal where the offices are situated.

I start my teaching career in a small village school in Cumbria, where I see Leslie through her primary education. During lunch breaks we go for walks in lanes and meadows and I am impressed by her knowledge of wild flowers. Together we admire their beauty, the swaying, whispering grasses and delicately-veined leaves and the gossamer silver wings of little insects alighting on them. We laugh at the sight of new lambs feeding, their tails rotating ecstatically. Standing on shallow stones in the little stream we watch tiny fish darting to and fro in the dappled water. We yearn over tall sunflowers and hollyhocks reaching to the sky in cottage gardens and dream of a cottage of our own.

Here in Kendal, where at last we have abundant space, we receive visitors from all over the world, as well as the strays whom Frank picks up or who come to our door asking for accommodation. In the summer holidays a French boy, Yvon, and his sister, Françoise come to us, and this starts an exchange that is to continue through the next generation. One day Frank announces that a group of Russian teachers has come to Kendal. For the first time they are being allowed to stay in pairs with families. Because of my unfortunate wartime experiences, I am eager to meet Russians in a time of peace, and so we offer to host two of them. It takes the whole of the first week of their stay to break down Valja's and Nadja's reserve. In the second week, however, we get to know them well and they respond to our goodwill towards them. When, at the end of their stay, we wave goodbye to them at the station, we thrill to hear Valja call impulsively out of the window of the departing train, 'We think you are wonderful people.' We keep in touch with them and from that time on I long to visit their country. Thirty-odd years later I realize my dream when, together with our fifteen-year-old granddaughter, Sandy, I travel to Moscow and Leningrad. By then *glasnost* and *perestroika* have given a new boost to our hope for a lasting peace between East and West and have paved the way for an event I had not expected to take place in my lifetime, the opening up of the Berlin Wall and East German borders for unhindered access. For me, who was born and lived in East Germany, this has been as momentous and moving an event as for those East Germans who set foot on West German soil for the first time in forty-four years.

Now that we are both earning, we are able to save enough to buy a caravan and on an extended holiday achieve our ambition to show the children the places where I grew up and where Frank and I met. We have a joyous reunion with Schnucki, now married with a daughter, go to the Wörthersee and travel all the way to Rome, my favourite capital.

When Leslie, at the age of nine and on the headmaster's recommendation, takes the eleven-plus examination and starts at Kendal High School, I take up an appointment at Casterton, a public school for girls, the school that the Brontë sisters attended.

I am happy teaching at Casterton. The girls, many of whom regard me as a substitute mother, are delightful and affectionate. Yet after nearly eight years of living in the area and despite the beauty surrounding me, I begin to feel oppressed by the seemingly constant rain, the dark days of clouds when the rain either drifts or comes straight down in a steady, never-ending stream — like the rain in Salzburg that the locals refer to as *Schnürdlregen*, because it looks like bootlaces falling from the sky.

Some days when I return from Casterton, a curtain of wet mist shivers like a grey veil over the hollow in which Kendal nestles. Behind me clouds of a purplish black hang over the scowling gloom of the barren fells, and on either side of the road sheep scuttle off on thin legs. Sometimes the clouds, swept by a savage wind, race with incredible speed across the sky. On those days the hills, which to me have always seemed stern and forbidding, look menacing and cruel, and the lakes, when they are whipped up by the bitter, relentless wind, resemble the angry sea.

Our eighth year in the district is a year of seemingly continuous rain, and my mind and soul begin to shiver in the damp. Endlessly the sky pelts the earth and the water collects in deep pools, burbling in the gutters, splaying and spurting from roofs, sluicing the trees and drinking up the daylight, and by two o'clock in the afternoon it seems to be evening. Great grey clouds, heavy with rain, hang so low in the thick wet air that they seem to touch the roofs. I am overwhelmed with grey desolation and fervently wish that I had been born with Frank's nature, which is unaffected by the vagaries of the weather.

To my mind rain has become so much a part of the area that a day when the sky is not sodden, when storms are not howling round the fells and when I am not blinded by sheets of water on the windscreen becomes unimaginable. I am becoming obsessed with the thought that I am imprisoned in grey: grey clouds, grey stone walls, grey torrents of water. I have completely forgotten my delight in the exquisite pastoral beauty of the scenery, the days when clouds of rose float in skies stained with jade and amethyst, when the hills and woods are on fire, when the dead bracken flames with colours of deep ruby, amber, orange and russet, when the water of lakes and tarns moves in tiny feathery waves, when the clear sky curves unbelievably blue over the craggy heather-purpled hills and the sun softens their severe outlines and grey bareness. So when we learn that Frank is being offered the post of regional secretary of the Midland Region, I am ready to welcome a move to anywhere. There has been severe flooding as the result of torrential rain and the cellars of our house have been flooded twice. Frank accepts, and I look forward to our move to Nottingham and a joyful reunion with our friends.

24
Loss

Time speeds on. Mother is participating fully in the life of our family, though she is withdrawn from outside activity. Inevitably there are times of sorrow and heartache, times of anxiety when I have to undergo a series of major operations, but throughout I am supported by the prayers offered for me by her and Frank and by their trusting faith.

Philip and Leslie have adjusted well to the move. Leslie has won a scholarship to Nottingham High School. Philip, despite being confronted by a complete change in set books, has obtained excellent A-level results and in consequence an unconditional offer of a place at Cambridge University, subsequently winning a scholarship there. I give thanks once again for the years of peace in which they have grown up and in which they are able to continue their studies, remembering my interrupted education and the years of endless study when already a wife and mother. Sometimes it seemed too much effort, too much work, unrelieved by the gaiety of the numerous diversions available to them — poetry, plays, music, games, balls, endless discussions over cups of coffee with other students. Instead there have been years of careful planning, for I was anxious that my family should not suffer. This meant the curtailment of sleep, meal-times and exercise, a relentless routine, leading by the time I sat the examinations to a mind that was feverish and blurred with work and to a sense of anticlimax instead of triumph when I learnt I had succeeded.

We enjoy our visits to Cambridge: services in King's College Chapel, hushed prayers by candlelight, the pure treble of boys' voices, plays directed by Philip, picnics by the river with sunshine chasing cloud shadows across the backs of the colleges, the soft splash of the water against the punt as we pole upstream. On the day of his graduation I look at Philip in the crowd of young people wearing their hired black gowns and see in him the recreation of Frank's youth, for they are most touchingly alike, not only physically but in their natures, disarmingly unaffected and of a true simplicity, with a delightful sense of humour and fun. Both he and Leslie have, in addition, inherited their father's conscience and intellect, his idealism, his concern for human social justice and his often fierce individualism.

After Philip has graduated, Leslie too leaves home to go to university. Mother misses them very much. I look with concern at her blue-veined temples, her bones worn so fine, her body delicate and weightless and am reminded of a husk of corn blown in the wind. I think of her goodness, of the weight of responsibility that she has taken upon herself for all unfortunates. Unceasingly she prays for all who suffer, enfolding them in love. In her room she spends long periods on her knees, focusing her mind on God. Always she returns strengthened to take up once more her daily self-appointed tasks; for the image of the cross of Christ eases her burden and, like John Bunyan's pilgrim, Christian, she can say, 'He hath given me rest by his sorrow, and life by his death.'

With a feeling of resentment, almost outrage, I see her growing feebler and older; but even though she is frail, I am aware as never before of her spiritual strength, which sustains her in her work, her fasting and the four-mile walk to and from Nottingham Cathedral on Sundays. In winter I often trail her surreptitiously in my car, in order to be on hand if she should slip or fall on the icy pavement, but she never does, for her feet, carrying so slight a weight, barely seem to touch the ground. I realize that the time must come when she must leave us for good, but I cannot bear the thought and resolutely dismiss it from my mind.

Father has been taken ill and is in the hospital at Neuwied. I have been sent for, and during my stay in Linz act mostly as chauffeur for the daily visits to the hospital. His second marriage is not a happy one. During a brief period of blind infatuation, when he had felt rejuvenated, he had imagined himself happy, but he had soon woken to bitter reality and had once more become the prey of melancholia, depression and recurrent headaches which he attributed to neuralgia. He has mellowed and is now anxious to show us how genuinely fond he is of us.

Several months after his discharge from hospital, I receive a phone call informing me that he has been readmitted, has for several days been in a critical condition and has asked for me. After booking my flight, I ring back and am told that he is dead. When I arrive in Linz, Father has already been transferred to Essen. Though he has often appeared hard and though I was bitterly hurt by his behaviour over Lutz and even more so by his divorcing Mother, I loved him. Though on those occasions I had doubted his love for me, I know that he loved me too.

On the day of the funeral I drive to Essen. I have asked to be allowed to see him alone. The sweet cloying scent of heavy perfume masking decay assails me. Soft music is playing over loudspeakers discreetly concealed in the long corridor from which the doors open into the tastefully decorated rooms in which the dead are lying. The sound seems an intrusion on the presence of death that weighs heavily upon the rooms.

I enter the room where Father lies, his head resting on a lace-edged satin pillow. He is wearing dress uniform and his waxen hands are folded around the hilt of the sword. His coffin is raised on a platform massed with flowers. At the sight of the waxen, strangely sharpened features that so soon will be beyond sight and touch for ever, pain, which has been anaesthetized by shock and the long hours of preparation for the funeral, tears at my heart and I am filled with desolation and incomprehension. To me he has been in turn a god, a cruelly used victim, a traitor and finally just a human being. But always his personality has been strong, at times overpowering; now it has instantly disappeared. I rebel against mortality that reveals the futility of human striving and contriving. His death has wiped out any lingering trace of resentment, leaving only love and pity, pity that he has moved from light into darkness.

Never again will he sit in the warm sunshine in his beautiful garden, never again drowse in half sleep by the fire, never again taste the golden wine of the Mosel. Like his father and grandfather before him, he will soon be no more than a whispered memory, and in generations yet to come he will be totally forgotten. In retrospect his life seems pathetically short. He and all of us are frighteningly insignificant in the immense universe, that great scheme that I cannot comprehend.

I look up at the window where a butterfly hovers and revolt at the implacability of 'never again'. Outside a rose sways in the breeze: the world is too beautiful to leave, and even in my grief I am glad and grateful to be alive and feel that to live in utmost hardship, privation, starvation and pain, as I did long ago, is still life. There is still the sky, there are trees, flowers and birdsong, colour and beauty, moonlight and starlight and sunsets . . . and I am seized by a feeling of exultation in living.

25

A Greater Loss

In January 1971 Frank commences work in London. We sell our house. Three days before we are due to move and a few days after her seventieth birthday, Mother has a coronary. She has been working hard, clearing up and packing in preparation for the move, and I have been unable to stop her from doing too much. Now I reproach myself bitterly. Knowing her dread of hospitals and having been implored by her never to make her go into one, I ask the doctor whether she can be cared for at home. In the circumstances, the doctor agrees. She will, so he tells me, soon be able to get up and, as long as she takes things easy, she should make a fairly good recovery. She is transferred by ambulance to the house where we shall stay until the end of the summer term. Our move takes place during the Easter vacation, and as a result I am able to look after her.

She is making good progress and we rejoice, but then she contracts a cold and cough and has to go back to bed. She becomes increasingly weak. The doctor shakes his head: just a common cold, he says, nothing much to worry about. I call him again, certain that something else is wrong, and he gives her a thorough examination. The verdict: pneumonia.

On impulse, Frank, who is in Edinburgh, decides to interrupt his return journey to London and spend the night with us. When he sees how exhausted I look, he insists on my going to bed while he sits up with Mother. I am reluctant to leave her. In the afternoon I had brushed the silky hair and had been unbearably moved by the frailty of her neck. A little later, she had suddenly appeared frightened and prayed aloud, 'Hail Mary, full of grace . . . the Lord is with thee . . . blessed art thou among women . . . pray for us . . . now and in the hour of our death.' I had listened fearfully. Could it be that after a lifetime of prayer and contemplation her strength of spirit was deserting her, that the thought of abandoning life was difficult even for a saint?

And under my breath I whispered fiercely, 'You are not going to die.'

Despite the doctor's assurance that Mother is in no danger, I am worried about her. At first I refuse to go to bed and leave her, but at last I give in. Sleep will not come. I lie there feeling light, disembodied with exhaustion. A few minutes later I hear Frank calling me from the bathroom, where I find him cradling Mother's head in his lap. She is in fearful convulsions and blood is foaming on her lips. I cry out in terror, clutching his arm. 'What is it, what is happening to her?'

'It's all right,' he says quietly, 'she is not suffering, does not feel anything.'

Suddenly her body relaxes, goes limp. After a few moments, Frank asks for a mirror. I am trembling so violently that I can hardly walk, but I obey. 'Is she. . . ?' He nods. The doctor comes to confirm what we already know.

In the morning the air is dancing in sunbeams that sparkle on dewy trees and grass. There has been torrential rain in the night, and at dawn a low mist clings to the ground. Tree tops rise out of it, some of them a froth of blossom. High above them tower clouds in shades of purple, crimson and rose that turn gradually to orange and then bright gold as the sun rises, lightening the sky and flooding the milky mist. I go into the room where Mother lies and look upon the lonely effigy, the shell from which the spirit has fled, the body that gave birth to me. As I look upon her worn beauty transfigured in death, disconnected phrases drift through my mind. 'She has desired a better country. . . God has prepared for her a city where she will be happy. . . Then shall the dust return to the earth as it was and the spirit shall return unto God who gave it. . . '

She had always regarded herself as sinful and expected to have to undergo a process of purification after death. 'O God,' I plead, 'she was a saint and throughout her life she has gone through refining fire: be merciful.' I touch her lips, closed for ever, never again to move in prayer, never again to smile tenderly at us, and once again I revolt at the implacability of 'never again'. The silence is unearthly yet alive, as though filled with a mysterious presence. Beside the bed lies the Bible, and I open it at random and read, 'The reward of humility and the fear of the Lord is riches and honour and life.' For a brief moment I feel reassured, then grief returns and in bitter pain I long to follow through darkness to where she has gone, long for our souls to meet. Yet, imprisoned by time and able to think only in finite terms, I find no relief.

Frank has had to go to London, will return as soon as he has settled affairs there. There are things I must attend to: I must go to see the undertaker, collect the death certificate from the doctor, register her death at the registrar's office, endure their professional air of compassion, receive the condolences of colleagues. People are kind, want to help, want to comfort; but sick with guilt and remorse, penitent and wanting to atone, I reject comfort. I accuse myself of insensitivity, of blindness, tell myself that I should have known how close to death she was. I am overwhelmingly conscious of my many failures, especially during the last days when I had felt overtaxed and had not given my last ounce of strength to sustain her, who had unceasingly given of herself to us. I reject, too, the terrible platitudes. 'It is better that she died quickly than had to endure the long-drawn-out weariness of old age,' people tell me, and 'Life must go on.' I know it must, I can see that it does, and my mind revolts at the terrible law that decrees that it must. I grieve at the pathos of her unfulfilled life. Over and over again I ask forgiveness for thoughtless selfishness, for not sufficiently returning her great love and tenderness. I refuse to listen to Frank, who assures me that she did not expect anything in return for love and devotion, that in loving she found joy, in giving she received. I reproach myself bitterly for not staying with her that last night. She had asked to go to the adjoining bathroom and Frank had tried to restrain her, had wanted to call me, when with super-human strength she had pushed him aside and staggered the few steps to the bathroom, where she collapsed. If I had been there I might have prevented her from getting up, and unceasingly I torture myself, sick with grief and recrimination.

Before going to the crematorium, we attend the simple service in the local Catholic church. Philip has come from London, Leslie from Durham. They and Frank are the only ones kneeling with me beside the narrow coffin on which lies one wreath from us and a bouquet of flowers sent by the staff of my department.

Fleetingly I remember the crowds at Father's funeral, the countless wreaths and flowers, the band playing *Ich hat einen Kameraden*. As we follow the hearse in our car, I see an old man stop and reverently remove his hat, a mark of respect to the dead. It is the last time that I am to see this gesture, once accorded to all on their last journey.

The dreadful finality with which the doors close behind the coffin on its way to the flames overwhelms me with unbearable anguish. Their fire will consume all that remains of the being without whom life is unthinkable. It is impossible that she has left me. She has always been there, from the moment when as an embryo I was enclosed in the warm darkness of her womb. Without her I shall be lost.

I am alone. Leslie, who had come down from university to help look after Mother in her last few days, had only just got back when she was recalled for the funeral. I remember how at her age, secure in youth's belief in immunity from death that is born of the instinct of self-preservation, I had shied away from death and grief. I wonder if she feels as I did. From Philip I receive a moving letter. He has taken with him a candle that was Mother's and watching its flame he reflects that it is like Mother, a still presence illumining all our lives. When I had phoned him to tell him that Mother was dead, he had asked for the actual time of her death, and then told me that at that moment he had been sitting on the top of a double-decker bus when suddenly he had experienced an overwhelming conviction that she was there with him.

I hate the house in which she died, torture myself with the thought that at the last she did not even have the comfort of our own home, of familiar surroundings. Mrs Burnham, a member of staff, immensely kind, understanding and practical, suggests that I move in with them. I am deeply grateful and am given a room in her beautiful home. She offers no spoken consolation, only remarks that guilt and remorse are part of the natural process of the experience of bereavement. The comfort I receive from her and her family comes in the form of loving care and sympathy that I shall never forget.

26

The Valley of the Shadow

We had already decided that we did not want to live in London, and after a long search we find a beautiful home in a village. Yet despite a new and exciting job and the thrill of having at last achieved my dream of living in the country, my depression deepens. I am still consumed by grief, guilt and remorse. No matter how often I tell myself how fortunate I am in Frank's love, in having bright, healthy children, I more and more often feel that all my life, my high hopes and endeavours and my achievements are hollow and empty, dust and ashes. The purpose has gone out of everything and there is no future to work for, to look forward to. Mother's life and death have become for me a symbol of the futility of all. We, all the countless millions of us, are here for such a brief space, and we breathe and suffer before our little flame is snuffed out and we are consigned to the soil or devoured by flames and forgotten. Soon my children and perhaps my grandchildren will stand as I have stood, seeing the coffin that holds my shell slide behind the doors; but life for them will go on as, so incredibly, it does, and I shall become a memory that gradually fades until no one at all remembers me and it will be as though I have never been.

As the weeks and months pass, my grief presses on me and chokes me and in time produces symptoms of an illness that is very real. They tell me that human nature can stand grief for but a limited time and that when the depths of sorrow have been plumbed, the mind turns with relief to concentrate on brighter things; but I know it is not true, for though I do obtain relief while my mind is occupied by day when I am teaching, as soon as I leave the college to drive home, I become once more lost in darkness, sorrow and guilt.

Once again I rebel against the essential apartness of the individual. One in body, mind and spirit with Frank, who is loving, kind and understanding, I still feel alone in my grief. Will it ever be possible to overcome this aloneness? Is the fact of one's yearning to overcome it an indication of its being possible in the beyond? With great grief holding me in a grip that causes physical and mental suffering I begin to think of mortality as a barrier that I long to cross.

I think of Mother's self-abnegation, her simple goodness that was natural and effortless, her humility, all the qualities that are wholly beyond my grasp, and I am filled with a sense of worthlessness and failure. I think again and again of how much I owe her, how now I can never make her comprehend my gratitude for all she has given us. In total forgetfulness of self she has been happy. When the children were making too many demands on her and I reprimanded them, she only smiled with great tenderness. And she had so often, when I was worried about petty little disasters, brought me back to a sense of proportion by reminding me how insignificant they were compared to the vast tragedies that wrench the world.

I had thought, too, that I had followed where she and Frank had led, had once again found the faith of my childhood; but I had never really sought the forgiveness of God or earnestly repented of my sins, never experienced the ardent longing for my Saviour, never loved God enough. All my love was given to those dear to me. And thinking of her saintliness I know that I am of this world, worldly. Anything of this world has always been more important to me than the God who wants my love. To rise each morning to yet another glorious day of being with Frank, to feel the deep contentment of falling asleep in his arms after a hard day's work, to feel the sun on my face, to travel and see again my beloved mountains . . . all this and more I thought of rather than thinking of God. Now once again in deep need, I cry to him.

Sixteen months after Mother's death, when I have reached rock bottom, Cecil Jackson-Cole, universally known as CJC, the chairman of the company that Frank has recently joined, comes to see us. I have briefly met him once or twice before, a small rubicund figure, retiring, diffident and shy. I have just been assailed by one of the terrible fits of weeping that have attacked me since Mother's death, often at the most inopportune moments, and my eyes are red and swollen. Embarrassed, he looks past me and enquires of Frank if he has called at an inconvenient time. While Frank reassures him, I withdraw into the kitchen to make coffee and bathe my face. When I return he tells me that he is sorry to hear that I have recently lost my mother, and to my surprise I find myself opening up to him, telling him about my grief, my guilt and my remorse.

He listens quietly, his small plump hands folded on his stomach; from time to time he inclines his head in sympathy, a kind father confessor. Then he tells me of the way he felt after the death of his mother and later of his wife, Phyllis, whose last words had been, 'It is so lovely,' and I feel strangely comforted.

He invites us to have tea with him at Burrswood, where he is staying at Chapel House, the guest house, and enquires if we have been to Burrswood. When he hears that, though we have now lived in Groombridge for over a year, we know nothing about it, he points through the window across the fields and the ridge to where I can just make out the tower of a church. 'This is the Church of Christ the Healer, the church of the Burrswood community,' he says. He goes on to tell us briefly about Dorothy Kerin, the founder, whom he himself has known and whose miraculous healing had in 1912 made headlines in all the national papers. After many years of illness she developed tuberculous peritonitis and meningitis, lay unconscious for two weeks and, on the point of death, was healed totally and instantaneously. My face must betray my incredulity and disbelief, for CJC hastens to add that several doctors who examined her before and after her miraculous healing had testified to it. She founded her first home of healing in Ealing, later moved to Speldhurst and eventually to Groombridge and Burrswood, the Christian Centre for Medical and Spiritual Care, with its nursing home, resident doctor, chaplain and trained nurses. There, too, the church in which services of healing are held was built.

The term 'faith healing' springs to my mind, and instinctively I recoil. I have a dread of fanatics, particularly those that indulge in overt displays of fervour. I cringe at the thought of evangelists who, in an atmosphere overcharged with spiritual emotion, induce mass hysteria. So now, on hearing of this place and its supernatural associations, I feel uneasy and only reluctantly accept CJC's invitation.

In my present frame of mind, the church to which he takes us seems a little too Italianate. I look critically at the little gilt cherubs and fatuous madonna with child, but when I kneel down to pray, I am aware of being gently enfolded in peace.

A few days later, strangely drawn to the place, though mostly motivated by curiosity, I ask Frank to come with me to one of the healing services. 'I have no intention of going up for the "laying-on of hands",' I tell him, 'I just want to have a look.'

As I kneel down in the hushed silence, I am conscious once again of being enfolded in peace, and into my mind slide the words from T.S.Eliot's *Little Gidding*.

> You are not here to verify,
> Instruct yourself, or inform curiosity
> Or carry report. You are here to kneel

Where prayer has been valid. And prayer is more
Than an order of words, the conscious
   occupation
Of the praying mind, or the sound of the voice
   praying.
And what the dead had no speech for, when
   living,
They can tell you, being dead: the
   communication
Of the dead is tongued with fire beyond the
Language of the living.

Though I had not intended to do so, when the time comes for people to go forward for the laying-on of hands, I go. I feel nothing, have no sensation of anything unusual taking place; quietly I return to the pew to be led deeper and deeper into the heart of peace. I become aware of love into which my whole consciousness is being absorbed until I lose every sense of my surroundings, even of myself, in prayer and praise, and time ceases to exist. I feel close to Mother, know that all is well. There is no doubt left at all, and I am filled with joy. For the first time, the words from Revelation that I have heard so often before have real meaning for me. 'He will wipe every tear from their eyes. There will be no more death or mourning or crying or pain, for the old order of things has passed away.'

Grief and bleak despondency have fallen away and with it my physical exhaustion and all the complaints from which I have suffered. And the joy is more wonderful than any joy I have ever known; it permeates every fibre of my being, making me feel wonderfully and gloriously alive, for, when I felt that grief could no longer be endured, God found me and I have at last found God.

My intense preoccupation with grief had degenerated into self-pity. I had mourned my loss, and part of my grieving for Mother had been grieving for my past, my memories of experiences shared. In prolonging my grief indefinitely I thought I was cherishing her, thought that in order to prove how dearly I loved her, I had to continue grieving, thought, too, that in grieving for her I was closer to her, when in fact the opposite was the case, for I feel infinitely closer to her now in gladness. I had grieved over her wasted life, thought of it as a failure. Now I think of Christ, who was crucified to take away the pain and suffering of the world, and know that her life has not been a failure, for it has affected the lives of all of us, and not only of us but the lives of all the others for whom she prayed. She had been aware of evil, pain and suffering, had taken it upon herself until the burden was taken from her by Jesus, who says, 'Come to me, all you who are weary and burdened, and I will give you rest. Take my yoke upon you and learn from me, for I am gentle and humble in heart, and you will find rest for your souls. For my yoke is easy and my burden is light.'

Now, with all my senses quickened, I am reminded of the sensations experienced when, after narrowly escaping death following my last operation, I felt reborn. My increased awareness and appreciation of the most commonplace objects has heightened the quality of everyday life, given a new and passionate intensity to all experience. I regard everything with wonder; see, taste, feel, smell and hear as though for the first time, desiring with all my heart to make others as aware of the wonder and beauty of God's creation as I am; for now I find the world exquisitely beautiful, and sometimes in the middle of performing the most mundane tasks, I fall on my knees to praise and give thanks. Knowing myself to be immeasurably rich I am filled with humility.

When, after a while, this increased awareness dims, I am desolate. Henceforth, however, life is never to be the same, even though I might never again feel as sensitively aware, never again recapture the experience, though I long for it with all my being. There is the occasional flash of exultation, of heightened awareness, but I cannot hold it. It slips from me, leaving me sad, and I remind myself of Eliot's words from 'Burnt Norton' that 'human kind cannot bear very much reality'.

My mind strays back over the years of my continuous search for faith. Even as a small child, secure in the love of the God who created me, I had asked the question, 'Why have I been born?' Throughout the years it persistently recurred as, 'Is there a purpose and if so, what is it? How do I fit into the pattern?' As I grew up, the earth, once so immense, began to shrink to a tiny sphere and I, once the centre of the universe, knew myself to be but one among the thousands of millions of its inhabitants and became frightened. Then the war, with its senseless destruction of millions of lives, with its cruelty and bestiality, had convinced me that there was no purpose. In those dark years, all that I had previously believed in fell away, for I judged God by the standards of mankind. And the more remote God became, the more insecure I felt.

As students, like countless students of our age before us, my friends and I had sat up late into the night and earnestly, though confusedly, discussed philosophy, sociology, politics and religion. We had debated on the nature of knowledge, the universe, perception, human aspiration, logical positivism. We had considered the doctrines of Nietzsche, Hegel and Kant. We had argued about the existence or non-existence of God, speculated about how the universe had come about, considered the cosmic boom and humanity as a cosmic joke.

In the end, full of arrogance and intellectual pride, we had decided that religion, 'the opium of the people', was for those whose intellect was low. Yet without God, without a purpose for life, existence itself seemed meaningless and monstrous. To grow old, lonely, unwanted and unlovely, to die and rot away underground or be eaten by flames were prospects too horrible to be true.

After meeting Frank I constantly met people of intellectual and spiritual power and of a deep abiding faith in God, who believed in a purpose. Busy and wonderfully happy and secure in Frank's love and the knowledge that he and Mother prayed for me, I had been content to lean on them and their faith. God for me was in the flower, in the sunset, on top of the mountain and deep in the music of the nightingale, of Beethoven, Mozart and Bach. Frank and Mother had totally committed their lives to God but I was frightened of total commitment, feared the loss of freedom that it meant — for what might be asked of me that I did not want to do? Even now I am apprehensive that God may ask more of me than I am capable of.

Burrswood has a bookstall, and eager for knowledge and anxious to learn, I get book after book. I read and read until the intellect tires and I remember the words of Ecclesiastes, 'The making of books is endless and much study is wearisome.' Then I lay them aside, take God's hand and trustfully walk with him, content to wait for his purpose for me to be revealed in his time.

27

A Glimpse of Reality

Freed from the burden that for so long has oppressed me and feeling well once more, I can fully appreciate Little Orchard, our lovely new home. Throughout our married life I have longed for a house in the country and now at last have realized my dream, have found my magic place away from the noise and clamour of the town. I feel that I have truly come home, will stay here until I die.

From the front of the house the view is of open country, filtered through the green luxuriance of old pine trees, magnolia and rhododendrons to a tree-covered ridge on which stands Burrswood. All the windows look out on gardens. A large hall leads into unusually spacious rooms that are full of light. Almost everyone who enters comments on the welcoming warmth of our home. It is a place for quiet reflection, reading, music and the enjoyment of a profusion of colour throughout the seasons, a tranquil and peaceful retreat from the turbulent crowds of commuters rushing along the platforms of railway and underground stations. The air is pure, without any town smells to pollute it and, in the stillness of early morning, Frank and I stand listening to the birds and take deep breaths of the scent of dew and earth and trees.

Almost daily new and delightful surprises await us. So, on an April evening, as dark purple shadows slowly lengthen behind the rhododendrons, I stand under the apple tree where petals lie in drifts. As always in blossom time, my thoughts fly back to the day so long ago now when we danced through the enchanted orchard. Suddenly, from the top of the old scots pine float long, clear, vibrating notes, low and tender, softly swelling and heart-rendingly beautiful. Thrilling with delight I listen to the power, clarity and purity of the notes and marvel at their variety as the long sweet notes break joyously and rapturously into phrases of liquid 'wheet' staves, punctuated by short bubbly 'tucs'. I want to call Frank but am afraid to move. When he comes looking for me, I put a finger to my lips and we stand close together while our eyes strain until, through a gap in the branches, we see the white breast of the small bird that we come to think of as 'our nightingale'.

We spend every weekend working in our garden. As the sun climbs higher and higher in the sky and the shadows shorten, we down tools and stretch out on the sunken terrace, inhaling the scent of grass from the newly-cut lawns, and watch through half-closed lids the bees that descend drunkenly through the trembling heat-haze as they crawl from one stamen to another. I think of how much Mother would have loved this garden and look forward to the time when our grandchildren will play in it.

Before long we get to know the members of the Burrswood community. I discover that the manuscript of the book *Called by Christ to Heal*, written by Dorothy Arnold, who usually sits in the pew in front of us, was typed in our present home by one of the two ladies for whom the house was built and I am once again astonished when I think of the remarkable number of coincidences that have brought us here. My mind strays back to the day when CJC, then unknown to us, had from out of the blue phoned to invite Frank to join his organization. He had used all his powers of persuasion, but Frank had refused, for he was content in the work he was doing and, knowing how happy I was in my post as head of a large language department, had no intention of uprooting me. However,

CJC was determined to have Frank. Many phone calls and several meetings later, and after much heart searching and prayer on our part, CJC had prevailed and Frank began work as personnel and training director of CJC's company, with a fifty per cent commitment to associated charities. This, I now recall, was the first step along the road that led us to Little Orchard and Burrswood.

CJC is a frequent guest in our home. He is unfailingly courteous and I find it hard to believe the stories told by some who know him well of his ruthlessness and terrible rages if opposed by anyone or when he is confronted with what he regards as inefficiency. He used to own furniture shops, and the story goes that on one occasion he entered one of these and found the assistants apparently engaged in gossip, whereupon he sacked them all there and then, including two customers.

He has a puckish sense of humour and on occasion reduces us to helpless laughter. Leslie enjoys his company and he and she are on the same wavelength from the start. She is impressed when she learns that he is a co-founder of Oxfam, founder of Help the Aged and Voluntary Christian Service and was honorary secretary of the Oxford Committee for Greek Famine Relief, the forerunner of Oxfam.

One day we are talking about my experiences in post-war Cologne and I express my admiration for Victor Gollancz who, though himself a Jew, had founded Save Europe Now and had shown such compassion for the suffering in post-war Germany. He tells me that Victor Gollancz was very influential in the work of the Oxford Committee, in which he himself was involved, and diffidently adds that he had placed the advertisement for donations of supplies to be sent to Europe.

The more I hear of his work, his vision, the more impressed I am with this homely little man whose activities have generated several hundred million pounds for his trusts and charities. He could own a magnificent home and several yachts, and yet he lives either in hotel rooms or in a modest flat and wears clothes that look as though they have come from one of the charity shops. He is very fond of Frank and often boasts to me that he has once again picked the right man for the right job. He tells me that he admires Frank for his absolute integrity and adds, with a wicked twinkle in his eyes, 'You see, he is not afraid to stand up to me when he thinks I am wrong.'

Philip, now married to a lovely girl, Danielle, is working in an advice centre in Harlesden, an area with a largely immigrant population. He leads a young team that he describes as 'the poor man's lawyers'. While at Cambridge, he became increasingly disturbed by remorse and scruples, became aware of social inequalities that had not troubled him before. Like his father, Philip has a sensitive conscience, a passion for justice and is ever open to the claims of human need. He is generous, uncalculating, kind, an innocent in many ways. He combines within himself the qualities of the dreamer and those of the social reformer. Again like his father, he cares little about money and, fortunately for him, Dany is not bothered by this.

In 1973 their daughter Sandy, our first grandchild, is born. We are thrilled to be grandparents and, as I look down at the tiny, exquisitely-shaped head, I pray, as in time I pray over each one of our grandchildren, that God will guard and protect them, keep them safe, enfold them in his limitless love and fill them with his divine Spirit.

The following year, on a glorious July morning, Leslie's wedding to a young graduate named David is, by special permission, taking place at Burrswood. The service, an unusually long one, is deeply moving. With all my heart I pray that Christ will strengthen them in their love for each other and their love of him. The young couple set up house in Oxford where they both continue with their postgraduate studies.

Exactly one week after Sandy's third birthday, her sister Stefanie is born. Our joy is muted only because she is born with a dislocated hip. She is fitted with a frame that she will have to wear for several months, and I am distressed at her obvious discomfort. When I return from London, where I have been looking after Sandy during Dany's stay in hospital, we place her name in the altar book in Burrswood on which the priest and others taking part in the healing service lay hands. A few weeks later Dany rings to tell me that Stefanie has kicked off the frame, and later gives us the joyous news that the consultant who has examined the baby has said that she will not have to go back into it.

A year after David has begun work, Leslie and he have a daughter, Kathy. When, after another interval of three years, their second little girl, Joanna, arrives, we have a quartet of granddaughters. When our home is filled with the laughter and noise of all our children and grandchildren, we look at one another and know that our lines have indeed 'fallen in pleasant places'.

From the moment when for the first time I look upon each tiny, vulnerable baby, through watching with delight the endearing toddler, so ineffably trusting, the noisy, sometimes unruly pre-teen, idolizing pop stars, to the surprisingly poised teenager, eager to accompany us to the opera, to the ballet and on foreign holidays, I find the role of grandparent a wonderful and deeply rewarding one. Family meals, which have always been festive occasions, become get-togethers of rollicking, uproarious fun.

There is the delight of having one or two of them with us for a week or a fortnight, when we totally forget the pressures of day-to-day existence and time rolls back as we build sand-castles on the beach, watch Punch and Judy, ride in the bluebell train or the ghost train or drive dodgem cars; and all these joys come with the extra bonus that, when we are tired of the youngsters' unceasing demands, we can relinquish all responsibility and hand them back to their parents.

From the moment of birth each of the four has had a

unique and distinctive personality, but all of them are generous and warm-hearted. The two eldest of our quartet are now quite grown up and are lovingly protective towards us. Thankfully, all of them are growing up secure in a background of stable relationships and love.

28

Divided Loyalties

England is truly my home, but there are times when I am made painfully aware of the feelings of many English people towards my native country and fellow Germans.

When they were young, I wanted both my children to have the assurance and security of totally belonging, and having experienced rejection and sometimes open hostility, I never spoke about the war. Nevertheless, neighbours and others were aware that I was German and very soon Philip was nicknamed 'Fritz','Jerry' and 'the Hun'. With radio plays and TV and cinema films about the war, in which the Germans were for the most part portrayed as inhuman monsters, children in the roads and on playgrounds were, not surprisingly, constantly re-enacting the war between Britain and Germany. I can recall one day I heard the children in the road taunting Philip and Leslie, calling them mongrels. My heart contracted, and then I heard Leslie's voice, clear and unafraid, 'Anyway, mongrels are much more intelligent than pure-bred dogs.'

There are also the occasional items in the national papers expressing hatred of Germany, the Germans and everything German. One such is an article in the *Guardian*, in which Germans are vilified by Geoffrey Moorhouse. In my reply to it, I try to point out that by the subtle viciousness of his article, Mr Moorhouse is undermining the continuous attempts that I and others were making to act as a bridge between decent people in England and Germany;

that to accept the possibility that the German people as a whole are not monsters does not exonerate past evil, but to imply that the German nation has a monopoly of evil then or at any time is hardly supported by the recent news columns of his paper.

I am very heartened when, in response to my published reply, I receive letters in support of what I have said, including a letter from a professor in America, a German Jew, who echoes Victor Gollancz in saying, 'Nothing can save the world but a general act of repentance instead of the self-righteous insistence on the wickedness of others.' And, on the fiftieth anniversary of *Kristallnacht*, I hear the Archbishop of Canterbury saying: 'We all have to repent, for without centuries of Christian persecution of the Jews, *Kristallnacht* could never have happened.' But there is also the memory of the dinner party when the wife of one of Frank's senior colleagues, who is spending a weekend with us, expresses the opinion that there is something inherently brutal and cruel in the German character.

The fact that people in Germany are conscious of feelings like these is brought home to me when, as part of my work as a college lecturer, I visit students who are spending time in Germany as part of their course.

The hotel in Cologne where I am staying is the venue for a conference and the restaurant is crowded. The waiter enquires apologetically whether I would mind joining a gentleman who is sitting alone at a table for two. During the meal we get into conversation and, when he hears that I live in England, he remarks that the British regard Germans as concentration camp criminals. As always, when I am in Germany I rush to the defence of the British, just as in England I do the same for the Germans. He looks at me earnestly. 'Does anyone over there ever talk of the concentration camps of the British in which during the Boer War over 26,000 Dutch women and children died?' Before I can point out that they died of disease and starvation and not in gas chambers, he continues, 'Look, we all know that the people who were pressed by Hitler into the army were not carefully selected individuals. All and sundry joined and potential criminals did not change on conscription. On the contrary, they revelled in the insanity of legalized slaughter, were honoured and decorated for it. Herr Hitler's thugs had no difficulty in finding the staff for their concentration camps among them.

'I am sick,' he groans, beating his chest with his fist, 'of striking my chest and confessing my guilt, of taking the blame. I was a little kid during the war, and the others, the grown men and women who were taken in by Hitler, were not the only ones to be duped by him. In 1935 Churchill expressed his admiration for the great man and Lloyd George described him as a born leader, a magnetic, dynamic personality. Why did we not get rid of him right at the beginning, they ask us now. Why don't *they* get rid of the IRA, of the people who are killing, maiming, murdering innocent people almost daily? In one day we killed twenty thousand Jews in Auschwitz, they tell us. Did I know this? Did the youngsters in the Hitler Youth, who hero-worshipped that man of honour and virtue, their Führer, know it? Of course we did not. And what about the three hundred thousand women, children, the old and infirm killed by *them* in one night in Dresden, the thousands killed night after night in Hamburg, in Cologne and other major cities?'

He gulps down some wine. 'Why always us, why always the Germans who are singled out as the pariahs? Millions died in Stalin's camps in peace time, millions were killed by Mao Tse Tung in China, in Chile more people were killed in six weeks than by the Gestapo in six years. I am not trying to exonerate what was done here, all I want to know is why they pillory just us?' He does not wait for an answer but continues, 'They might equally ostracize the inhabitants of a whole road because in it at one time lived Jack the Ripper.'

I look at him helplessly. How can I even begin to tell him

what I feel, with my divided allegiance, my divided loyalties, my love for the country of my birth and my love for the country of my adoption and my ardent desire to bring about healing and reconciliation between the two.

Suddenly, impulsively, he reaches across the table. 'I am sorry, I had no right to unload my ire on to you; after all, you are German too and I guess you have to put up with quite a lot, living over there.'

So then I tell him about my experience of the kindness of British people, their compassion and generosity. I tell of those who have told me that they admire the Germans, of others who have expressed distress about what happened during the obliteration bombing of German cities. And I remind him of the exchanges between German and English cities and towns to forge links between the people in them, and I mention the broadcast that took place on the fortieth anniversary of the bombing of Dresden in which both German and English people took part. When we part he has calmed down and I hope that he is feeling less bitter.

29
Moving On

Frank has now retired from gainful employment and, though he is no longer active in Action Aid, the children's charity that he, together with CJC and another colleague, founded, he is giving more time to the other voluntary organizations in which he is involved. He is deputy chairman of 'Help the Aged', trustee of Voluntary Christian Service, is on the board of trustees and chairman of the Personnel Committee at Burrswood and also preaches there on a regular basis.

At the end of a service in the Church of Christ the Healer one Sunday I sit up and see that Bishop Morris Maddocks, the bishop visitor at Burrswood, and his wife, Anne, are kneeling behind me. Though I had not intended to do so, I feel moved to ask them to come and see us before they return to their home that afternoon. They are taken somewhat by surprise by my sudden and unexpected invitation to come and have tea before they leave, but nevertheless they accept.

While we sit round the tea table, Morris confides in us and tells us that he feels that he has been called to devote himself totally to the Christian healing ministry and the renewal of the ancient partnership between doctors and clergy. The problem that he has to solve is that, in order to do so, he will have to give up his bishopric of Selby and will be without any financial support. Frank and I have been praying for guidance about our future commitments and we exchange a quick glance. Are we to be part of this?

In the discussion that follows, Frank advises the setting up of a trust to support Morris and Anne in their work and ensure an income for them. Morris tells us that he has already received one offer of financial help from a friend. Frank arranges for Morris to see the chairman of one of CJC's trusts, who promises support. Shortly afterwards the Acorn Christian Healing Trust comes into being with Frank as chairman and Charles Longbottom and Lord Hylton as trustees. In due course Morris is appointed adviser to the archbishops of Canterbury and York on the ministry of health and healing.

By now the time is approaching when I am due to retire. Leslie and I are talking about the possibility of our living near each other after I have retired. Her family is planning to move nearer to London to suit David's work. Frank roundly declares that he has no intention of moving from Groombridge and Little Orchard. I do not want to leave Little Orchard either, but the thought of being near Leslie and her family and nearer to Philip and his family is irresistible, and I continue to work on Frank until he eventually gives way. Having done so, he never once looks back with regret. Perversely, when the time comes for us to leave I am assailed by serious misgivings and am desolate at leaving the home I love.

I walk slowly down the drive, past the magnolia that is now devoid of its waxen blooms, the rhododendrons, the quince and the forsythia, passing my hand over each as I move towards the gate. Before me stretch the fields where sheep are grazing with this year's lambs, now almost as big as their mothers. Beyond them the trees on the ridge stand like sentinels beneath the sun, green deepening to ebony where cloud shadows sail over them. Above them rises the bell tower of the Church of Christ the Healer that has come to mean so much to us.

Under the large old conifer by the gate our little wren darts rapidly to and fro, and on one of its branches a blackbird lifts his throat in a long, low, chuckling trill, undeterred by the squirrel that leaps from branch to branch. Thrushes, robins, chaffinches, goldfinches and tits are singing less riotously now that summer is moving towards autumn. I turn reluctantly and move towards the porch where hydrangeas in unprecedented luxuriance all but cover the small leaded window of the cloakroom.

From the hall and through the patio doors of the dining-room, I see the loveliness of the garden Frank has created. Light fills the house, and I am reminded of the day when I first entered here nearly fifteen years ago. It will not be put out with our going, but we are leaving it behind to move back into urban life, from which I had longed to escape for so many years.

All our married life I had faith in my vision of our home in the country and it has come to life here. For three years I have battled to persuade Frank to leave it, and the more he opposed me the stronger was my will to conquer until at last I won. Now that the fight is over, a thrill of panic courses through me. Suddenly I feel that I cannot bear to leave. All the other places where we have lived have been but stations on the way, where we rested for a while before journeying on. This is the home where we wanted to spend the rest of our lives. Its spirit is reaching out to me now, claiming me, and I know that it is here that I belong. Yet it is irretrievably lost to us, everything has been signed. In the large playroom that we have built in the attic, Frank is tying up the last boxes in readiness for the removal men.

The sense of bereavement once again confronts me with the implacability of 'never again'. I shall never again be able to fill a house with flowers as I have done here, where throughout the changing seasons the garden has provided them in such prolific abundance. Never again shall I have as much light as here, where the sun sliding from east to west sends its shafts through patio doors and windows all day long. Nor, in the heady peace of a summer afternoon, in the silence when birdsong is stilled, shall

I watch the burly bumble-bees steering their zigzag course among the flowers on the terrace wall, plunging their furry heads deep into each honeyed calyx. I shall never again watch the glorious rose and amber sunsets smouldering behind the dark pines or listen to the liquid call of the owl that comes swinging along the moon-silvered trees in the incandescence of the garden. Instead of the moonlight and starlight and soft blue shadows, there will be the harsh yellow and orange glare of street lights; instead of silence, the roar of traffic. My sentimental reverie is interrupted by the sound of splintering wood as the removal van turns into the drive, wrenching the gate off its hinges.

I am now teaching one final term at college before retiring at Christmas. A former mature student of mine, Stefanie, and her husband, Gerry, who have become friends, have kindly lent me a small flat in their house. I travel to our new home in Caversham at weekends and hate being away from Frank during the week.

Our house, just a few minutes' walk from Leslie and David's home, is situated in a tree-lined private road. Nevertheless, cars that are taking a short cut from one main road to another pass fairly frequently. The rooms seem small compared with the very spacious ones of Little Orchard, and the garden, just one fifth of an acre, a fraction of the size of the one we are leaving, strikes us as minute.

Now that retirement is almost on me, I view it with alarm. In the phantom silence of night, in the cold little attic bedroom, I lie sleepless for hours. The life left to me looms ahead as an oppression and a terror. The autumn seems to have become a symbol of my life, now moving towards its final stage. There is still warmth and colour but there is also the scent of decay. The year is moving richly and lingeringly towards death. Pale gold leaves tremble against the blue sky and, weakened by night frosts, come spinning down when the breeze touches them. In the peculiar stillness that autumn brings, blue smoke drifts over scarlet dahlias and the pungent scent of bronze chrysanthemums mingles with the scent of fallen leaves. Apples that should have been picked hang crimson and gold high up on almost bare branches, and bushes are brilliant with ripe berries.

Sometimes, when I look at the beauty, the pomp of glorious colour and of brightly burning foliage there are moments of joy in the midst of my melancholia, but in the mornings, when shrubs and bushes look grey, festooned in cobwebs, I gloomily ruminate on their resemblance to the hair of old women and the aptitude of the word *Altweibersommer*, the German designation for this part of the autumn season, which means old wives' summer and which introduces a poignant note of sorrow into the drifting golden gentleness.

Everything seems to contribute to my low spirits. At the weekend I look from the window of the train that crawls along, stopping at every station, at the fields brimming in late afternoon with the lambent brightness of autumn and revealing everything with an almost painful clarity, at once rich and wistful. Like them I stand empty handed, waiting for death. Yet such a very short time ago, life stretched ahead endlessly, held such promise, such opportunities for achievement. There was so much to be done, so much to be seen and experienced. I was needed by the children and by Mother, was important, felt solidly based. Now they have all gone, and soon I shall no longer be needed by my students either. My job will be a thing of the past and I shall be drifting, hopelessly and without purpose. I have been so busy being happy, have savoured each moment, have ceaselessly driven onwards and upwards; from now on I shall be looking down towards the end.

Goethe speaks of abnegation and renunciation, words suggesting the willing sacrifice of all. But what does one gain by sacrificing? Peace? Wisdom? Eliot says in *Little Gidding*, 'Do not let me hear of the wisdom of old men, but rather of their folly.' What then is left? There is love, and love endures, but there might even come the time when I shall be completely alone. The thought is intolerable, unbearable and unthinkable, for Frank is the pivot of my life, infinitely reliable, the rock upon which my life is built. Without him there can be no life for me. And in this mood of dejected nostalgia my mind ranges over the qualities that make him lovable and for which he is respected by many. We are opposites: he impetuous, I cautious; he an optimist and ever cheerful, I tending to pessimism and melancholia. A man of strong convictions, a non-conformist and a rebel, he is always on the side of the underdog. Whatever he cares for, he cares for very deeply, for he is a man of deep loyalties and idealism. His inherent courtesy makes it impossible for him to inflict pain consciously but, if he should unwittingly do so, he is contrite and anxious to put right any harm he might have done. His clear truthfulness and his strength of spirit have increased over the years. Slow to judge, he is always ready to give people the benefit of the doubt, whereas I, being a perfectionist, tend to expect perfection in others, even though I am aware that I myself fall far short of my own stringent expectations. His absolute sincerity, integrity and honesty, to which he sticks no matter what the consequences to himself, have on occasion made him enemies; in one case he has caused dear friends to react in a very hurtful way because he will not give way on a principle he knows to be right. Because of marriage to me, he has strong bi-national affiliations, and his defence of Germany when faced with certain statements, often based on ignorance, has sometimes landed him in deep waters.

He has a great sense of humour and loves a story told against himself. It is fortunate that I am the only occupant of the compartment in which I travel, for at this point in my reflections I laugh out loud at the thought of how he would mock, quip and wisecrack if he could read my thoughts. He might even remind me of how in the early days of our marriage some of the qualities I have just enumerated to myself had on occasion irritated me. Often, when exasperated by some trivial incident, something he had or had not done, I had lost my temper and had longed for him to meet my temper with his. His unfailing generosity and forbearance had infuriated me because it made me feel so beastly. We do, of course, have the occasional quarrel, mostly sparked off by explosions of temper on my part, usually about trifles or imagined hurt, but always they already contain the sweet anticipation of the joyous reconciliation which is to follow, for even the slightest estrangement is unbearable for both of us.

As the distance between us slowly lessens, I anticipate the big smile with which he will welcome me when this terrible tortoise of a train eventually reaches Reading. He is as full of vitality as ever, his joy in life as intense, his stride as buoyant and eager as when I first knew him. And when I see his laughing face, I am always reminded of Richter's description of Theisse: 'His face is a thanksgiving for his former life, and a love letter to all mankind.'

30
Commissioned

Even before the children were of school age, Leslie kept busy by writing and translating. Now that they are at school, she has once again taken up the pursuits that had dynamically interested her at university. Both she and Philip belong to the Campaign for Nuclear Disarmament and she is very active in it. She believes that she must express her religious beliefs in a practical way and does so ardently and intelligently, not only through her writing but also in the many other activities that she initiates. I realize that I, albeit unintentionally, have been the catalyst that has caused her to campaign so ardently, for though I have always been careful to conceal my insecurities, both she and Philip have been aware of the fact that there has been discrimination against me in my career, not only on account of my sex but also because of my nationality at birth. This has inspired her to work for justice for victims of both sexual discrimination and racial oppression.

I understand the conviction that drives her to take part in campaigns with those who are prepared to make sacrifices and even to endanger their careers in the cause of world peace. I admire her dedication to CND, for she has taken up a position against the common mind that is intent on defending the country by any means, against those who feel that the nuclear deterrent is the only practical way of dealing with aggression and who claim that pacifism is totally impractical. They are convinced that they are right, must be right, since they are in the majority and believe that history has proved them right.

It is with something of a shock that I realize that our adorable little girl has grown up into a formidable young woman who is pursuing her work for the cause she has adopted with passion and pertinacity. I admire her courage in challenging the validity of the law and, even though I do not entirely agree with her on this point, I understand her commitment. She is seeking out in every country and in every city she visits, from Tokyo to Vienna, those who share her vision, are united in their one desire, the desire for peace. She knows where she wants to go and is possessed of the strength and determination that will take her there. She faces up to the issues and works to realize her dream.

I too want to build a living peace but am aware that we must first remove from our own souls anything that militates against peace. Christ's message was peace. It has been abused throughout the ages by those who consider themselves to be his followers. I myself am doubtful about the efficacy of demonstrations. Growing up in an atmosphere of enthusiasm for what were then considered ideals and great purposes has given me a perhaps irrational aversion to ardours and causes and any outward display of support for them. The result is that I am inclined to view them with suspicion and at times even with cynicism. I desire peace as passionately as she does, but feel that even prayers for peace cannot be answered until each one of us lives according to the message from Galilee, until we prove our desire for peace by our own sincerity, by living the message and by demonstrating it in our private lives day by day.

Leslie, now so intensely occupied with many affairs, has no time for cosy little chats over cups of coffee; nor, I discover in due time, would I have enjoyed spending my remaining years measuring out my life in coffee spoons. The adjustment to a situation that is so entirely different from what I had envisaged is at first painful, but I am now less concerned with authority and dignity, which just a few years earlier I had been anxious to defend. Things that were then of supreme importance now seem much less so. This is a help in bridging the gulf between generations. Gratefully I reflect, however, that nothing has changed over the years in the relationship between Frank and me and that with the passing of youth, strength and beauty, our love has not lessened but increased. Now, for the first time in many years, we have more time to enjoy each other's companionship.

When I have recovered from the morbid preoccupations of the pre-retirement period, I begin to appreciate my prolonged holiday. The days slip by and we greet each morning with profound thanks for the gift of yet another day. I look forward more eagerly than ever before to spring, for, with the awareness that any spring could be the last, it has become infinitely precious. At first I delight in the freedom from mental effort, the delicious feeling that, while others are slogging away in school or college, I can linger over breakfast, sipping my coffee. I find great satisfaction in manual work and its results — a sparkling clean house, shining silver and brass. However, this soon palls and the need for other occupation reasserts itself. Though I have resigned from one examinations board, I remain chief examiner for another, and this entails trips to London for meetings, as well as setting the papers for various stages of the examinations. This, however, is not sufficient; and I am not fulfilled by the contribution I can make as trustee of the Acorn Christian Healing Trust, in which Frank as the chairman is working very hard.

Then, almost before I realize it, I am drawn with Frank into active participation in the ministry of healing. The prospect fills me with dismay. Though we have supported the work of the Christian healing ministry for years now, we have never sought personal ministry. I fiercely resist the idea of active involvement. I want to serve but I want to do it quietly and unobtrusively.

Despite the commitment I made at Burrswood, despite the fact that we have been praying for guidance, have been waiting for a call, now that it seems to come I argue and try my very best to wriggle out of it. I am more than ready to assist and support others in what they are doing, I tell Frank, but I myself want to remain in the background. I have always been reluctant to explain what happened at Burrswood, knowing it to be inexplicable. Even if I tried no one would understand, for the language needed to convey such an experience would have to be the language of another sphere of being. The faint apprehension, the glimpse of reality that I have had can only sound foolish if put into ordinary words. It might, moreover, cause antagonism in some. I am not worthy, I plead.

Even though we are not worthy, God uses us as channels, comes the reply.

I continue to argue and plead but it is no use. At a service at Wells Cathedral, Frank and I are asked to assist Morris Maddocks and the Bishop of Wells, John Bickersteth, members of the clergy and several others working in the healing ministry.

In our new church of St Peter's in Caversham, we have received a wonderful welcome. During a beautiful service arranged by the rector, Richard Kingsbury, Frank has been relicensed as lay reader for the parish. It is Richard who asks us to minister with him to a young man with a lovely wife and three children who has cancer.

The first time we visit J., the only demand made on us is to listen for the best part of two hours while he pours out his fears, his hopes and his doubts and speaks about his past, his resentments and his guilt. He and his family are lapsed Christians, but J. is eager to pray with us and anxious for us to come again. During our subsequent visit his wife is present and at the end of it we ask them to pray for us. When next we see them he is eager to let us know that he and his wife now pray regularly together, 'holding married hands'. From this results forgiveness and reconciliation with people and events from the past.

J. has had a colostomy and now has a secondary cancer of the pelvis and cancer of the liver. After we have known him for some months, we are told that the cancer of the liver is no longer there and he is strong enough for chemotherapy for the cancer of his pelvis. By now we have come to know and love the whole family, including J.'s mother-in-law, who lives with them. Our hopes that he will be completely restored to health and wholeness are high. Then he falls and fractures his pelvis. He is taken to hospital and dies there nine days later.

Times like this are hard, when we pray for faith for those who cannot find faith, or pray for the sick who seem to get no better or for the tormented who remain in agony. At such times I fear that there is no power in my praying and so no power to help those asking for aid. Then, when God seems far away and I am weary, depressed and discouraged, I turn to Frank. He reminds me of the broken marriages that have been healed by prayer, the people who have been granted release from fear, from feelings of resentment, guilt and rejection, and those who have been healed of sickness. And he reminds me too of the apostle Paul's words in his letter to the Ephesians that 'we wrestle not against flesh and blood but against principalities, against powers, against the rulers of darkness of this world'.

There is always renewal for me at Burrswood, where I can lay all at the foot of the cross in prayer and wait in silence and tranquillity, in a spirit of peace and recollection, knowing that, even if all other supports were to go, I have this, which is all I need. Here I am enfolded in peace, even before I enter the church, from the moment when I open the door of the car and set foot on the drive. From the window of our room I look across the valley, drinking in the beauty. At night I drift into deep refreshing sleep

274

and wake joyously to the dawn chorus of praise that drifts through the open window.

It has been a long journey, during which I have been prayerfully supported by Mother and Frank, from childhood faith through faithlessness to faith regained, when in his immeasurable love, God, whom I in my pride and arrogance had rejected, found me and welcomed back, the prodigal.

31

View from the Mountain Top

After our fortieth wedding anniversary, which we celebrate quietly with the family, and just before Frank's seventieth birthday, we revisit Velden and Graz. As the plane dips from a sky of pink and lavender towards the lights of Klagenfurt that glitter in the distance, I try to pick out landmarks and cannot find them. Into my mind crowd images of childhood and youth, the faces of loved ones, friends and acquaintances, most of them gone now. There are memories of love and suffering, of ambitions and hopes. When the lights of the runway come closer, I turn to Frank, who has taken my hand in his, and a wave of gratitude sweeps over me for our years together, for though the incredible rapture of the first years has calmed, love's music has deepened and never ceased.

In Velden we pass through the archway of the Schloss Hotel and, after telling the receptionist of the occasion when I last stayed there, we are led to the most delightful suite of rooms with a vine-covered 'Romeo and Juliet' balcony. The view from the dining-room of the lake and the Karawanken is unchanged, except for many new buildings along the shore and windsurfers and motor boats that, to my inward-looking eyes, seem an intrusion.

In Graz we have a joyous reunion with Schnucki and her sister Gretl. We go to see our old house and walk round the corner to the house where Schnucki used to live. I seem to see the young ghosts of ourselves walking ahead of us.

Suddenly I am overwhelmed with yearning for the time so long ago, when we first walked here together. I long to step back into youth and beauty, into the marvellous, enchanting springtime of our lives, to recapture the poetry and ecstasy of being in love for the first time, to rediscover our innocence, our eagerness, the thrill of recognition and wistfully I ask, 'Wouldn't it be wonderful if, just for one day, we could time-travel?' Then we laugh, calling each other hopeless, incurable romantics.

On Sunday we go to the service in Graz Cathedral, where to our incredulous delight we find that the choir of the Graz Academy of Music and the Pro Arte Ensemble Graz are singing Schubert's Mass, the one that the chorus and soloists of the Graz Opera House sang on New Year's Day in 1946 when we last worshipped here. Now, so many years later, the pure sound that fills the cathedral and wings upwards to the vaulted roof miraculously brings back the emotions of that morning, when together we had sat where the morning sun, shining through the stained glass windows, had splashed the aisles with deep pools of jewel colours. It seems to me that the voices that rise triumphantly in the 'Gloria' now speak of love's victory, the fierce strong joy that has banished fear and sorrow.

We wander hand in hand through pine woods, take great breaths of the sweet scent that rises from the resinous needles of the conifers, mingled with the smell of pine gums, meadow flowers and moss. From the top of the mountain we look upon the world spread out below and exclaim with delight at the host of alpine flowers all around us and, high up where the snow lies, a drift of small crocuses. One evening, on returning after many hours of walking and a particularly steep climb, we reflect on our extreme good fortune at being still fit enough to do this. Then we give thanks to God, who has so abundantly blessed us.

Sandy

I am grateful to you for making me write this brief
account of my life, for, in the late autumn of my days, I
have lived once more in springtime and summer-time and
have been able to pay tribute to two of the finest people,
my mother and my husband. As I look back with deep
gratitude, I see how tenderly I have been protected and
how lovingly led, and know that the joy and happiness
that has been mine is as nothing compared to that which
is still to be.

Your loving
Grandma

GHETTO
Poems of the Warsaw Ghetto 1939-43

Jenny Robertson

Fifty years have passed since the beginning of
World War II. But there are some things which can
and should never be forgotten.

On 15 November 1940 half a million people
were sealed within the Warsaw Ghetto. It was the
first step towards their extermination.

Very few people lived to bear witness; but
written words live on. The diaries and papers
which survived bear witness to a basic human
hope: that those who cry in the night will be heard
beyond the dark.

This book is intended neither to moralize nor to
theorize, but simply to allow eyewitnesses to
speak.

*'These poems, written because I have walked where
the Ghetto once stood, distil the pain and loss I sensed.
I have tried to give voice to those who were silenced, to
make a memorial kaddish, to light a frail candle flame:
because we need to mourn and not to forget.'*

JENNY ROBERTSON is the author of a number of
books of poetry as well as novels and plays. Her
life-long love of Poland, its language, literature and
people stems from student years when she worked
among Nazi victims in displaced persons camps.
She then did postgraduate studies in Warsaw
where the tragedy of the Holocaust became deeply
imprinted in her experience.

ISBN 0 7459 1804 2

A TOUCH OF FLAME
An anthology of contemporary Christian poetry

Compiled by Jenny Robertson

This book brings together more than 100 poems by
contemporary Christian poets. Some are well
known. Many are little known. All deserve wider
recognition.

The selection is not confined to 'religious'
poems. Its broad themes offer rich variety:
nativity, incarnation, commonplace, laughter and
tears, landscape, beatitude, way of the cross,
resurrection . . . And the poems themselves touch
and delight the reader. They restore to a hungry
world the lost dimension of wonder.

ISBN 0 7459 1509 4

IRINA

Dick Rodgers

In 1983, Irina Ratushinskaya, one of Russia's
leading poets, was sentenced to twelve years in a
strict-regime prison camp. Her crime was 'anti-
Soviet agitation in the form of poetry'.

In prison, she was kept in degrading conditions.
Her diet was bread and water, with rotten cabbage
soup every other day. Her hair was shaved off. She
spent months at a time isolated in the punishment
cell, with only a few thin clothes to protect her
against the sub-zero temperatures. Her husband,
Igor, began to plead for her release.

His pleas were heard in England by Dick
Rodgers, a surgeon and priest living in
Birmingham. Like many others, he lobbied for
Irina's release. But unlike others, he spent forty-
six days in a cell matching Irina's to bring her
plight before the eyes of the Western world.

This is the story of what happened when a group
of determined individuals confronted a
superpower.

ISBN 0 7459 1367 9

KILLING TIME

Noel Fellowes

Imagine your worst nightmare.

Arrested and interrogated for a murder you know nothing about.

Sentenced to years behind bars for a crime you did not commit.

But there's a final, chilling detail to this nightmare. You are an ex-policeman, hated by everyone in the 600-strong prison.

This nightmare is the true story of Noel Fellowes.

'It would be an understatement to say that this is an extremely disturbing case.'
The Lord Chief Justice, Lord Lane

'It is clear that police officers handling the case either ignored or deliberately withheld vital evidence.'
Sunday Express

ISBN 0 7459 1051 3

CHARNWOOD

Grace Wyatt with Clive Langmead

Charnwood is the name of a very remarkable
nursery centre which gives handicapped and
normal children the opportunity to play, learn and
grow up together, and provides much-needed
support for parents. Today the experts readily
acknowledge the all-round benefits, to both
normal and handicapped children, of this kind of
integrated education. In the 1960s, when Grace
Wyatt's pioneer work began, it was frowned on
and even considered harmful — and there were
many battles to fight before the Charnwood centre
earned the recognition it so obviously deserved.

This is a story, especially, of handicapped
children and their families, the agonies and the
triumphs. It carries a strong message of hope for all
who are in any way involved with handicap, and for
the 'normal' too — a way through the initial
embarrassment so many feel, to real relationship.
There is joy in loving a child purely for who he or
she is, and great reward in seeing children with
different abilities play together in a child-world
untouched by labels and restrictions.

ISBN 0 7459 1137 4

WHO PROFITS?

Richard Adams

In the 1970s Richard Adams started a company. Along the way he conquered coffee cartels, the rag trade, import quotas, public flotation, boardroom battles and a cold store full of rotting green peppers. He learnt the hard way how to make a success of trading with developing countries — steering his company through birth, growth, crash and turnaround.

Adams uses his company, Traidcraft, as a case-study. It is now Britain's largest independent alternative trading organization — a multi-million-pound Public Limited Company. He shares his passionate commitment to the need for producers in the developing world to get consistent outlets and fair profits if trade is to develop.

All this really means good management. Adams highlights the principles and reflects on the struggles of working out management and trading methods.

This book is not only a remarkable inside story. It also shares a wealth of ideas, thinking and experience in how to tackle this crucial and fast-developing area of trade.

ISBN 0 7459 1606 6

A selection of top titles from LION PUBLISHING